Foundations of
Catholic
SOCIAL TEACHING

Living as a Disciple of Christ

AVE MARIA PRESS AVE Notre Dame, Indiana

The Subcommittee on the Catechism, United States Conference of Catholic Bishops, has found that this catechetical high school text, copyright 2015, is in conformity with the *Catechism of the Catholic Church* and that it fulfills the requirements of *Elective Course C: Living as a Disciple of Christ* of the *Doctrinal Elements of a Curriculum Framework for the Development of Catechetical Materials for Young People of High School Age.*

Nihil Obstat: Reverend Monsignor Michael Heintz, PhD
              Censor Librorum

Imprimatur: Most Reverend Kevin C. Rhoades
             Bishop of Fort Wayne–South Bend

Given at   Fort Wayne, Indiana, on 21 July 2014

The *Nihil Obstat* and *Imprimatur* are official declarations that a book or pamphlet is free of doctrinal or moral error. No implication is contained therein that those who have granted the *Nihil Obstat* or *Imprimatur* agree with its contents, opinions, or statements expressed.

Other references cited as Notes beginning on page 335.

Founded in 1865, Ave Maria Press is a ministry of the United States Province of Holy Cross.

Engaging Minds, Hearts, and Hands for Faith® is a trademark of Ave Maria Press, Inc.

www.avemariapress.com

Paperback: ISBN-13 978-1-59471-467-2

E-book: ISBN-13 978-1-59471-468-9

Author
Sarah Kisling

Project Editor
Michael Amodei

Pedagogical Consultant
Dr. Michael Boyle
Assistant Director, Center for Catholic School Effectiveness
Clinical Assistant Professor, Research and Psychology in the Schools
Loyola University Chicago

Cover image © Superstock, © Thinkstock, © Wittman Photography.

Cover and text design by Andy Wagoner.

Printed and bound in the United States of America.

ENGAGING MINDS, HEARTS, AND HANDS FOR FAITH

ENGAGING MINDS, HEARTS, AND HANDS FOR FAITH®

ave maria press

An education that is complete is the one in which hands and heart are engaged as much as the mind. We want to let our students try their learning in the world and so make prayers of their education.

Bl. Basil Moreau
Founder of the Congregation of Holy Cross

In this text you will find:

 a well-referenced survey of Catholic social teaching, from its Gospel roots through the Church's collection of doctrine since *Rerum Novarum* in the nineteenth century

 an examination of challenging social issues faced by people today, always examined through the lens of God-given human dignity

 ways for teens to respond to the injustices in today's world effectively and with compassion

CONTENTS

SOCIAL PERSONS CALLED TO JUSTICE

EACH LIFE MATTERS

The Guadalupe Clinic, founded by the Diocese of Wichita, Kansas, has the mission to "provide access to necessary health care for those in need, work for social justice in health care, and call upon the entire Church and other people of goodwill to join in these efforts."

A woman named Vicki experienced the charitable justice of this organization. Although she had a full-time job, her $7.15 per hour pay was not enough for health insurance. Meanwhile, she had not been feeling well; she could hardly walk up stairs without struggling to breathe.

Her son heard about the Guadalupe Clinic and urged her to go there. Regarding her experience when she walked into the clinic, she said, "They only asked for five dollars, but treated me like a million dollars!"

After some tests, the doctor informed Vicki she needed surgery. She said that she could not afford surgery. The doctor replied, "It's not an option, it's your life." Once again, she reiterated that she couldn't afford surgery. The doctor insisted, "It is taken care of."

Vicki received the surgery and made a full recovery. She said she couldn't have asked for better treatment than she received at the clinic. "The Guadalupe Clinic gave me my life back, and with dignity!" she said.

Vicki didn't want a handout, but she realized she needed help. Now she extends that help to others in need. She has returned to the clinic as a regular volunteer.[1]

FOCUS QUESTION

How does living as a **SOCIAL BEING** lead you to pursue justice?

INTRODUCTION
The Human Pursuit of Happiness

Have you ever looked forward to the weekend and the enjoyment it promises, only to be left disappointed in the end? Have you ever been excited about seeing an upcoming movie that ended up being not nearly as good as you expected? Has a close friend ever let you down?

Has anything for which you had high hopes left you dissatisfied or unhappy? And then you tried to find something else to fill the void, only to be disappointed again?

Everyone wants to be happy. In fact, almost every action people take is aimed at finding happiness. Even the simple act you took today of getting up and going to school is somehow linked with a desire for happiness—whether just for the short-term happiness (or absence of unhappiness) that comes with not getting in trouble for skipping class, or for the anticipated future happiness connected with receiving good grades, getting into college, and earning a degree to establish a secure career and income.

Everyone spends a whole lot of energy on what they *think* will make them happy. Almost every marketing campaign is somehow built upon this reality. Think about all the advertisements you saw the last time you watched TV or were online: you were promised better hair, a faster car, delicious food—all things that are intended to increase your "happiness" in some way.

The ache for happiness is bottomless. Just as humanity will always be pursuing more money, the faster-speed computer, or the "smarter" phone, so too,

NOTE TAKING

Naming and Classifying Attributes. Make a table like the one below. In the first column, list several human attributes described in this section. In the second column, write a description of each attribute.

Human Attributes	Description
Made in God's image	Humans are persons, modeling the Blessed Trinity, who is Three Persons in One God.
A union of body and soul	

GOD'S ATTRIBUTES

List five qualities that you have learned are essential characteristics or attributes of God. Some examples would be loving, compassionate, creative, just, beautiful, intelligent, understanding, and so forth. For each of these qualities, provide a real-life example of a person with the quality, knowing that all good human qualities come from God.

no one here on earth could honestly think, "Now I am as happy as I could ever be." It seems that even a moment that seems to provide the ultimate happiness could always be improved upon. For example, why be happy to win a hundred dollars when it's possible to win a thousand or a million or mega millions?

You can see where this is going. If the thirst for happiness is never-ending, only a source of infinite goodness—that is, God—can satisfy it. St. Augustine of Hippo, one of the Church's great theologians, knew this. He said, "We all want to live happily; in the whole human race there is no one who does not assent to this proposition, even before it is fully articulated."

St. Augustine had spent his early life looking for happiness in all the wrong places. He embraced many false philosophies. He lived with a woman outside of marriage. Nevertheless, he remained unsatisfied and continued to look for happiness. Finally, inspired by Scripture, St. Augustine came to know God. He discovered that only in God was his desire for happiness quenched. He was baptized and became a Christian. He was later ordained a priest, and became a bishop. St. Augustine famously offered this prayer in thankfulness to God: "You have made us for yourself, and our heart is restless until it rests in you."

> **soul** The innermost spiritual part of a person. The soul is the subject of human consciousness and freedom. Body and soul together form one human nature. The soul does not die with the body. It is eternal and will be reunited with the body in the final resurrection.

Achieving Lasting Happiness

How is true, everlasting happiness achieved? Everything in this world works better when it acts in accordance with its nature. The nature of the physical makeup of a fish means that it will function better when it is in water. A fish is free to jump onto land, but because this type of environment goes against its nature, it will not thrive there, and will probably die. A tree needs sunlight to grow. Deprived of sunlight, the tree will gradually wither and die.

And so, to understand how humanity is happiest, you have to understand the nature of the human person. Consider these attributes of human persons:

- Humans are made in the image of God. Each person is not just something, but truly some*one*. Humans are rightly called "persons," because they are made in the image of the one God in the Blessed Trinity.

- Humans are a union of body and **soul**. Humans are not purely spiritual beings like the angels, or purely corporal like the matter of the earth. Humans are physical beings who have an inner life called the soul. The soul is not "trapped" in the body, but rather united with it. The reality of a person's soul is expressed through the body.

- Humans possess free will. Humans can make choices based on more than just instinct or impulse. Through this self-determination, they are able to weigh options and foresee consequences.

- Humans possess a rational intellect. Humans can think in a way that animals cannot. They can engage in self-reflection and perform abstract, conceptual reasoning.

- Humans are able to enter into communion with others and, ultimately, with God. Humans are capable of going outside of themselves to enter into relationships.

This isn't all, of course. You also know that humanity is in a fallen state because of **Original Sin**. Humans have a darkened intellect and a weakened will. All personal sin after man's first sin has been disobedience toward God and a lack of trust in his goodness. Because of this, not only is it difficult for people to *see* the good, it is often challenging to *choose* good over evil as well. Surely, everyone can relate to this.

However, humanity is not overcome by its fallen nature. While Original Sin wounded the human soul and a person's faculties of intellect and will, it did not destroy them or leave them in complete darkness.

Through Christ's Passion, Death, Resurrection, and Ascension, humanity was redeemed and transformed. The **Paschal Mystery** accomplished even more. In Jesus, you have a glimpse of what it means to be human, for Christ "fully reveals man to himself."[2] God has given you the Holy Spirit and his many graces to combat **concupiscence** and the temptation to commit personal sins in your own life. Disciples of Christ have the divine image "restored, renewed, and brought to perfection in them," said St. John Paul II. Indeed, only in being conformed to the image of Christ "can man be freed from the slavery of idolatry, rebuild lost fellowship and rediscover his true identity."[3]

Take a few moments to let that sink in: *only in Christ can you find your true identity*. This reality of being made in the image of God—an image restored by Christ—drives the pursuit of happiness. In other words, the more you are like God, the happier you will be.

> **Original Sin** The sin of the first human parents, by which they lost their original holiness. Original Sin is transmitted to every person born into the world, except Jesus and Mary.
>
> **Paschal Mystery** Christ's work of Redemption, accomplished principally by his Passion, Death, Resurrection, and glorious Ascension. This mystery is commemorated and made present through the sacraments, especially the Eucharist.
>
> **concupiscence** The human inclination toward sin, caused by Original Sin. More specifically, it means "the rebellion of the 'flesh' against the spirit" (*CCC*, 2515).

SECTION ASSESSMENT

NOTE TAKING
Use the chart you completed to answer the following questions.
1. Name and describe five attributes of the human person named in this section.
2. How do these attributes differentiate human beings from any other living creature?

COMPREHENSION
3. What did St. Augustine mean when he said, "You have made us for yourself, and our heart is restless until it rests in you"?
4. What does it mean to say that Christ "fully reveals man to himself"?

APPLICATION
6. Explain why it makes sense to say that the more a person is like God the happier he or she is.

SECTION 1
People Are Individual and Social Beings

Although human beings share one nature, each person has a unique individuality. Each person is not some-*thing*, but some*one*. There is no other *you* in the entire universe, and there never will be. Even if you were to discover an identical twin you never knew you had, this person would not be you. St. John Paul II said:

> A human being is an object to be counted, something considered under the aspect of quantity, one of many millions. Yet at the same time he is a single being, unique and unrepeatable . . . somebody thought of and chosen from eternity, some called and identified by his own name. (*Urbi et Orbi*, Christmas Message, 1978)

This individuality is absolutely essential; however, it is also important to note that each person is also a social being. Now, this does not mean "social" in the conventional understanding of the word—that is, outgoing and eager to interact with peers and other people. Instead, being social beings means that you are called to *be with others*. Just by being born, you have a connection with other beings—most fundamentally, your family.

Your social nature is absolutely vital to your quest for happiness. Adam realized this. Looking at all the animals, he recognized that none of them were like him. God said in regard to Adam's dilemma: "It is not good for the man to be alone" (Gn 2:18). God took care of Adam's loneliness by giving him Eve; together, they formed the first human society.

NOTE TAKING

Fill In the Blanks. As you read the text section, fill in the words that best complete the sentences below.

1. A human person is made in the image of _____. Therefore, he is an individual, but also a _____ being.

2. Denying this image leads to _____.

The Importance of Society

The *Catechism of the Catholic Church* defines *society* as a group of persons bound together organically by a principle of unity that goes beyond each one of them (see *CCC,* 1880). This definition is deliberately general. Applying it to your life, you can see that you are a part

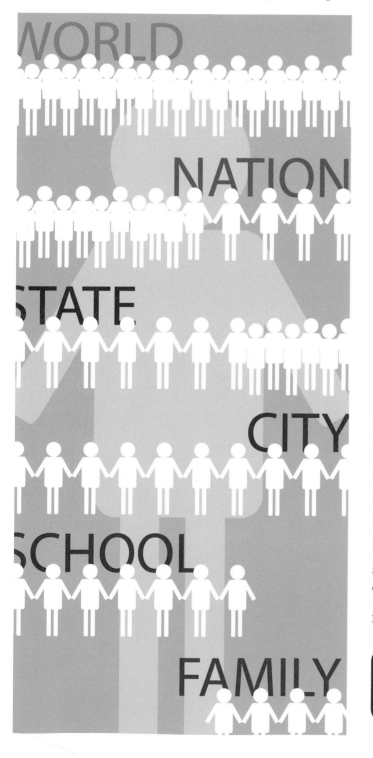

of many societies. Foremost, you have the society of your family. You are also part of a school society and the larger societies of your city, state, and nation. Ultimately, you are a member of the society made up of the entire world, bound together by the fact of a shared humanity of all people.

Living in society is essential to being a human person. The *Catechism of the Catholic Church* teaches: "Through the exchange with others, mutual service and dialogue with his brethren, man develops his potential; he thus responds to his vocation" (*CCC,* 1879). Although each person is an individual, no one is truly isolated; the call to communion is inherent to human nature. Pope Benedict XVI put it this way:

> Our lives are involved with one another, through innumerable interactions they are linked together. No one lives alone. No one sins alone. No one is saved alone. The lives of others continually spill over into mine: in what I think, say, do and achieve. And conversely, my life spills over into that of others: for better and for worse. (*Spe Salvi,* 40)

Your social nature is rooted in the Trinity. It's not irrelevant that the Trinity is a **communion of Persons**. You learned in the Introduction that the more you are like God, the happier you will be. Because "God is love" (1 Jn 4:8), he is an eternal exchange of Persons. The Father loves the Son; the Son loves the Father; and the Holy Spirit *is* that love. Just as the Trinity is an eternal self-gift, you too are called to give of yourself to others. The exchange of the gift of yourself to God and others is at the heart of what it means to be human.

> **communion of Persons** A complete giving-of-self, shown perfectly in the life of the Trinity. The Trinity, as a communion of divine Persons, is a model for human relationships.

The Second Vatican Council taught that

The Lord Jesus, when praying to the Father, "that they may all be one . . . even as we are one" (Jn 17:21–22) has opened up new horizons closed to human reason by implying that there is a certain parallel between the union existing among the divine persons and the union of the sons of God in truth and love. It follows, then, that if man is the only creature on earth that God has wanted for its own sake, man can fully discover his true self only in a sincere giving of himself. (*Gaudium et Spes*, 24)

Everyone is created for communion with others; ultimately, each person's destiny is communion with God, who himself is the perfect communion of Father, Son, and Holy Spirit. Only in relationship with God can man and woman fully discover "the authentic and complete meaning of their personal and social lives."[4] Since being made in God's image marks the life of every human, the more one is like him, the greater is one's happiness.

The Church Goes Beyond Human Society

As part of Christ's plan to draw everyone to himself (see Jn 12:32), he assembled the People of God from the ends of the earth and gave her the name Church. "The Church is in Christ like a sacrament or as a sign and instrument both of a very closely knit union with God and of the unity of the whole human race."[5] The Church draws her life from Christ himself and becomes his Body. Essentially, the Church shows the way to unity with God, and therefore communion with other humans. The Church is thus a guide and a sign of the unity to which our human societies must aspire. The Church is the source of Salvation and truth.

This unity of the Church is expressed in many ways:

- *The Church is the Mystical Body of Christ.* Christ intimately identified himself with his people: "Abide in me, and I in you. . . . I am the vine, you are the branches" (Jn 15:4–5). And St. Paul boldly proclaimed, "Now you are Christ's body, and individually parts of it" (1 Cor 12:27). And so, it is Christ himself who is the source of unity. The *Catechism of the Catholic Church* reiterates this: "Not only is [the Church] gathered *around him*; she is united *in him*, in his body" (*CCC*, 789). And, "in the unity of this Body, there is a diversity of members and functions. All members are linked to one another, especially to those who are suffering, to the poor and persecuted" (*CCC*, 806).

- *The Church is the Family of God.* This expression of the Church is modeled when you pray the Our Father. Those reborn by water and the Spirit in Baptism are united as brothers and sisters, with God as their loving Father.

Icon of Christ the True Vine (Athens, sixteenth century)

- *The Church is the Community of Sanctified Believers.* What this means is that through the Church's union with Christ, Catholics also have a common activity: that is, sanctification (to make holy). "All the activities of the Church are directed, as toward their end, to the sanctification of humanity and the glorification of God."[6] Those in the Church are not only united in who they are, but also in what they are moving toward.

- *The Church is Teacher.* St. John XXIII said, "To [the Church] was entrusted by her holy Founder the twofold task of giving life to her children and of teaching them and guiding them—both as individuals and as nations—with maternal care."[7]

- *The Church is Listener.* Through a true spirit of ecumenism with other faith communities, she always seeks a common bond rooted in what is authentically human.

In all of these expressions, the Church helps both individuals and societies to reach their full potential.

SECTION ASSESSMENT

NOTE TAKING

Use the fill-in-the-blank notes you made as a reading guide to answer the following questions.

1. What are the implications of being made in God's image?
2. When a person denies this image, what are the consequences?

COMPREHENSION

3. Why is being a part of society essential to your humanity?
4. Why is the Church a guide and sign of unity to which all other societies must aspire?
5. Name five ways the Church expresses her unity.

APPLICATION

6. Explain how the following statement provides a guide to full human living: "There is a certain resemblance between the unity of divine persons and the fraternity that men are to establish among themselves in truth and love" (*CCC*, 1878).

JOURNAL

7. St. Francis de Sales famously said, "Be who you are, and be it well." What does this statement mean?
8. In what "societies" of your life are you most fully yourself? Why?

SECTION 2
What Is Justice?

MAIN IDEA
Justice means "giving others their due." The three main types of justice are commutative, distributive, and legal. Social justice is the overarching justice that ensures the other three.

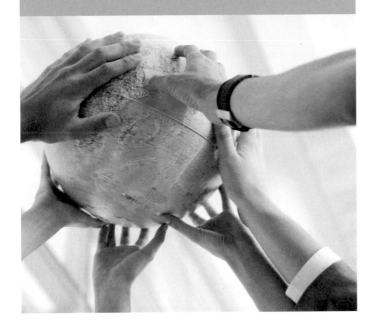

Human societies are not perfect. Consider three examples from the society made up by the United States of America:

- More than 1.5 million babies are legally killed from abortion every year in the United States alone.

- Every year in the United States, some 700,000 children are victims of abuse or neglect.

- Fifteen percent of US citizens live below the poverty level.

Failings such as these point to the need for **justice**. The *Catechism of the Catholic Church* defines justice as, "the moral virtue that consists in the constant and firm will to give their due to God and neighbor" (*CCC*, 1807). Simply put, justice is "giving others their due."

This need for justice is common to the human experience. From a young age, a child is sensitive to inequalities, and that sense of justice grows into adulthood. A mature sense of justice wants to see

> **justice** The cardinal or moral virtue that consists in the constant and firm will to give God and neighbor their due; the actions that flow from that virtue.

NOTE TAKING

Summarizing Information. Create a diagram like the one below to help you outline the main content of this section. Record the definitions of each type of justice in the appropriate rectangle.

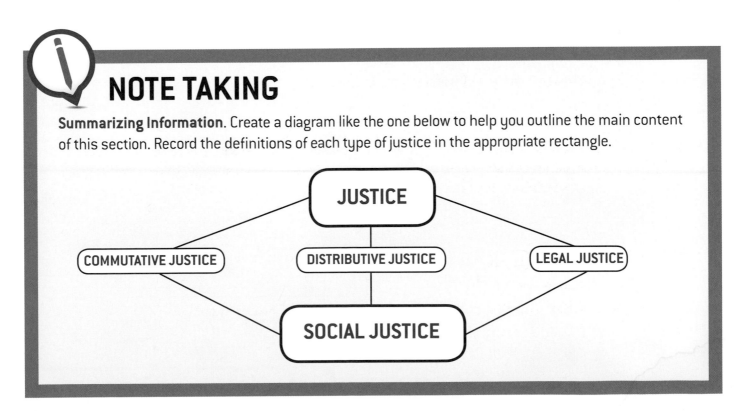

"A way has to be found to enable everyone to benefit from the fruits of the earth, and not simply to close the gap between the affluent and those who must be satisfied with the crumbs falling from the table, but above all to satisfy the demands of justice, fairness, and respect for every human being" (Pope Francis, *Address to the Food and Agricultural Organization, June 2013*).

the criminal punished, the good rewarded, and the deprived satisfied. St. John Paul II spoke about the need for justice:

> How can it be that even today there are still people dying of hunger? Condemned to illiteracy? Lacking the most basic medical care? Without a roof over their heads? . . . And how can we remain indifferent to the prospect of an ecological crisis which is making vast areas of our planet uninhabitable and hostile to humanity? Or by the problems of peace, so often threatened by the specter of catastrophic wars? Or by contempt for the fundamental human rights of so many people, especially children? Countless are the emergencies to which every Christian heart must be sensitive. (*Novo Millennio*, 50–51)

The human need for justice does not go unacknowledged by God. In God is perfect justice, which gives hope amid experiences of profound injustice. Indeed, God's justice is clearly revealed throughout Scripture. "The Lord does righteous deeds, brings justice to all the oppressed" (Ps 103:6). Also, Christ promises to satisfy this "hunger and thirst for righteousness" (Mt 5:6).

Three Types of Justice

Society can participate in bringing justice to the oppressed and satisfying the thirst for righteousness through different forms of justice. The three types named in this section are commutative justice, distributive justice, and legal justice. A fourth definition is also included: social justice, which is the overarching type of justice that ensures the other types.

Commutative Justice

Commutative justice is the type of justice that deals with relationships between persons and private social groups (*commutative* means "reciprocal"). It involves the justice within families, friendships, and work relationships. It includes paying back debts (big or small), making restitution for damaging others' goods, and

> **commutative justice** The type of justice that governs exchanges between individuals and private groups.

A fender bender requires the parties involved to agree to and complete a fair resolution.

fulfilling contracts or promises. It calls for fairness in agreements and exchanges between individuals or private social groups. Commutative justice requires that you get what you pay for. It also obliges you to give others what is rightly theirs and to earn what you are given.

For example, if you're hired as a cashier at a retail store, you have an obligation to give a fair amount of work and not stand around and talk to coworkers while customers are left unattended. Conversely, your employer must pay you a just wage for your work. Or if a mother hires you as a babysitter to watch her toddler, then in justice you should do a good job of caring for the child and not spend the time distracted with texting your friends. Similarly, the mother should pay you the agreed-upon wage and not renege on her part of the agreement.

Commutative justice requires that both sides respect the dignity of the other and responsibly fulfill their obligations. Without commutative justice, a society could not function. It would be riddled with theft, fraud, and disregard for others and their property. The fundamental principles of commutative justice lead to other forms of justice.

Distributive Justice

Distributive justice regulates what a society owes its members in proportion to what they need and what they contribute. It sees to the just distribution of created goods that God intends for all to use and share. The Second Vatican Council taught:

> God intended the earth with everything contained in it for the use of all human beings and peoples. . . . Thus, . . . attention must always be paid to this universal destination of earthly goods. . . . The right of having a share of earthly goods sufficient for oneself and one's family belongs to everyone. (*Gaudium et Spes*, 69)

The individual right to car ownership would be fruitless without supporting the common need for shared highways and roads.

Distributive justice is an obligation for all people and all societies. However, its application varies from nation to nation. Distributive justice certainly is not in opposition to private ownership of goods and services, but it requires individual citizens to support the common needs of all. For example, the private ownership of cars and homes is part of the so-called American dream. Yet Americans must also support programs, either public or private, to provide transportation and housing for those who can't afford ownership of either.

> **distributive justice** The type of justice that governs what the greater community owes individuals based on their contribution and needs.

JUSTICE CHEAT SHEET

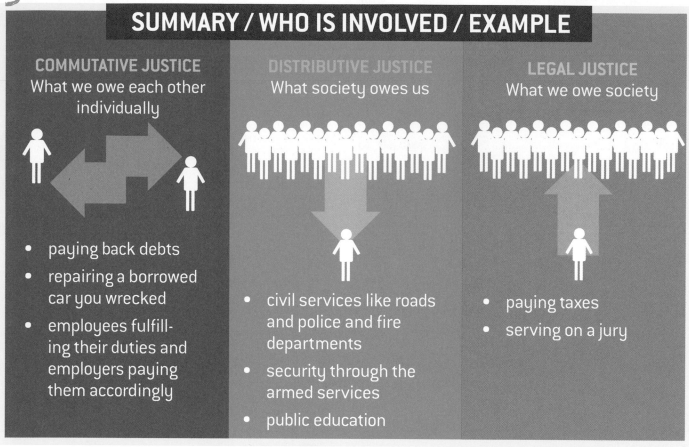

SUMMARY / WHO IS INVOLVED / EXAMPLE

COMMUTATIVE JUSTICE
What we owe each other individually

- paying back debts
- repairing a borrowed car you wrecked
- employees fulfilling their duties and employers paying them accordingly

DISTRIBUTIVE JUSTICE
What society owes us

- civil services like roads and police and fire departments
- security through the armed services
- public education

LEGAL JUSTICE
What we owe society

- paying taxes
- serving on a jury

Taxes are one way this support is given. In the case of transportation, taxes not only help to fund transit service, but also the costs of road repair, snow removal, and the like—services that benefit all people.

The previous example shows distributive justice based on someone's *contribution*. Distributive justice, as you will learn in ensuing chapters, can also be based on someone's *need*.

Legal Justice

Legal justice involves citizens' responsibilities to society. It includes paying taxes, obeying just laws, and offering help in times of crisis. What constitutes legal justice is usually spelled out in laws and legal documents.

To review the three types of justice, examine the chart on this page.

Social Justice

The term **social justice** was first employed in Church documents by Pope Pius XI in 1931 in his encyclical *Quadragesimo Anno* ("On Reconstructing Social Order"). But the practice of social justice has always been part of the Church's work and is rooted in Christ's very mission of service. The Church's modern body of teaching on social justice began with Pope Leo XIII in 1891, when he issued the first **social encyclical**,

> **legal justice** The type of justice that governs what individuals owe their country and society.
>
> **social justice** The application of the virtue of justice. The defense of human dignity by ensuring that social structures and institutions on all levels—including political, cultural, and economic—provide for essential human needs and protect human rights.
>
> **social encyclical** A letter from the Pope to the Church on issues related to human rights, social justice, and peace.

Rerum Novarum ("On the Condition of Labor"). Social justice applies the Gospel message of Jesus Christ to the structures, systems, and laws of society in order to guarantee the rights of individuals. Social justice demands that everyone has a right to a fair say in the social, political, and economic institutions of society.

The *Catechism of the Catholic Church* teaches that "society ensures social justice when it provides the conditions that allow associations or individuals to obtain what is their due, according to their nature and their vocation" (*CCC*, 1928). Theologian Fr. John Hardon, S.J., explained social justice as a person working in concert with others, through organized bodies, as a member of a group whose purpose is to identify the needs of society, and, by the use of appropriate means, to meet these needs locally, regionally, nationally, and even globally.[8]

Social justice is an overarching type of justice that ensures the practice of the other types of justice described in this section. Social justice is most closely related to legal justice, although it does, indeed, address all types.

SECTION ASSESSMENT

NOTE TAKING

Use the graphic organizer you created to complete the following questions.

1. What is the difference between commutative justice and distributive justice?

2. Which type of justice is social justice most like?

VOCABULARY

3. Define the terms *justice* and *social justice*.

4. What is the difference between justice and social justice?

CRITICAL THINKING

5. What are the basic responsibilities of citizens in society?

6. Conversely, what are the basic responsibilities of society toward citizens?

7. Why is justice both a personal obligation and a social necessity?

SECTION 3
Other Justice Topics

Several other topics are crucial to an initial understanding of justice and what it means to live a truthful and happy life. Three of these topics are (1) the need to commit to the common good, (2) the practice of charity and justice, and (3) awareness of how sin—specifically, social sin—affects people collectively and individually. These topics are addressed in the next subsections.

The Common Good

The term *common good* refers to the sum total of social conditions which allow people, either as groups or as individuals, to reach their fulfillment more fully and more easily.[9] Three essential elements of the common good are:

1. Respect for the life and dignity of every person.

2. A commitment to the social well-being and development of the group, especially by ensuring that individuals' basic needs are met.

3. The establishment of a peaceful and just society.

The common good always begins with the needs of individuals. Starting from the needs of individuals, society builds structure and methods that meet these needs, benefitting everyone. It is the role of the state to defend and promote the common good of civil society and its citizens. The common good is always oriented toward the *progress of persons*. This order is founded on truth, built up in justice, and animated by love. A just society is relentless in its efforts to maintain the dignity

NOTE TAKING

Word Webs. Create word webs around each of the following concepts. To make a word web draw lines from the circle to key words and phrases that will help you understand the meaning of the concept.

Common
Good

Justice &
Charity

Social
Sin

of the individual human person, both for his or her own benefit and for the common benefit of all. In using the word "common," the Church does not reject the needs of the individual for the sake of the greater community, but rather exactly the opposite. The Church recognizes that because of the social nature of human beings, the good of the individual is inseparable from the communal good. The *Compendium of the Social Doctrine of the Church* explains how the well-being of the individual human person is integral to the common good:

> A society that wishes and intends to remain at the service of the human being at every level is a society that has the common good—the good of all people and of the whole person—as its primary goal. The human person cannot find fulfillment in himself, that is, apart from the fact that he exists "with" others and "for" others. (*CSDC*, 165)

Actions aimed at the common good should always begin with the human person. Economies, governments, private organizations, and other societies should spring forth from the dignity of the human person. Pope Benedict XVI explained that the common good is linked to love of others:

> It is the good of "all of us," made up of individuals, families and intermediate groups who together constitute society. It is a good that is sought not for its own sake, but for the people who belong to the social community and who can only really and effectively pursue their good within it. To desire the *common good* and strive toward it *is a requirement of justice and charity*. The more we strive to secure a common good corresponding to the real needs of our neighbors, the more effectively we love them. (*Caritas in Veritate*, 7)

AFFIRMING DIGNITY

Society's emphasis on outward beauty, popularity, and financial success are three things that can take a toll on a person's true sense of human dignity. Make a promise to yourself to affirm the dignity of another person and, in doing so, affirm your own dignity as well. Make a list of some things you can do, such as the following:

- Be truly grateful for the important people in your life. Say "thank you" on a regular basis, especially to your parents.

- When you smile at others, make it authentic.

- Be a courteous driver. For example, allow the driver of another car to merge in front of you in traffic. Give a wave when someone does the same for you.

- In conversations, look people in the eye and sincerely pay attention to what they are saying.

- Give up your seat on the bus for someone who needs it more.

- Visit with someone who is lonely. Really take time to listen.

Charity and Justice

Note that Pope Benedict XVI declared that serving the common good is a requirement of both charity and justice. **Charity** is the theological virtue of love for God and neighbor. Charity involves loving God above all things and loving others out of love of God. Love is intrinsic to the Christian life, and thus to social relations among people. Just as the Trinity is a relationship of love between Father, Son, and Holy Spirit, so too are you to place charity at the center of your interpersonal relationships.

Jesus said that the greatest commandment is to love God with all of your heart, soul, and mind (Mt 22:37). In conjunction with this Jesus also clarified the second greatest commandment: to love your neighbor as yourself (Mt 22:39). Loving your neighbor out of love for God has obvious social implications. No

one is merely an isolated individual, and the basis of your relations with others is charity; therefore, charity is "at the heart of the Church's social doctrine."[10] Charity requires that you have a loving gaze toward the poor that compels you to give food to the hungry, drink to the thirsty, and clothing to the naked (see Mt 25:31–46).

The *Catechism of the Catholic Church* echoes Jesus' teaching, defining charity as the "greatest social commandment" (*CCC*, 1889). Charity is a requirement of justice and in fact makes one capable of true justice. The *Compendium of the Social Doctrine of the Church* further explains the necessity of charity within the practice of justice: "Only love is capable of radically

> **charity** The virtue by which people love God above all things for his own sake, and their neighbor as otherselves for the love of God.

transforming the relationships that men maintain among themselves. This is the perspective that allows every person of good will to perceive the broad horizons of justice and human development in truth and goodness" (*CSDC*, 4).

Sometimes a dichotomy exists in any discussion that includes charity and justice. You may have heard people express perspectives like the following: "We do not need to be generous with the poor (charity); instead, we need to create social systems, so there will no longer be any poor (justice)."

Yet from a Catholic perspective, these realities are not mutually exclusive. You are not to aim for justice *or* charity, but rather justice *and* charity: they are mutually dependent. Yes, you need to give food, shelter, and clothing to the poor (charity). However, with these acts, you also need to ask why the poor are in such conditions, and what you can do to bring justice to end this situation. Acts of justice do not exclude the acts of charity, and vice versa. Just as faith, without works, is dead (see Jas 2:17), so too justice, without charity, is empty.

In summary, remember this: justice always needs to be animated by charity, because like all Christian

> **social sin** The effect that every personal sin has on others; sin that violates the freedom, dignity, or rights of others; the collective effect of such sins, which can affect society and its institutions to create structures of sin.

actions, it needs to be aimed at love of God and love of neighbor.

Social Sin

Sin is deeply personal. Because of your free will, you are individually responsible for your acts, especially those that reject God's invitation to follow him. That said, personal sin affects society, and thus can affect societal injustice. For example, a Catholic politician may reject the Church's teaching prohibiting abortion, and thus be personally culpable; however, if he votes for laws to make abortion more available, he has contributed to a *social* injustice. Many persons collectively performing acts such as these repeatedly contribute to **social sin**.

Social sin includes attitudes, actions, and structures that foster unjust treatment. Unfortunately, the effects of social sin can be passed on to future generations, a reality that has contributed to 1.5 million abortions in the United States per year, for example. The personal sins of previous generations led to the

INJUSTICE IN THE NEWS

Choose a current prominent news story of injustice. Analyze at least four news sources that cover the same story. For example,

1. The local newspaper
2. A local television news program
3. A national network or cable news program
4. A website of a major news organization

Assignment: Write an assessment of the coverage. What makes the issue an injustice? Rate the seriousness of this injustice on a scale of **1** to **10** (10 being most unjust). Next, analyze the news coverage. How fair or unfair do you think the coverage is? What are some other local, national, and international injustices that were ignored?

federal ruling *Roe v. Wade*, the 1973 Supreme Court decision that legalized abortions nationwide.

Never forget that the root of social sin is always personal sin. For social sin to be transformed, each individual must personally reject sin and gravitate toward the truth of the Gospel, accept it, and convert. Can you see how this personal transformation would alter a nation's acceptance, or lack thereof, for abortion?

Because the importance of your practice of individual morality cannot be understated, another way to define social justice is "personal morality lived in society." In fact, all of the Ten Commandments, the cornerstones for a moral life, have a *social* dimension. The first three commandments address your relationship with God, which is a supernatural social reality. The last seven commandments show how you should act in your relationship with others—reminders that personal morality must be lived through all of your human interactions.

SECTION ASSESSMENT

NOTE TAKING
Use the word webs you created for this section to complete the following questions.

1. What is the common good?
2. How are charity and justice related?
3. How can individual sin lead to social sin?

APPLICATION

4. Read 1 Corinthians 13:1–13. Why is love superior to the other two theological virtues?
5. Explain from personal experience how your sin can affect others.

Section Summaries

Focus Question

How does living as a social being lead you to pursue justice?

Complete one of the following:

 Name a specific way you can be more charitable in the following societies: your family, your school community, your parish, and your city, and describe how this charity can be modeled on the charitable work of the Guadalupe Clinic.

 Pick a social injustice that strikes you deeply. Write a letter or an e-mail to a member of Congress, state legislator, or local government official that addresses the injustice, noting actions that need to be taken to correct the situation.

 Explain this quotation from St. Thomas Aquinas as it relates to acts of charity within a society: "Justice is love serving God alone, and consequently governing aright all things subject to man."[11]

INTRODUCTION (PAGES 3–6)

The Human Pursuit of Happiness

All human beings long for happiness; every action you take in some way or another is directed at this pursuit. The ache for happiness is limitless, and so only God, who has no limits, can satisfy it.

 Find one example from history or literary works of a person or people pursuing happiness. How did their efforts lead to their ultimate happiness? Explain.

SECTION 1 (PAGES 7–10)

People Are Individual and Social Beings

Humans are made in the image of a Trinitarian God. This means that people have a social nature and are made for communion with others. Societies' rejection of this truth results in injustices that attack the dignity of human life, such as abortion and poverty. The Church as the assembled People of God, the Body of Christ, is a community of faith that can guide people in establishing social relationships that honor human dignity.

 Read St. Paul's treatise on the Mystical Body of Christ (1 Cor 12:12–31). Then answer the following: What is *your* role in the Church? How do you both share in the sufferings and in the joys of other members of the Body of Christ?

SECTION 2 (PAGES 11–15)

What Is Justice?

Justice is giving others their due, first to God, but also in and through relationships among people. In relationships among people, the three forms of justice are commutative justice (between or among individuals), distributive justice ("top down" between society and the individual), and legal justice ("bottom up" between the individual and society). Social justice works to eliminate structures of sin, which are often the result of personal sin.

 Explain how the following are evidence of an unjust society: high unemployment, children bullying a classmate, a parent agreeing to work for less than the minimum wage, a water supply polluted to the point where it is unsafe to drink. Which type of justice (commutative, distributive, or legal) is needed for each?

SECTION 3 (PAGES 16–20)

Other Justice Topics

The common good ensures that the needs of individuals are met for the good of all. Charity—loving God above all else and loving your neighbor as yourself—is essential, but it must work alongside justice. One's personal sins can affect society; thus becoming "social sin."

 Name three examples from current world events of social sins. What are some actions *you* can take today that would work to rectify these societal sins?

Chapter Assignments

Choose and complete at least one of the three assignments assessing your understanding of the material in this chapter.

1. Summarize a Papal Encyclical

 Read the first seven paragraphs of *Caritas in Veritate* by Pope Benedict XVI. For each paragraph, write a two- to three-sentence summary in your own words. You can access the encyclical at www. vatican.va.

2. Write a Letter Addressing a Social Issue

 Writing a letter is an effective way to take a stand on a social justice issue, seek more information on a particular topic, and encourage those who are working for justice to continue their good work. Follow the directions below for choosing a social justice topic of interest to you and writing a letter to a person or agency that either needs to be informed about the issue or may benefit from hearing of an effort you may be able to suggest to help with this issue. Your letter should be at least one page. Bring your completed letter to class and have at least three classmates critique and edit it. Rewrite the letter and mail it to the appropriate person or organization. Follow the directions below:

1. Choose a topic.

- Pick out some issue related to social justice that interests you. (For ideas, page through the rest of this text.)

- Learn enough about your topic so you can write meaningfully and with authority.

2. Decide to whom you will write. Examples include:

- Governmental officials, for example, legislators;

- Newspapers expressing your opinion on a topic;

- Nongovernmental organizations, for example, the Red Cross;

- Experts in the field to get more information;

- Social justice advocates, including Church workers, to encourage them in their work.

3. Determine style and format.

- Address your letter properly. Find the recipient's correct address at your local library or online.

- Preferably, type your letter. If you don't type it, write it legibly. Follow an accepted style manual for business letters. Check your English grammar book.

- Keep the letter short and use your own words. One page is enough.

- Be clear.

- Focus on one issue.

- If expressing your opinion, support your opinion with facts.

- Be constructive.

- Be specific when requesting information.

- Share some research findings, if appropriate to your letter.

- It is quite appropriate to share Church teaching; for example, you might quote one of the relevant documents on social justice.

- Don't be afraid to ask questions, and politely ask for responses to them.

4. Follow specific writing guidelines.

- In the first paragraph, identify yourself and explain why you are writing.

- In the second paragraph, make your point or request information.

- In the closing paragraph, thank the reader for his or her kind consideration.

- If you receive a response, be sure to write a thank-you note.

3. Take Part in "Two Feet of Love in Action"

Research the "Two Feet of Love in Action" program at the United States Conference of Catholic Bishops' website www.usccb.org. Two Feet of Love in Action describes two ways to aid society through social justice (addressing systemic, root causes of problems that affect many people) and charitable works (short-term, emergency assistance for people). Choose one of the program's suggestions for addressing either root causes of problems (social justice) or providing immediate assistance (charity). Develop a plan for how you will take part in that suggested activity. Then put the plan into action. Prepare a two- to three-page report covering the following information:

- A summary of the Two Feet of Love in Action program;

- The suggested activity you chose to participate in;

- An explanation of why you chose this particular activity. The explanation should detail what motivated you to choose the activity and what outcomes you hoped your participation would yield.

- A description of your experience along with any new insights you gained from the experience.

Faithful Disciples

St. Vincent de Paul and St. Louise de Marillac

Sometimes God brings together two souls with similar callings, effecting great results through their shared vision. Such is the case of St. Vincent de Paul and St. Louise de Marillac, two saints whose lives are marked by extraordinary charity.

Vincent was born in 1580 in southern France into a poor farming family. Because of his predilection for intellectual pursuits, his father sold some of the family's livestock so that Vincent could be educated. Vincent studied theology and was ordained a priest at the age of nineteen. Although at first Vincent's goal was to live out his priesthood with prestige and in comfortable wealth, after a long spiritual struggle he abandoned this quest. He instead made a promise to God to dedicate himself to the service of the poor.

Fr. Vincent began traveling around France to preach missions and establish charities for the poor. He also worked in the prisons serving the inmates, who lived in squalid physical and moral conditions. Eventually, he founded a community of priests to aid in these charitable works called the Congregation of the Mission, known as the Lazarists or the Vincentians.

Women from wealthy and aristocratic families wanted to help Vincent in his service, so he founded the Ladies of Charity. Although these women made great financial contributions, many of them were not comfortable with direct contact with the poor. Vincent knew that some women would take a more direct role in service to the needy. This is when his mission became entwined with that of Louise de Marillac.

St. Louise de Marillac came from a very different background than St.

St. Vincent de Paul speaks to St. Louise de Marillac and the Ladies of Charity.

Vincent. Although her mother died shortly after she was born and her father passed away when she was in her early teens, Louise was still raised in the world of the upper class and was well educated. Although at the age of fifteen Louise desired to enter a cloistered convent, her spiritual director advised against this. Louise eventually married a successful man named Antoine Le Gras, with whom she had one child, Michel. She was a devoted wife and mother, even as her husband coped with a long and debilitating disease that ultimately led to his death.

St. Louise moved to Paris, where St. Vincent was serving at the time. Believing she was not called to remarry, Louise dedicated her life to prayer and service of the poor. Even before she met St. Vincent de Paul, Louise had had a vision of his face as the one to give her spiritual guidance. They began exchanging letters and having meetings, in which St. Vincent aided St. Louise in her pursuit of holiness. St. Louise joined Vincent de Paul's Ladies of Charity. Vincent saw in Louise not only a heart of prayer, but also talents in leadership and organization.

In time, a few women came to St. Vincent from rural areas with a desire to give their lives to the less fortunate. These women moved into St. Louise's home, where they were trained in service to the sick and poor. With guidance from St. Vincent, they began helping in hospitals, institutes for the elderly and mentally ill, orphanages, prisons, and on the battlefield. They wore the dress of peasants and lived a life of simplicity. Others slowly joined them. St. Louise and St. Vincent eventually drew up an official rule of life for the women and renamed them the Daughters of Charity. Louise exhorted the women: "Love the poor and honor them as you would honor Christ himself."

When St. Louise died in 1660, the Daughters had more than forty houses in France. St. Vincent died six months later. His legacy is carried on most notably through the Society of St. Vincent de Paul, a charitable organization founded in 1833 by Bl. Frédéric Ozanam. Today, the society carries out its mission in more than 130 countries. St. Louise de Marillac's feast day is March 15. St. Vincent de Paul's feast day is September 27.

Reading Comprehension

1. Compare and contrast the backgrounds of St. Vincent de Paul and St. Louise de Marillac.
2. What were some of the ways St. Vincent and St. Louise served the poor?

Writing Task

- St. Louise de Marillac told her fellow sisters: "Certainly it is the great secret of the spiritual life to abandon to God all that we love by abandoning ourselves to all that he wills." What do you think this means? How do the lives of St. Louise de Marillac and St. Vincent de Paul model this quotation? How can you model this quotation in your own life, especially in the pursuit of charity and justice? Answer these questions in a short essay or journal entry.

Explaining the Faith

Free will is part of human nature. Does that mean everyone is free to do whatever he or she wants?

When talking about free will, it is important to address the notion of true freedom. Freedom is "the power, rooted in reason and will, to act or not to act" (*CCC*, 1731). It is the uniquely human ability to choose. Maintaining human freedom, especially freedom of one's conscience, should be essential to any society. However, many people confuse freedom with license, which is "the arbitrary and uncontrolled exercise of one's personal autonomy."[12] In other words, *true* freedom is more than merely "doing whatever you want." For example, drinking poison is a free, human act. However, it would cause you to become sick or even die, and thus your humanity becomes limited; indeed, you become *less* free. Hence, license—merely doing whatever you feel like in the moment—often leads one to an enslavement of some sort.

The greatest freedoms exist when you use your free will to *choose the good*, that which is best for your humanity. For example, not engaging in premarital sex may seem like a restriction on the surface, but in reality it frees one not to have to worry about sexual diseases, untimely pregnancy, unhealthy emotional dynamics, and so on. True freedom is more than doing whatever moves you in the moment, but rather it is choosing the *good*, which is always more freeing.

 Further Research

- Read paragraphs 199 and 200 from the *Compendium of the Social Doctrine of the Church*, which you can access at www.vatican.va. Answer the following questions: How is freedom expressed in pursuit of one's personal vocation? Why must freedom include the capacity to reject what is morally offensive? What is the relationship between individual free will and the common good?

Prayer
Prayer for Justice and Peace

Almighty and eternal God,

may your grace enkindle in all of us

a love for the many unfortunate people

whom poverty and misery reduce

to a condition of life unworthy of human beings.

Arouse in the hearts of those who call you Father

a hunger and thirst for justice and peace,

and for fraternal charity in deeds and in truth.

Grant, O Lord, peace in our days,

peace to souls, peace to families,

peace to our country, and peace among nations.

Amen.

—Pope Pius XII

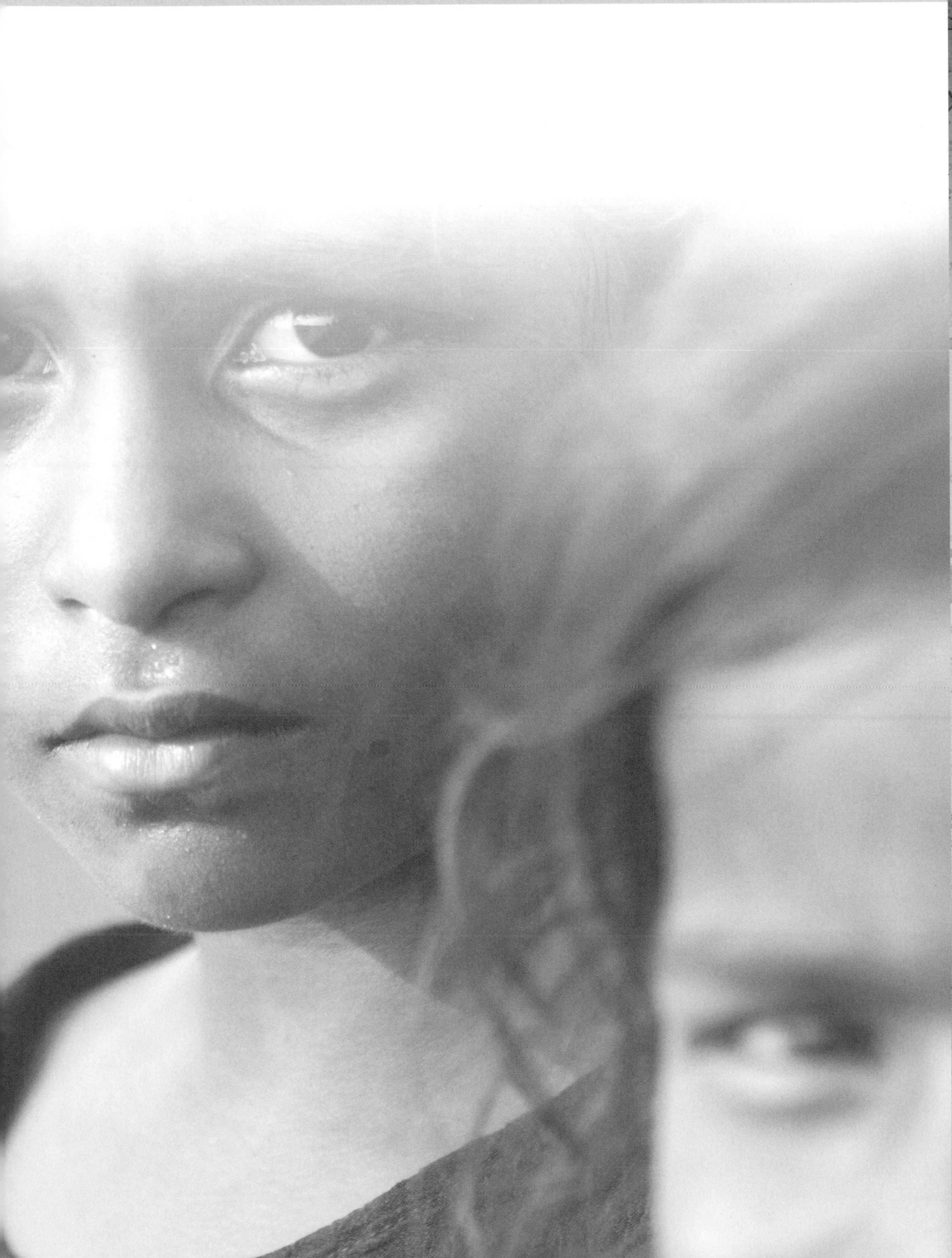

CATHOLIC SOCIAL TEACHING: DEFINITION AND HISTORY

Pope FOR THE POOR

It wasn't long after Cardinal Jorge Mario Bergoglio, S.J., of Argentina was announced as Pope Francis in 2013 that the media began to take note of his lifestyle of simplicity. The press discovered that in Buenos Aires, Cardinal Bergoglio had chosen to live in a small apartment, cook his own meals, and take public transportation rather than enjoy the conveniences and assistance afforded to him as cardinal. He continued this modest lifestyle as pope. Rather than live in the grand papal apartments at the Vatican, he opted to live in a modest suite in a Vatican guesthouse.

But the pope's interest in humility and a spirit of poverty extended beyond his own daily life. True to the example of his namesake, St. Francis of Assisi, a saint known for his radical poverty and love for the poor, Pope Francis turned his own, and the world's, attention to the plight of the poor and suffering. In one of his first public addresses, Pope Francis spoke about the need for Christians to "dedicate themselves to helping the sick, orphans, the homeless, and all the marginalized, thus striving to make society more humane and more just." He also said the Church needs to address those who suffer from

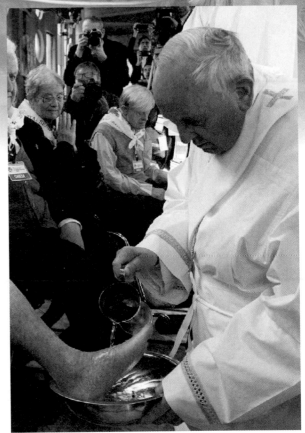

In a break with tradition, Pope Francis has washed the feet of non-priests—inmates, the disabled, and the elderly—on Holy Thursdays since his election as pope in 2013.

spiritual poverty, those for whom peace can be achieved only through obedience to the truth.

What was often *not* noted by the media coverage was the reality that the words and actions of Pope Francis, though news, were not really new. Indeed, the Catholic Church has a long history of being a voice for the poor, even among the papacy. For example, during his first Holy Week in Rome, Pope Francis "shocked" the world by washing the feet of inmates at a juvenile detention center on Holy Thursday; and yet, his predecessor, Pope Benedict XVI, visited the same center just six years before. Yes, Pope Francis's message that he wants "a poor Church for the poor" is, indeed, newsworthy, but certainly not "new"!

FOCUS QUESTION

How can you participate in the Church's MINISTRY OF SERVICE?

INTRODUCTION
Roots of Catholic Social Teaching

MAIN IDEA

The Church is a guide in your pursuit of justice. The Church's social teaching is based on the natural law.

Do you have a stirring in your heart to work for justice, but do not know where to begin? Have you ever felt confused between the right and wrong course of action? Have you ever wondered which issues in your own personal life, or the life of society, should take priority?

The Church is your guide in answering these types of deep questions about how you should live personally and how you should participate in society. The Second Vatican Council taught that "Christian revelation . . . promotes deeper understanding of the laws of social living."[1] Because the Church has received from God the full Revelation about what it means to be human, she has a special authority to speak the truth about the social relationships that encompass life on earth. You can think of the Church as a light and guide in your life as a social being.

Sometimes the Church is criticized for being involved in worldly matters. Governments from all eras, including today, have attempted to narrow the Church's influence while directing her to only minister to her own members. You may have heard of recent attempts to modify the language in the First Amendment of the United States Constitution from "freedom of religion" to "freedom of worship." Pause for a moment and think about how the two descriptions differ. Worship is something religious congregations do at defined times with their own members. Religion, on the other hand, is practiced at *all* times among people within, and outside of, the community of faith. Regarding the Catholic Church, many believe that this change in language is an attempt by government to limit the Church's ministry to only Catholics, not all people. This is an impossible demand on the Church.

Because the Church is a sacrament—that is, a sign of "communion with God and of unity among all"[2]— she must be involved in worldly matters. This does not mean that the Church is a political community.

NOTE TAKING

Summarizing Material. Create an outline like the following in your notebook. As you read the text section, use the outline to help you summarize the material.

I. Catholic Social Teaching

  A. Definition: _____
  B. Three Elements of CST
    1. _____
    2. _____
    3. _____

II. Natural Law

  A. Definition: _____
  B. Three Characteristics of the Natural Law
    1. _____
    2. _____
    3. _____

Instead, the Church is concerned with temporal activities, in that they are ordered to God, who is the ultimate end for all people.

But the Church's real concern is not politics, but to bring about Salvation of souls. This mission does not separate the Church's work from the everyday lives of people who are not Catholic. And the Church does not insist that the people she serves become Catholic in order to benefit from her ministry. Indeed, the Church teaches that the unique earthly life of all people is the very pathway to Salvation. You "work out your salvation" (Phil 2:12) in the here and now of this life. It is the Church who gives the daily activities of individuals and society a deeper meaning.

A Catholic who brings the presence of Christ to his or her daily life contributes to the better ordering of human society and to the building of God's Kingdom. However, it is important to note that even with all the good that you and others contribute to the world, even the best human societies are not, and will never be, perfect. Because of sin, human societies will always carry elements of injustice. The Church responds to this reality by engaging with the world, with the goal of bringing Christ's love and mercy to those most in need of it.

The Church's encounter with human societies over the centuries has formed the basis for her social doctrine. With the ultimate aim of leading people to Heaven, the Church provides for all of humanity instructions on how to approach and act within the society. This body of **Catholic social teaching** includes:

- *principles for reflection*: The Church helps people understand the realities of their social nature and the need for justice.

- *criteria for judgment*: The Church gives people the means to look at the world and judge what does not serve the dignity of the human person and embrace that which does.

- *guidelines for action*: The Church instructs people not just to reflect upon the state of humanity, but even more to put these concepts into action.

The Origins of Catholic Social Teaching

Catholic social teaching is deeply rooted in Divine Revelation. God has guided his people to justice throughout Salvation History and the history of the Church. And from studying and reflecting upon this history, the **Magisterium** has formed the Church's social doctrine under the guidance of the Holy Spirit.

Moral law provides the foundation for the Church's social teaching. Moral law accounts for a person's duties and essential rights. Interestingly, much of the Church's social teaching can be known and understood without special revelation from God. **Natural law** is that which is written into the very nature of humanity and established by reason so that all men and women can come to know it without any special external revelation, though natural law ultimately comes from God. Natural law allows people to know what is true. Even across a variety of cultures, the natural law is both universally accessible and binding in its laws and authority.

Quoting St. Thomas Aquinas, St. John Paul II defined natural law as "the light of understanding infused in us by God, whereby we understand what must be done and what must be avoided. God gave this light and this law to man at creation."[3]

> **Catholic social teaching** The Church's social doctrine, which is articulated as she interprets events in the course of history, with the assistance of the Holy Spirit, in the light of the truth of Revelation.
>
> **Magisterium** The official teaching authority of the Church. Jesus bestowed the right and power to teach in his name on Peter and the Apostles and their successors, that is, the pope and College of Bishops. The authority of the Magisterium extends to specific precepts of the natural law because following these precepts is necessary for Salvation.
>
> **natural law** Moral knowledge written in every human heart and that every human person innately possesses. It is universal, permanent, and unchanging.

The natural law and Divine Revelation are closely related. For example, consider that the Ten Commandments that God revealed to Moses were already present in the hearts and minds of the Chosen People in the form of natural law. The Fifth Commandment—"Thou shalt not kill"—is a value or tenet accepted by all humans and all societies in every age. Put another way, left on your own, you and others can come to an understanding that indiscriminate killing is wrong. Similarly, you and others can identify right and wrong around issues of dishonesty, theft, adultery, and so forth. Because of Original Sin, you still need the light of God's Revelation to follow and live out the Ten Commandments. However, the presence of natural law leads you to discover their moral truths.

Truly, every thinking person is capable of discovering the natural law (cf. Rom 2:14–15). Therefore, even people without faith can use the natural law as a source of moral guidance. People of good will, believers or not, can draw on the natural law to discover how God intends for them to live in society. This leads to three essential teachings about the natural law:

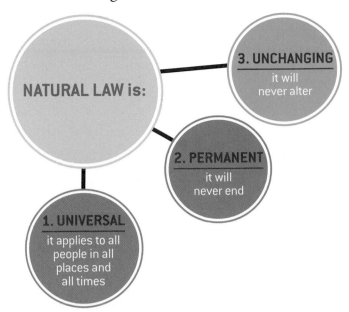

NATURAL LAW is:

1. UNIVERSAL
it applies to all people in all places and all times

2. PERMANENT
it will never end

3. UNCHANGING
it will never alter

Understanding Divine Revelation and the natural law is important in a course on Catholic social teaching. As you study in more depth, you will see how Catholic social teaching is indeed rooted in the truth God has made known to the human heart.

APPLYING NATURAL LAW:

Natural law is applied differently in various cultures, but its core remains the same. For example, all societies have laws to protect their citizens from being killed. Consider driving regulations designed to minimize car accident deaths by limiting the age of the driver, speed limit, and when to stop and go. Of course, the regulations may differ across societies. For example, one nation may have cars drive on the right side of the road, another on the left side. Nevertheless, the goal is the same: to protect human life.

SECTION ASSESSMENT

NOTE TAKING

Use the outline you created to answer the following questions.

1. Name three elements of Catholic social teaching.
2. What are the three characteristics of the natural law?

COMPREHENSION

3. Why is Catholic social teaching rooted in the natural law?
4. How is the natural law related to Divine Revelation?

CRITICAL THINKING

5. Explain how each of the following would violate the natural law:
   - using weapons of mass destruction
   - slavery
   - the sexual abuse of children
   - drinking to become intoxicated

SECTION 1
The Scriptural Roots of Justice

The Bible contains a wealth of imagery and insight on the subject of justice. For example, Amos 5:24 describes justice as a fast-moving stream like the stream in the photo on the left: "Then let justice surge like water, and goodness like an unfailing stream." This mountain stream is meant to eradicate all injustice in its path—poverty, neglect of widows and orphans, discrimination against foreigners, and the like.

Scripture presents justice as a burning concern of God. Justice is never described as simply a "balancing of scales," but a deep commitment by God to uphold his relationship with his people. God made, formed, and loves his people. God revealed his justice by being faithful to them. The biblical description of justice involves fidelity to what relationships require. And God is always faithful.

The next sections point out some other images of justice found in the Old Testament and the New Testament.

Justice in the Old Testament

The theme of justice is present in the Old Testament from the very first verses of the Book of Genesis. The Creation stories of Genesis emphasize the dignity of humans, created by God as male and female, and with a social nature written into their very beings. God in

NOTE TAKING

Summarizing Key Concepts. Make a table like the one below and use it to highlight key scriptural elements of this section. In one column, write a Scripture citation (e.g., "Gn 1:1–5"). In the second column, write a short summary of how the verse(s) address justice.

Verse	Summary
Am 5:24	God eradicates all injustice.
Lv 25:35	

The perfect order of God's creation points to the harmony of humankind and of all the world.

Three Divine Persons as Holy Trinity is relational. So too, he expects people to be with one another, and he with them. The relationship between God and humans is formalized in several places throughout the Old Testament in God's continual promise of a covenant that not only binds God to his people, but also his people to each other.

The nature of the relationship that people are to have with one another is expressed often in the Old Testament. The Genesis story of Cain and Abel and the call to be your "brother's keeper" (Gn 4:9) is not only another reminder that humans are relational, but correlates to the necessity for ensuring the common good (see pages 16–17).

Catholic social teaching emphasizes the need for special attention due the poor and oppressed. In the Book of Deuteronomy, God performs justice for "the orphan and the widow, and befriends the alien [foreigner], feeding and clothing him" (Dt 10:18) and exhorts humans to do the same: "You too must befriend the alien, for you were once aliens yourselves in the land of Egypt" (Dt 10:19). Deuteronomy also instructs God's People to share their food and possessions with the poor, depositing them on a regular basis "in community stores" so that "the alien, the orphan and the widow who belong to your community, may come and eat their fill" (Dt 14:28–29). Likewise the Book of Leviticus points to a sharing of goods with the less fortunate:

> When one of your fellow countrymen is reduced to poverty and is unable to hold out beside you, extend to him the privileges of an alien or a tenant, so that he may continue to live with you. (Lv 25:35)

In the account of the Israelites' Exodus from Egypt, the Old Testament details the care of God himself for the oppressed:

> But the LORD said, "I have witnessed the affliction of my people in Egypt and have heard their cry of complaint against their slave drivers, so I know well what they are suffering. Therefore I have come down to rescue them from the hands of the Egyptians and lead them out of that land into a good and spacious land, a land flowing with milk and honey. . . ." (Ex 3:7–8)

This spirit of justice from the Book of Exodus continued within the legal tradition of the Israelites. Justice is a theme throughout the Decalogue (The Ten Commandments): the first three commandments deal with justice toward God, and the last seven commandments clearly point to justice among the social relations of people. The codified structure of justice is a practice that is maintained in the Church today.

God's justice and the call of all people to model such justice are also reiterated in the wisdom literature.

In Psalms

The maker of heaven and earth, the seas and all that is in them, who keeps faith forever, secures justice for the oppressed, gives food to the hungry. The Lord sets prisoners free; the Lord gives sight to the blind. The Lord raises up those who are bowed down; the Lord loves the righteous. The Lord protects the stranger, sustains the orphan and the widow, but thwarts the way of the wicked. (Ps 146:6–9)

In Proverbs

Open your mouth, decree what is just, defend the needy and the poor! (Prv 31:9)

In Sirach

My son, rob not the poor man of his livelihood; force not the eyes of the needy to turn away. A hungry man grieve not, a needy man anger not; Do not exasperate the downtrodden; delay not to give to the needy. A beggar in distress do not reject; avert not your face from the poor. From the needy turn not your eyes, give no man reason to curse you; For if in the bitterness of his soul he curse you, his Creator will hear his prayer. Endear yourself to the assembly; before a ruler bow your head. Give a hearing to the poor man, and return his greeting with courtesy; Deliver the oppressed from the hand of the oppressor; let not justice be repugnant to you. (Sir 4:1–9)

The Old Testament prophets also ring out some of the clearest calls for responsibility to embrace justice. For example, Isaiah says to "make justice your aim: redress the wronged, hear the orphan's plea, defend the widow" (Is 1:17). The prophet Micah sounds a warning to practice justice that can be heard through the ages:

> You have been told, O man, what is good, and what the LORD requires of you: Only to do the right and to love goodness, and to walk humbly with your God. (Mi 6:8)

Justice in the New Testament

God's action in the Old and New Testaments is unified. He is not a God of strict justice in the Old Testament only to be a seemingly different God of love in the New Testament. Rather, God's justice and charity are inseparable. God's proclamation of justice is fulfilled in

In the first Beatitude, Jesus preached the requirement to care for, and serve, the anawim.

Jesus Christ in the fullness of his Revelation: "For God so loved the world that he gave his only Son" (Jn 3:16). From the onset of his ministry, Jesus embodied perfect justice infused with charity. Coming to his hometown synagogue in Nazareth, Jesus picked up the holy scroll and read from the prophet Isaiah:

> The Spirit of the Lord is upon me, because he has anointed me to bring glad tidings to the poor. He has sent me to proclaim liberty to captives and recovery of sight to the blind, to let the oppressed go free, and to proclaim a year acceptable to the Lord. (Lk 4:18–19)

Indeed, Christ fulfilled these words of Isaiah with his very life, specifically in his public ministry. You are familiar with Jesus' compassion toward the poor and outcast, and his instructions to his followers to do the same. You may have heard these stories of Jesus so often that you don't always really take note of what they really say; however, the reality that Christ came to "seek and save the lost" (Lk 19:10) is crucial to your understanding of social justice. Here are some familiar stories and teachings that express this fact:

- The Sermon on the Mount (Mt 5–7), especially the Beatitudes, fosters the need to care for and serve the *anawim*, the name for the poor in the Jewish Scriptures. These were people without material possessions who kept a positive attitude, realized their helplessness, and sought out God for all of their needs. It was the *anawim* whom Jesus spoke of when he said: "Blessed are the poor in spirit, for theirs is the kingdom of heaven. . . . Blessed are those who hunger and thirst for righteousness, for they will be satisfied" (Mt 5:3, 6).

- The Greatest Commandments (Mt 22:37–39) tell of the necessity to love God above all else, and also your neighbor as yourself.

- The parable of the Good Samaritan (Lk 10:30–37) defines your neighbor as the one in need of your mercy.

Justice in the Gospels

The Gospels speak of justice. In words and through his example, Jesus teaches the way to serve those in need. Read the Gospel passages indicated. Then, answer the questions.

John 13:1–17: The Washing of the Disciples' Feet
1. What is the basic meaning of this passage?

2. List three ways you can symbolically wash others' feet.

Mark 2:1–12: The Healing of the Paralytic
1. How did Jesus heal the paralyzed man?

2. List four sins in the world today that desperately need healing.

Matthew 14:13–21: The Feeding of the Five Thousand
1. How did Jesus respond to the needs of the gathered crowd?

2. List three ways you can respond to the hungry in today's world.

- The parable of the Last Judgment (Mt 25:31–46), in which you are told that your very Salvation is bound in how you show love for Christ by the way you treat the least of his people:

> Then the king will say to those on his right, "Come, you who are blessed by my Father. Inherit the kingdom prepared for you from the foundation of the world. For I was hungry and you gave me food, I was thirsty and you gave me drink, a stranger and you welcomed me, naked and you clothed me, ill and you cared for me, in prison and you visited me." Then the righteous will answer him and say, "'Lord, when did we see you hungry and feed you, or thirsty and give you drink? When did we see you a stranger and welcome you, or naked and clothe you? When did we see you ill or in prison, and visit you?" And the king will say to them in reply, "Amen, I say to you, whatever you did for one of these least brothers of mine, you did for me."

The importance of Christ's model of justice cannot be overemphasized. As the *Compendium of the Social Doctrine of the Church* explains:

> Jesus, in other words, is the tangible and definitive manifestation of how God acts towards men and women. . . . Jesus announces the liberating mercy of God to those whom he meets on his way, beginning with the poor, the marginalized, the sinners. He invites all to follow him because he is the first to obey God's plan of love, and he does so in a most singular way, as God's envoy in the world. . . .

For Jesus, recognizing the Father's love means modeling his actions on God's gratuitousness and mercy; it is these that generate new life. It means becoming—by his very existence—the example and pattern of this for his disciples. Jesus' followers are called to live *like him* and, after his Passover of death and resurrection, to live *in him* and *by him*, thanks to the superabundant gift of the Holy Spirit, the Consoler, who internalizes Christ's own style of life in human hearts. (*CSDC*, 28–29)

This quote from the *CSDC* elucidates a crucial reality. It is important to realize that Christ's words and actions of justice are not merely an example. In other words, Christ doesn't just show you the way; he *is* the Way (cf. Jn 14:6). Christ calls you to more than merely "doing acts of justice." Instead, you are to conform your life to Christ in his justice. Indeed, because

God's justice is made manifest in him (see Rom 3:21–22), no true justice is possible apart from him. This is the greatest of justices:

You cannot perform acts of true justice and charity apart from Christ; you need his grace.

By living out the justice that Christ embodied in his earthly life, you become an "other Christ." You continue Christ's presence in the world today.

SECTION ASSESSMENT

NOTE TAKING
Using the Scripture passages you summarized and recorded in your table, complete the following assignments.

1. Write one to two paragraphs comparing and contrasting one of the biblical images of justice with the secular understanding that justice is only a "balancing of scales."

2. Choose one description of justice from the Old Testament and one from the New Testament that particularly strike you. Why did these descriptions stand out for you? How can you live justice like they describe in your daily life?

COMPREHENSION
3. Explain how justice is directed differently between the first three and the last seven of the Ten Commandments.

JOURNAL
4. Explain this statement: "It is important to realize that Christ's words and actions of justice are not merely an example. Christ didn't just show you the way; he *is* the Way."

SECTION 2
Justice in Sacred Tradition

MAIN IDEA
Through the guidance of the Holy Spirit, the Church's mission of justice has continued through the centuries and is embodied in the lives of countless saints and holy people.

Jesus' mission and ministry did not end with his Death. The Church's history records and Sacred Tradition teach the ongoing sharing of Christ's justice with the world. In the early Church, the Apostles instructed Christians to practice charity by sharing in common necessary material goods: "All who believed were together and had all things in common; they would sell their property and possessions and divide them among all according to each one's need" (Acts 2:44–45). The Letter of James reminds the Church to allow justice to not be merely a sentiment, but an action:

> What good is it, my brothers, if someone says he has faith but does not have works? Can that faith save him? If a brother or sister has nothing to wear and has no food for the day, and one of you says to them, "Go in peace, keep warm, and eat well," but you do not give them the necessities of the body, what good is it? So also faith of itself, if it does not have works, is dead. (Jas 2:14–17)

The practice of serving those in most need is evident throughout Church history. In the fourth century, St. Ambrose wrote, "You are not making a gift of what is yours to the poor man, but you are giving him back what is his. You have been appropriating things that are meant to be for the common use of everyone. The earth belongs to everyone, not to the rich."[4]

In the fifth century, St. Augustine shared a connection between charity and justice: "You give bread to a hungry person; but it would be better were no one

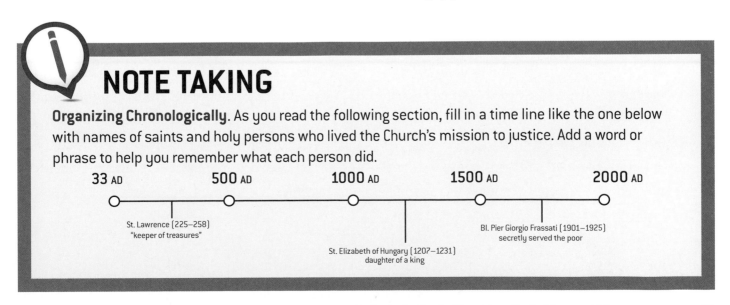

NOTE TAKING

Organizing Chronologically. As you read the following section, fill in a time line like the one below with names of saints and holy persons who lived the Church's mission to justice. Add a word or phrase to help you remember what each person did.

33 AD	500 AD	1000 AD	1500 AD	2000 AD

St. Lawrence (225–258)
"keeper of treasures"

St. Elizabeth of Hungary (1207–1231)
daughter of a king

Bl. Pier Giorgio Frassati (1901–1925)
secretly served the poor

"Laundry Love" is a ministry in Huntington Beach, California, that collects money for detergent and quarters so that the poor can wash their clothes at a local laundromat. Said one volunteer: "It is probably the best way to be involved in other people's lives, not just handing out food in a soup kitchen, or whatever. We get to know them very well, and that's probably the best part of this whole deal."

hungry, and you could give it to no one. You clothe the naked person. Would that all were clothed and this necessity did not exist."[5]

St. Thomas Aquinas, in his famous *Summa Theologiae,* wrote extensively on justice; his wisdom from the thirteenth century is the basis for many of the Church's modern-day teachings on justice.

Other Catholics—men and women, ordained, religious, and laypeople—have set remarkable examples for their service to justice. Read and view the photo essay detailing the lives of some of these remarkable saints on pages 46–47.

The Magisterium Responds to Justice Issues

The Magisterium, the official teaching office of the Church, has decried injustice from the earliest centuries to the present. For example, consider a few of the many issues the Church has spoken out about (e.g., in encyclicals, documents, letters, and audiences) in recent times:

- human trafficking
- universal access to health care (as part of the principle of the human destination of goods)
- immigration reform
- religious persecution of all kinds
- war
- the protection of life in the womb

Through the ebb and flow of history, the Church never neglected Jesus' call to compassion. As the structure of the Church became more organized throughout the centuries and thrived under the direction of Church leadership, she established hospitals, homes for battered women, orphanages, a school system that educated the poor, homes for the aged and dying, and countless other institutions that addressed people's needs. In fact, many of the world's leading human service agencies have their roots in the Church's mission to serve the needy. One such example is Catholic Charities, which is the largest private charitable organization in the United States, raising countless millions of dollars in support of those in need. Similarly, Catholic Relief Services, founded in 1943 by the Catholic Bishops of the United States to serve World War II survivors in Europe, now reaches more than 100 million people in ninety-one countries on five continents.

Anti-war protestors march in a rally in Washington, DC

MEN AND WOMEN LIVING JUSTLY IN CHURCH HISTORY

The Church's formal teachings on justice and charity have been embodied in the lives of countless saints throughout the ages. Here is a small sampling of the innumerable saints who gave their lives to the Church's mission of social justice.

ST. LAWRENCE (225–258)

St. Lawrence lived during the persecution of Christians by Emperor Valerian, in which many Christians were being sentenced to death without a trial. The Prefect of Rome seemed to think the Church had hidden wealth, so he demanded that Lawrence—a deacon whose title was "keeper of the treasures of the church"—hand over the riches. Lawrence spent three days gathering all of the poor and neglected in the area, brought them to the prefect, and announced: "This is the Church's treasure!" St. Lawrence was burned on a gridiron for the act.

ST. ELIZABETH OF HUNGARY (1207–1231)

The daughter of the king of Hungary, St. Elizabeth devoted herself to a life of simplicity. She gave food to the poor who would come to the gate of her home. Upon her husband's death, she gave up all of her earthly possessions to become a Secular Franciscan. She founded a hospital and spent the remainder of her days serving the sick.

ST. MARTIN DE PORRES (1579–1639)

Born in Peru to a Spanish father and a freed slave of African descent, St. Martin was a lay Dominican. Martin and other Dominicans lived in extreme frugality, so they would have more provisions for the sick in the monastery infirmary, where St. Martin primarily worked. As a person of mixed race, he was often persecuted. He offered all of the ridicule up to God as a sacrifice.

ST. ELIZABETH ANN SETON (1774–1821)

St. Elizabeth was the first American-born canonized saint. She was a convert to Catholicism. After her husband passed away, Elizabeth took religious vows and helped found the first free Catholic schools in America as well as two orphanages.

ST. GASPAR (1786–1837)

In the nineteenth century, St. Gaspar founded the Congregation of the Most Precious Blood. He and his priests went to the most dangerous areas of Italian cities and preached the Gospel. They also served the needs of the most vulnerable, especially the sick and impoverished.

BL. FRÉDÉRIC OZANAM (1813–1853)

A great academic, Bl. Frédéric Ozanam realized he needed his intellectual faith to be concretized in his life. He founded an organization to serve the poor modeled on the life and work of St. Vincent de Paul, naming it the St. Vincent de Paul Society. The organization is active around the world in the service of the poor today.

ST. KATHARINE DREXEL (1858–1955)

St. Katharine gave up her inherited fortune to devote her life to the disadvantaged persons in the United States, especially Native Americans and African Americans. During her lifetime, the religious community she founded established more than sixty schools. Most were devoted to educating Native and African Americans.

BL. PIER GIORGIO FRASSATI (1901–1925)

Although he was born into privilege with agnostic parents, Bl. Pier Giorgio Frassati led a life of deep prayer and simplicity. He drew many people to himself through his cheerful disposition and vibrant personality. His sister said of him: "Catholic social teaching could never remain simply a theory with Pier." He was politically active, but even more, Pier Giorgio humbly spent time in the slums to serve the neediest of his city. He gave away his food, clothing, and anything those in need would ask of him. Upon Pier's death from polio, which he contracted from working with the poor, his parents were shocked to see the thousands of people who turned out for his funeral. Many of them were the poor and needy Pier had served.

ST. GIANNA BERETTA MOLLA (1922–1962)

St. Gianna is known for upholding the dignity of life, even at its very beginnings. As a wife, mother, and doctor, St. Gianna saw her work in the medical profession as truly a mission, and she gave special attention to mothers, babies, and the elderly. Her pregnancy with her fourth child had complications. She chose to forgo measures that would save her life but endanger the life of her unborn child. She insisted, "If you must decide between me and the child, do not hesitate: choose the child. I insist on it. Save him." Soon after giving birth to a daughter, she passed away.

DOROTHY DAY (1897–1980)

Once an atheist and socialist, Dorothy Day was drawn to the Catholic Church as "the church of the immigrants, the church of the poor," and converted to Catholicism. She lived a life of solidarity with the poor. She began the Catholic Worker movement, the hallmark of which was a newspaper to make public the social teaching of the Church and suggest ways to transform society in peaceful, just ways. She fought for civil rights and preached nonviolence, especially against the arms race. She was a voice of conscience that called Catholics to works of justice, for "comforting the afflicted and afflicting the comfortable."

BL. MOTHER TERESA OF CALCUTTA (1910–1997)

In the modern world, Bl. Mother Teresa is synonymous with charitable works. A woman of deep prayer and holiness, she founded the Missionaries of Charity. Depending completely on the providence of God, Mother Teresa and her religious sisters served those experiencing dire poverty, no matter how deplorable their state seemed, and treated them with utmost dignity, respect, and compassion. The Missionaries of Charity continue this work around the world today.

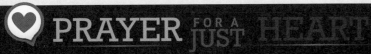

PRAYER FOR A JUST HEART

Ask for the intercession of these great saints by writing a prayer in your journal or notebook to help you commit to a life of justice and charity.

SECTION ASSESSMENT

NOTE TAKING

Refer to your time line of saints and holy people committed to social justice to complete the following assignment.

1. Name four saints committed to social justice who interest you the most. Tell what attracts you to their stories.

CRITICAL THINKING

2. What are some common themes in the lives and work of the saints mentioned in this section?

RESEARCH

3. Research more about the lives of the saints you listed in your response to the Note Taking assignment above. Answer the following question: How did the particular time periods in which those saints and holy people lived influence their paths to sainthood?

SECTION 3
Catholic Social Teaching in the Modern World

MAIN IDEA
The Church has developed systematized Catholic social teaching to meet the particular needs of the modern world.

The past 150 years have seen extraordinary development in the Church's body of social doctrine. The body of documents that forms modern Catholic social teaching is detailed on pages 51–54. The documents remind you and all people that working for justice is an essential dimension of Christian living and that ignoring it is sinful. For example, to treat a person with a disability with less respect than any other person is sinful. Not to speak out against corporate practices that put profits ahead of people is wrong. Ignoring government policies that increase defense budgets while slashing aid programs for the needy is immoral in most circumstances. Correcting such behavior requires a change of heart, repentance, and restitution when necessary. Pope Paul VI reminded the Church that the "teaching and spreading of her social doctrine are part of the Church's evangelizing mission."[6]

The Development of Modern Catholic Social Teaching

The body of the Church's modern social teaching that Catholics study, learn from, and put into practice originates with Pope Leo XIII (1810–1903; pope from 1878

NOTE TAKING

Summarizing Key Points. Create a wheel like the one here with the seven themes from the USCCB document *Sharing Catholic Social Teaching*. In the appropriate writing bubbles, write a word or two for each principle to remind you of its meaning.

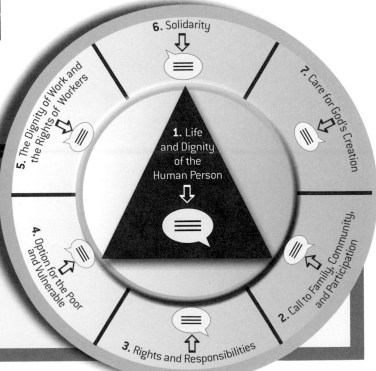

to 1903). With the nineteenth century's Industrial Revolution and "its new structures for the production of consumer goods, its new concept of society, the state and authority, and its new forms of labor and ownership," (*CCC*, 2421) new offenses against human dignity, most notably in the abuse of workers, emerged.

Pope Leo XIII lived at a time when the ideas of Karl Marx (1818–1883) were gaining a strong following among the world's working masses. Marx was reacting to the abuses of laissez-faire **capitalism**, an unbridled economic system that so often exploited workers simply for profits. In particular, industrial barons often trampled on workers' rights. Little or no social security system existed for retired workers. Workers were denied decent wages and reasonable working hours. Pensions, health insurance, and so many other rights were unheard of. Marx preached revolt against these deplorable conditions. He claimed a workers' paradise, a utopia, would result from his ideas, which were labeled *Marxism*. In his view, the state should see to it that everyone would be treated equally.

Pope Leo XIII saw in *both* Marxism and unbridled capitalism tremendous dangers for the individual dignity of people. He believed that Marx's brand of **socialism** subordinated the individual to the state, thus undermining human dignity. This fear proved well founded when atheistic **communism**, a descendant of

Pope Leo XIII

Marxism, took hold in the former Soviet Union and its satellite nations in the twentieth century. In 1891, Pope Leo wrote an encyclical entitled *Rerum Novarum* ("On Capital and Labor") to condemn the abuses of both Marxist socialism and unbridled capitalism. This encyclical became a benchmark. The document is summarized on page 51. In addition to the brief summary given here, you can read this important document in its entirety online. It is available at the Vatican website. Since its publication, many papal encyclicals and statements from the Church's Magisterium have addressed social justice issues. In addition, the Second Vatican Council issued the Pastoral Constitution *Gaudium et Spes* ("On the Church in the Modern World"), which addressed the dignity and rights of all people.

Take some time to survey the Catholic Church's key social justice documents on pages 51–54. Rooted in Sacred Scripture and Sacred Tradition, these teachings help form the core of Catholic social teaching.

capitalism An economic and political system in which trade and industry are controlled by private owners for profit.

socialism A social-economic system based on the common ownership of the means of production and exchange of wealth.

communism A social or political system in which all economic and social activity is controlled by a totalitarian government dominated by a single political party.

CATHOLIC SOCIAL TEACHING

DOCUMENTS

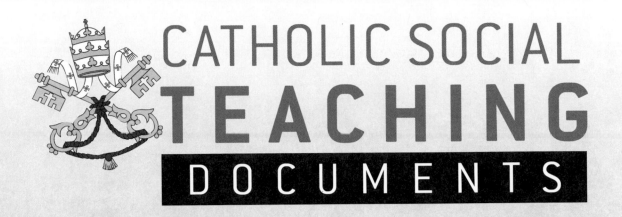

POPE LEO XIII

1891

Rerum Novarum
("On Capital and Labor")

- historical context: the effects of the Industrial Revolution
- addresses the dignity of the worker
- looks at the rights and obligations of both workers and employers
- upholds right to private property
- condemns socialism and unrestrained capitalism

POPE PIUS XI

1931 40TH ANNIVERSARY OF *RERUM NOVARUM*

Quadragesimo Anno ("On the Reconstruction of the Social Order")

- historical context: immediately after the economic crisis of 1929; post-World War I, in which totalitarian regimes are gaining power in many European countries
- expands *Rerum Novarum's* look at work, in light of current conditions
- introduces the principle of subsidiarity
- looks at not only the needs of the worker, but also the family

ST. JOHN XXIII

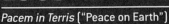

70TH ANNIVERSARY OF *RERUM NOVARUM* ## 1961

Mater et Magistra
("On Christianity and Social Progress")

- the historical context: post-war recovery and the beginnings of decolonization
- explains how the social question involves relations between countries
- focuses on community and socialization
- denounces the disparity between rich and impoverished nations: instructs wealthier and more advanced countries to help those less so, but without oppression

1963

Pacem in Terris ("Peace on Earth")

- historical context: development of the nuclear age
- first time a Church document is addressed to "all people of good will" (not just Catholics)
- details rights and responsibilities between people, between individuals and the state, and the global community
- reiterates importance of the common good and addresses the problems with the arms race

VATICAN II

1965

Gaudium et Spes
("On the Church in
the Modern World")

- focuses on the human person as the starting point for all society and its structures—cultural, economic, political, familial
- emphasizes the importance of the Church in dialogue with the world

POPE PAUL VI

1967

Populorum Progressio
("On the Development of Peoples")

- builds upon *Gaudium et Spes*'s teachings on economic and social life
- teaches about the development, progress of humans in all their capacities, but not just economically and technologically, but also the cultural and social capacities, most especially the capacity to know God
- encourages international relations

SYNOD OF BISHOPS

1971

Justicia in Mundo
("Justice in the World")

- defines justice as an essential ingredient of the Gospel and the Church's mission
- cites modern injustices, especially against the poor and powerless for whom the Church should speak in a special way
- encourages the Church itself to be an exemplar of justice in the way it treats its own members

1971 | 80TH ANNIVERSARY OF *RERUM NOVARUM*

Octogesima Adveniens
("A Call to Action")

- focuses on issues such as urbanization, the condition of young people, the condition of women, unemployment, discrimination, emigration, population growth, influence of social communications, ecological problems
- says that ideologies alone are not enough to answer these problems

ST. JOHN PAUL II

90TH ANNIVERSARY OF *RERUM NOVARUM* | 1981

Laborem Exercens
("On Human Work")

- a theological and philosophical reflection on work
- stresses that work is a fundamental expression of the human person
- explains that work has dignity, in that it aids in fulfilling the human vocation

1987 | 20TH ANNIVERSARY OF *POPULORUM PROGRESSIO*

Sollicitudo Rei Socialis
("On Social Concern")

- reiterates that true development involves not just goods and services, but rather that it must contribute to the development of one's humanity, especially his moral nature
- explains how many of the hopes of *Populorum Progressio* have not been fulfilled, especially in the great disparity of wealth between nations
- calls out "structures of sin" within nations—condemns the West for materialism and the East for attacks on basic human dignities

1991
100TH ANNIVERSARY OF *RERUM NOVARUM*

Centesimus Annus
("On the Hundredth Year")

- historical context: collapse of communism in many countries
- emphasizes solidarity, or "social charity"
- looks at the "new things" that have emerged socially in the one hundred years since *Rerum Novarum*
- condemns socialistic countries for their atheistic view of the human person
- supports free markets, but condemns unbridled consumerism

PROMULGATED BY ST. JOHN PAUL II
1992
20TH ANNIVERSARY OF *POPULORUM PROGRESSIO*

The Catechism of the Catholic Church

- a compendium of Catholic doctrine on faith and morals that serves Catholics as a norm for teaching the faith and as an authentic reference text
- offers a succinct presentation of the Church's teachings on social justice in both the introduction to the Ten Commandments and specifically in the treatment of the Seventh and Tenth commandments

1995
Evangelium Vitae ("The Gospel of Life")

- reiterates the most important human right; namely, the right to life
- addresses specific attacks against human life, such as abortion, euthanasia, and capital punishment

1998
Fides et Ratio ("Faith and Reason")

- explains the connection between faith and reason in searching for truth
- shows how the search for knowledge is a search for God, and that Christians find the ultimate meaning in life in the Paschal Mystery of Christ
- warns against some modern philosophies that lead to nihilism, which denies ultimate truth, and states firmly that humans have the ability to find the truth

PONTIFICAL COUNCIL FOR JUSTICE AND PEACE
2004
Compendium of the Social Doctrine of the Church

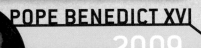

- offers a summary of the Church's social teaching, addressing and analyzing economic, political, and social realities

POPE BENEDICT XVI
2009
Caritas in Veritate ("In Charity and Truth")

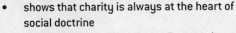

- shows that charity is always at the heart of social doctrine
- draws much upon *Populorum Progressio*
- highlights that truth is key to the development of peoples; it always must be aimed at the common good
- explains that a spirit of gratitude to God is necessary in our economic world

Pope Francis's first encyclical *Lumen Fidei* ("The Light of Faith"), 2013, is not explicitly connected to social justice themes, though from faith always comes the practice of charity. "Faith is no refuge for the fainthearted, but something which enhances our lives," Pope Francis wrote. "It makes us aware of a magnificent calling, the vocation of love. It assures us that this love is trustworthy and worth embracing, for it is based on God's faithfulness which is stronger than our every weakness."

PASTORAL LETTERS

The Catholic bishops of the United States have issued numerous letters to the Catholic of the United States on issues of social justice. The following chart lists a few of these letters, with a brief summary of each.

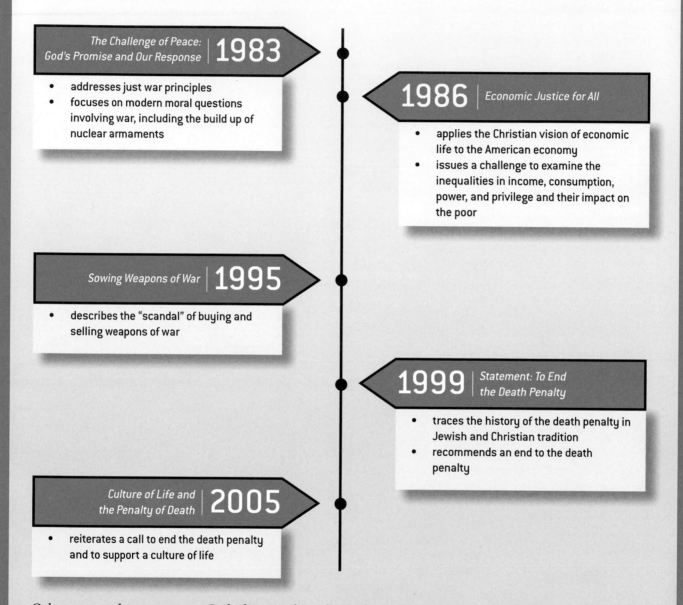

The Challenge of Peace: God's Promise and Our Response | 1983
- addresses just war principles
- focuses on modern moral questions involving war, including the build up of nuclear armaments

1986 | Economic Justice for All
- applies the Christian vision of economic life to the American economy
- issues a challenge to examine the inequalities in income, consumption, power, and privilege and their impact on the poor

Sowing Weapons of War | 1995
- describes the "scandal" of buying and selling weapons of war

1999 | Statement: To End the Death Penalty
- traces the history of the death penalty in Jewish and Christian tradition
- recommends an end to the death penalty

Culture of Life and the Penalty of Death | 2005
- reiterates a call to end the death penalty and to support a culture of life

Other recent documents on Catholic social teaching also merit mention and encourage you to deeper reading: the Christmas message of Pope Pius XII (1942), the Second Vatican Council's *Dignitatis Humanae* ("Declaration on Religious Freedom," 1965), Pope Paul VI's *Evangelii Nuntiandi* ("Evangelization in the Modern World," 1975), St. John Paul II's *Redemptor Hominis* ("Redeemer of Mankind," 1979) and *Dives in Misericordia* ("Rich in Mercy," 1980), the Congregation of the Doctrine of Faith's *The Participation of Catholics in Political Life* (2002), Pope Benedict XVI's *Spe Salvi* ("In Hope We Are Saved," 2007), statements from the Vatican's Peace and Justice Commission, key documents of other national and regional conferences of bishops, and the like.

The Seven Themes of Catholic Social Teaching

Another important organizational thread of Catholic social teaching will be used as an outline for the remaining chapters of this text. These seven themes are a good summary of the Church's social teaching. They are drawn from a 1998 document of the United States Conference of Catholic Bishops titled *Sharing Catholic Social Teaching: Challenges and Directions—Reflections of the US Catholic Bishops*. The seven principles are briefly introduced in the next subsections.

1. Life and Dignity of the Human Person

A person in every stage of human life—womb to tomb—is precious and worthy of respect and protection. Unless human life is treated as sacred and respected as such, there is no way for a society to be just. "Every person, from the moment of conception to natural death, has inherent dignity and a right to life consistent with that dignity" (*Sharing*, 1–2).

2. Call to Family, Community, and Participation

This principle states: "In a global culture driven by excessive individualism, our tradition proclaims that the person is not only sacred but social. . . . The family is the central social institution that must be supported and strengthened, not undermined. . . . We believe people have a right and duty to participate in society, seeking together the common good and well-being of all" (*Sharing*, 4–5).

Related to this principle, governments must guarantee and protect human life and dignity and promote the common good and well-being of all citizens, especially the poor and weak of society.

3. Rights and Responsibilities

"The Catholic tradition teaches that human dignity can be protected and a healthy community can be achieved only if human rights are protected and responsibilities are met" (*Sharing*, 5). The essential fundamental right is the right to life—the right that makes all other rights possible. Every person also has a right to the necessities that make for human decency—religion and family life, food and shelter, education and a job, and health care. Rights have corresponding responsibilities to family members, to friends and neighbors, and to the larger society.

4. Option for the Poor and Vulnerable

Jesus taught in the parable of the Last Judgment (see Mt 25:31–46) that the needs of the poor and vulnerable must come first. Why? The principle of the common good and an authentic response to our Christian vocation requires that the poor must be protected, or society will fragment and all will suffer. The poor and vulnerable person, as a brother or sister, is Christ in disguise; all people deserve respect, the protection of their rights, and the ability to participate and to share in God's good creation. In other words, they deserve justice. The most basic test of the justness of a society is the answer to this question: "How are our most vulnerable members doing?"

5. The Dignity of Work and the Rights of Workers

Work helps people to make a living so that they might participate in the life that God has given them. The purpose of the economy is to serve the people, not the other way around. The dignity of work is safeguarded when workers' rights are respected. These rights include having productive work, decent and fair wages, union participation, private property, and economic initiative. "Respecting these rights promotes an economy that protects human life, defends human rights, and advances the well-being of all" (*Sharing*, 5).

6. Solidarity

Catholic teaching requires a commitment to the common good—the good of each and every person. Why? "Because we are all really responsible for all," St. John Paul II explained in *Sollicitudo Rei Socialis* ("On Social Concern"). All people are members of the same human family (*SRS*, §38). Therefore, the principle of **solidarity** helps to remind you and everyone else "that we are our brothers' and sisters' keepers, wherever they live. . . . 'Loving our neighbor' has global dimensions in an interdependent world" (*Sharing*, 5). Also, the principle of solidarity requires all people to work for peace and justice in a world marked by violence and war.

7. Care for God's Creation

Care for God's creation, or **stewardship**, refers to the proper use of the gifts God has given to humankind, in particular, the care for creation that will allow the earth and its resources to flourish and be long-lasting. The document states: "We are called to protect people and the planet, living our faith in relationship with all of God's creation" (*Sharing*, 6). In short, you can show respect for God by being good stewards of the earth.

Two Other Principles of Catholic Social Teaching

In addition to the seven themes of Catholic social teaching, two others appear frequently in Catholic social teaching.

First, the principle of *equal dignity* holds that although people have different talents, all have the same fundamental dignity as God's children, made in his image and likeness. Therefore, any form of discrimination or prejudice that contradicts the rights that

flow from this equality is unjust. (What it means to be equal in dignity is examined in Chapter 3.)

Second, the principle of **subsidiarity** deals with "the responsibilities and limits of government, and the essential roles of voluntary organizations" (*Sharing*, 6). Under the principle of subsidiarity, the lowest level of an organization should handle a function if it is capable of doing so without the higher level intruding. The idea is that individuals or groups closer to the problems should be given the first opportunity to solve them without higher levels (e.g., the government) intruding. Subsidiarity will be examined at length in Chapter 5.

In whatever way the fundamental principles of Catholic social teaching are organized, it is important to always keep in mind the relationship of each principle to human dignity. As the United States Conference of Catholic Bishops pointed out in *Sharing Catholic Social Teaching*:

> These principles build on the foundation of Catholic social teaching: the dignity of human life. This central Catholic principle requires that you measure every policy, every institution, and every action by whether it protects human life and enhances human dignity, especially for the poor and vulnerable. (6)

solidarity The virtue of social charity, friendship, and responsible sharing whereby the interdependence among all people is recognized.

stewardship The proper use of the gifts God has given us, in particular, the care for creation that will allow the earth and its resources to flourish and last for future generations.

subsidiarity The moral principle that large organizations or governments should not interfere with, or take over, responsibilities that can be administered by individuals and local organizations, but rather should support them, always with a focus on the common good.

SECTION ASSESSMENT

NOTE TAKING

Use the wheel with themes of Catholic social teaching to answer the following questions.

1. Which theme of Catholic social teaching interests you the most? Why?

2. Which theme of Catholic social teaching seems most difficult to follow? Explain.

COMPREHENSION

Regarding the first modern encyclical of Catholic social teaching:

3. What was its title?

4. When was it written?

5. Who wrote it?

6. What were the historical reasons it was needed?

APPLICATION

7. Review the chart on pages 51–54. Identify at least four themes common to all the documents.

Section Summaries

Focus Question

How can you participate in the Church's ministry of service?

Complete one of the following:

 Explain how you can bring Catholic social teaching to the various societies to which you belong: your family, your school, your local community, and your country.

 Carefully read the parable of the Last Judgment (see Mt 25:31–46). Which phrases did you connect with the most? Why? How does Jesus' command in this parable apply to practical service in the world today? Explain.

 Investigate papal encyclicals and the documents of the Second Vatican Council at www.vatican.va and statements of the United States Conference of Catholic Bishops at www.usccb.org. Write three "notable quotes" on some aspect of the Church's social teaching that you found in one or more documents at these sites. Tell how you can apply these quotes to your own practice of social justice. Be sure to note the original source of the quote.

INTRODUCTION (PAGES 33–36)

Roots of Catholic Social Teaching

As a light to humanity, the Church has developed her social teaching to guide all people through their social relations here on earth, with the ultimate aim of a life of communion in Heaven. Catholic social teaching is rooted in Scripture and Tradition, and in the natural law. The natural law is the moral knowledge every human person innately possesses. It is universal, permanent, and unchanging.

 Cite two examples of the natural law being violated in today's society. Explain your choices.

SECTION 1 (PAGES 37–42)

The Scriptural Roots of Justice

Throughout Salvation History, God's justice and your call to model this justice is evident. It culminates in Christ, who is both the example of justice and the Way to it.

 Carefully read the parable of the Good Samaritan (Lk 10:30–37). In what ways do you identify with each of the various characters in the story (the victim, the passersby, the Samaritan)? Give personal examples to support your answers.

SECTION 2 (PAGES 43–48)

Justice in Sacred Tradition

The call to practice justice was not limited to Christ's first disciples or to the early Church. The Church has served the most vulnerable in society throughout her history. This practice of justice through love for others is seen most visibly in the lives of the saints.

 Name at least four ways in your daily life that you can emulate the lives of the saints you learned about in this section.

SECTION 3 (PAGES 49–57)

Catholic Social Teaching in the Modern World

In response to the unique social challenges of the modern era, the Church has developed a body of social teaching to guide the people of God in responding to these challenges.

 Look up the text of *Rerum Novarum* at www.vatican.va. Read paragraph 37 and write a two-sentence summary of the paragraph.

Chapter Assignments

Choose and complete at least one of the following three assignments to assess your understanding of the material in this chapter.

1. Helpers of the Poor

 Create a notebook listing Catholic religious orders and communities whose primary apostolate is to serve the poor. You should include at least five different communities. For each community, address the following:

- Who is the community's founder? When was it founded? Where?

- What kind of work does the community do?

- How many professed members does it have?

- In what parts of the world does the community serve?

- Other interesting facts about the community.

2. Identifying Rights and Responsibilities

 Read Sections 11 to 36 of St. John XXIII's encyclical *Pacem in Terris*. You can access the document at www.vatican.va. List five rights discussed in these sections and five corresponding responsibilities. Next, list three rights necessary to ensure a peaceful and cooperative atmosphere at your school and their corresponding responsibilities. What would it take for students at your school to live up to the responsibilities for each right?

3. Living Examples of Social Teaching Principles

 Create a multimedia presentation of the seven themes of Catholic social teaching (see pages 55–56). In the presentation, identify a Catholic saint, either from this chapter or not, who embodies each theme. Follow these instructions:

- Use a different saint for each theme.

- Make one slide for each theme that includes these elements: the name of the theme, the name of the saint, a quote from the saint or a brief description of his or her work, and a photo or portrait of the person.

- In the Notes section of the multimedia presentation, include brief biographical information on the saint and notes about the theme he or she represents. Plan to share this information with your classmates.

Faithful Disciple

St. Peter Claver

Catholic social teaching looks at both the spiritual and physical needs of people; it embraces both charity and justice. St. Peter Claver embodied this unity of charity and justice.

Born in Verdu, Spain, Peter Claver studied at a Jesuit university and was ordained a Jesuit priest in 1616. St. Peter had a strong calling to serve the people of the New World. He answered this missionary call in 1610 by traveling to Cartagena, which is in modern-day Colombia.

Cartagena was near a major port for the African slaves arriving in South America; about ten thousand slaves arrived every year. St. Peter Claver was shocked by the treatment of the African people, who would be transported in deplorable conditions. Many died on the way or contracted terrible diseases.

St. Peter Claver begged for food to bring to the slaves. As soon as a ship arrived, he would go aboard with a translator and minister to every single African slave. Along with the food, he also provided medical care and worked diligently to meet the captives' other physical needs. Peter Claver dedicated himself

A stained glass window depicting a man kissing St. Peter Claver's hand.

by a special vow to the service of the African slaves brought to the New World. Along with ministering to the slaves, he called on their masters to treat them humanely and worked to bring an end to slavery.

Peter Claver's care for the slaves extended beyond their physical needs. He also attended to their spiritual care. He instructed them in the catechism and administered the sacraments. Through his efforts, more than three hundred thousand slaves received the Sacrament of Baptism.

St. Peter Claver worked unceasingly in the service of the enslaved Africans in Colombia for more than forty years, until his death in 1651. St. Peter Claver was canonized in 1888 by Pope Leo XIII. In 1896 Pope Leo declared him the patron of missionary work among all African peoples. His feast day is September 9.

Reading Comprehension

1. What were some of the abuses of human dignity the African captives endured?

2. How did St. Peter Claver meet both the physical and spiritual needs of the African slaves?

Writing Task

- In one of his journals, St. Peter Claver wrote about the African slaves: "This was how we spoke to them, not with words but with our hands and our actions." What do you think this means? How can you model this example in your own life? When *is* it necessary to speak with actions and not just words? Respond to these questions in a short essay or journal entry.

Explaining the Faith

What makes the actions of Christians different from nonreligious people who serve the poor or fight against other social injustices?

For a Christian, acts of love are indispensable, but they are merely one piece of a larger picture. The Christian performing works of charity or justice sees them as part of a higher calling, namely his or her own eternal Salvation and the Salvation of those served. An atheist does not have such an eternal destiny in mind.

For Christians the motivation to serve others is Christ himself. They are impelled by Christ's love and animated by his Holy Spirit. They understand that they are part of Christ's Body acting on earth. They follow Christ's commandment concerning love of neighbor, and also see Christ in the people whom they serve.

 ## Further Research

- Read paragraphs 62 and 75 from the *Compendium of the Social Doctrine of the Church*, which you can access at www.vatican.va. Write a one-paragraph explanation of this quotation: "Since the mystery of Christ illuminates the mystery of man, it gives fullness of meaning to human dignity and to the ethical requirements which defend it."

Prayer
Prayer for the Ability to Serve

Dearest Lord, may I see you today and every day in the person of your sick, and, while nursing them, minister unto you.

Though you hide yourself behind the unattractive disguise of the irritable, the exacting, the unreasonable, may I still recognize you, and say, "Jesus, my patient, how sweet it is to serve you."

Sweetest Lord, make me appreciative of the dignity of my high vocation, and its many responsibilities. Never permit me to disgrace it by giving way to coldness, unkindness, or impatience.

—Bl. Mother Teresa of Calcutta

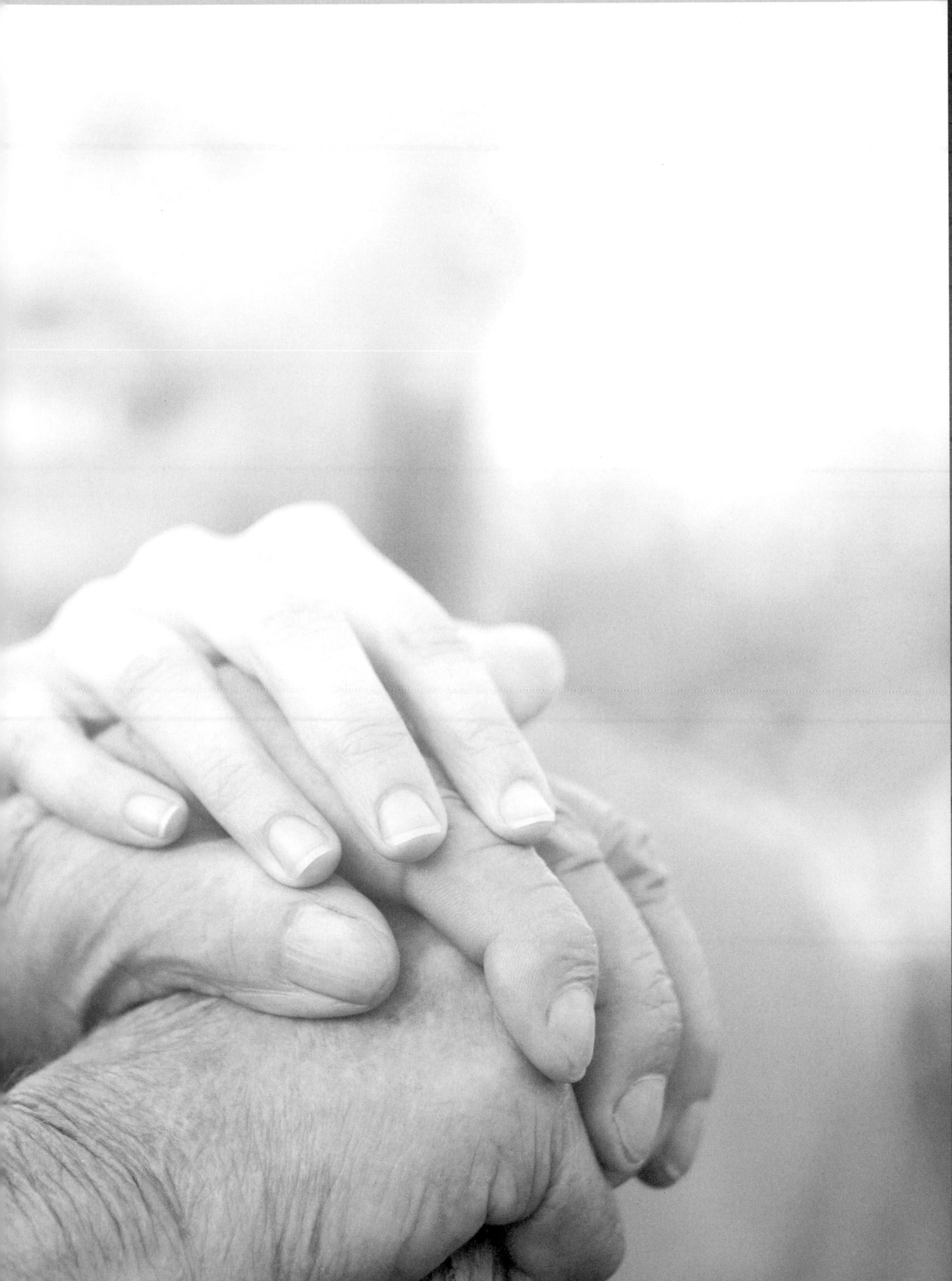

CHAPTER REVIEW

LIFE & DIGNITY
OF THE HUMAN PERSON

3

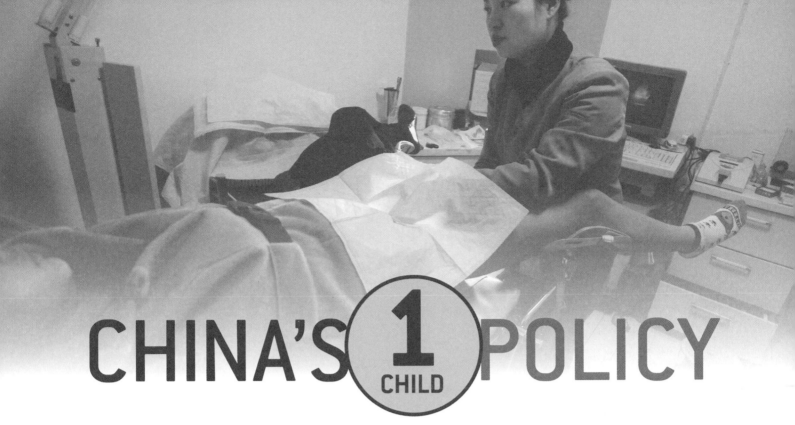

CHINA'S 1 CHILD POLICY

In 1979, China introduced a one-child policy, in which many families—especially those in urban areas—are limited to a single child. Failure to meet this requirement results in fines and other legal repercussions. Since its implementation, this policy has resulted in approximately 250 million fewer births in China through 2010. The policy has had strong demographic consequences as well, such as a disproportionate elderly population.

Also, because many couples want a male child, some choose to abort unborn baby girls. In fact, for every one hundred girls born in China, there are 119 boys. Again, this has drastically affected demographics: for example, it is predicted that by 2020, more than twenty-four million men in China will not be able to find a spouse to marry because of the gender imbalance.[1]

Another dramatic result of the one-child policy is numerous reports of women being forced to have abortions and undergo sterilizations. This reality made international news in June 2012 with the case of Feng Jianmei, a woman living in rural northwest China.

Feng was in her seventh month of pregnancy with her second daughter. She and her husband were asked to pay a fee of 40,000 yuan (about $6,000) for violating the one-child policy. They could not pay; as result, Feng was arrested. She was forced into signing an agreement for an abortion. She was held down and injected with a drug that killed her unborn child and induced a stillbirth labor. She said, "I could feel the baby jumping around inside me all the time, but then she went still."[2] Feng was traumatized both physically and emotionally from the incident.

Although this type of occurrence is reportedly widespread in China, Feng's case made international headlines because a photograph a family member took went viral. The photo depicted Feng lying unconscious in the hospital bed with her dead baby in a plastic bag next to her.

Although the one-child policy was eased in late 2013, strict regulations regarding childbearing are still in effect in China, often with severe and even inhumane measures taken to enforce them.

FOCUS QUESTION

How do you witness to the DIGNITY OF EVERY PERSON?

Chapter Overview

| Introduction | The Human Person |

| Section 1 | Abortion |

| Section 2 | Other Beginning-of-Life Issues |

| Section 3 | End-of-Life Concerns |

INTRODUCTION
The Human Person

It is only natural that the first theme of Catholic social teaching is the "life and dignity of the human person." There would be no norms for social behavior without people! This first theme appears to be in two parts (life *and* dignity), but you really can't have one without the other.

Consider, first, the simple right to life. Before you can even address the dignity due the human person, you must first be clear in your beliefs about the right for a human being to live. It is only when you understand the inherent dignity of *all* human life—from its earliest beginnings at conception to the final breath a person takes before death—that you can really appreciate the right to life itself.

As you recall from Chapter 1, God's image is reflected in each person, from the richest to the poorest, youngest to oldest, healthiest to most ill. God's image is reflected in both genders—male and female—and in every race and ethnicity. This gives each person inherent dignity and makes each person worthy of profound respect.

NOTE TAKING

Identifying Main Ideas. Create a two-column chart like the one below to help you organize the content in this section. Fill in the second column with further details. Add rows and ideas as needed.

MAIN IDEA	DESCRIPTION
The first theme of Catholic social teaching	
Definition of *personalistic norm*	
The root of equality among people	

The Personalistic Norm

A person with dignity is not to be a "means to an end," but rather is to be given the freedom, respect, and love he or she is due. This sacredness of the human person was affirmed in the Incarnation, when God became human in the person of Jesus Christ. This principle is sometimes referred to as the **personalistic norm**, which seeks to affirm the unique value of each human person in the world of nature.

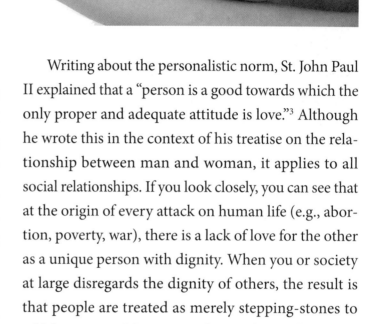

According to the personalistic norm, people are not just *there*, like rocks or plants. Instead, God created you and handed you over to yourself. Thus, you are your own person. Because of this, you can accept or reject things yourself. In freedom, you can, in a certain sense, create your own self. To truly respect you and others who make up a society, society has to step back and let you and everyone else live life as a self-determining being.

Psalm 139 expresses well the unique nature of each person:

> You formed my inmost being; you knit me in my mother's womb. I praise you, so wonderfully you made me; wonderful are your works! My very self you knew; my bones were not hidden from you, when I was being made in secret, fashioned as in the depths of the earth. (Ps 139:13–15)

> **personalistic norm** The principle that maintains that a person is to be treated as a unique individual, never a means to another's end.

Writing about the personalistic norm, St. John Paul II explained that a "person is a good towards which the only proper and adequate attitude is love."[3] Although he wrote this in the context of his treatise on the relationship between man and woman, it applies to all social relationships. If you look closely, you can see that at the origin of every attack on human life (e.g., abortion, poverty, war), there is a lack of love for the other as a unique person with dignity. When you or society at large disregards the dignity of others, the result is that people are treated as merely stepping-stones to selfish interests. This is not what God intended.

The ultimate end or ultimate purpose of society is not the society itself. The ultimate purposes of society are the lives of the people who make up the society. In other words, a person is never to be used for another's, or society's, gain. This is why slavery is wrong and sinful; it is also why blind loyalty to a government leader or ideology (consider Nazi Germany or contemporary North Korea) is wrong.

By asserting that the human person is the "ultimate end" of society, the Church teaches that people are the very purpose of society. Therefore, all other social activity—such as family life, work life, and political life—should always serve the dignity of the human person:

"Social justice can be obtained only in respecting the transcendent dignity of man" (*CCC*, 1929).

Applying the personalistic norm to Catholic social teaching means being less driven by "issues" than by the people affected by issues. For example, one should not be just concerned with "hunger," but rather with *the person who is hungry*. The personalistic norm in Catholic social teaching is not merely about being on a certain "side" of a controversial topic; instead, it is about vigilantly upholding the dignity of the human person in all of your social relationships.

Dignity and Equality

Because every man and woman is made in God's image and likeness and called to happiness in him, every person is equal *in dignity*. "Since something of the glory of God shines on the face of every person, the dignity of every person before God is the basis of the dignity of man before other men."[4] It is important to note that

Bethany Hamilton survived a shark attack while surfing in 2003. Her faith in God and story of perseverence have inspired many people. She was the subject of the 2011 movie Soul Surfer.

this dignity is inviolable; that means it can never be lost or taken away.

That said, your daily experiences show you that not everyone is equal in every aspect. For example, some people are more gifted in mathematics; some are more athletic. Some have been born into relative economic comfort with the opportunities that affords, others are born into poverty and the deprivation that accompanies it. Many people are born with physical or mental disabilities; some are born into environments of abuse or neglect. Some of these inequalities can be overcome through hard work and effort, others are permanent; some are the result of natural circumstances, others are the result of structures of sin.

These differences between people should never be the basis of discrimination, nor should they leave a person with a sense of inferiority or feeling condemned to a certain state of life. Instead, the differences should have a positive effect, by pointing to everyone's social nature. All people *need* others to recognize their God-given goodness to help them thrive. "These differences belong to God's plan, who wills that each receive what he needs from others, and that those endowed with particular 'talents' share the benefits with those who need them" (*CCC*, 1937).

Assaults on the Dignity of Human Life

Unfortunately, the equal dignity of every person is often ignored in today's world. Whether in everyday occurrences, such as in the gossiping of classmates or disrespect of a parent, or on a larger scale, such as child abuse or war, a lack of respect for the dignity of others persists.

The clearest assaults on the dignity of the human person are those that end the life of another. The Fifth Commandment states, "You shall not kill." This commandment prohibits murder, the deliberate killing of an innocent human being—an intrinsic evil; that is, an action that is always morally wrong. The Fifth Commandment also demands profound respect for the dignity of every human life. The remainder of the chapter will look at some of these attacks on the right to life and on the dignity of human life that are prohibited by the Fifth Commandment.

SECTION ASSESSMENT

NOTE TAKING

Use the notes from the chart you created to respond to the following items.

1. Explain the personalistic norm.

2. What is the root of everyone's equality?

3. What is the first theme of Catholic social teaching?

COMPREHENSION

4. What does the Church assert by teaching that the human person is the "ultimate end" of society?

JOURNAL

5. Describe an occasion from the past week when you recognized the dignity of another person and treated that person with respect.

CRITICAL THINKING

6. St. John Paul II wrote that a "person is a good towards which the only proper and adequate attitude is love." Connect this statement with the definition of the personalistic norm and explain its meaning.

SECTION 1
Abortion

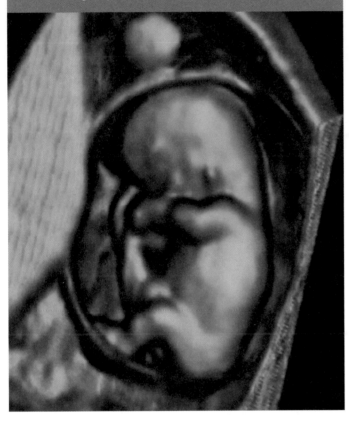

Every human person, no matter the stage of his or her development, has the right to life. The *Catechism of the Catholic Church* clearly states that

> Human life must be respected and protected absolutely from the moment of conception. From the first moment of his existence, a human being must be recognized as having the rights of a person—among which is the inviolable right of every innocent being to life. (*CCC*, 2270)

Nevertheless, human dignity is often denied at the earliest stages of life. Abortion is a horrendous outrage plaguing society. Each day in the United States, approximately 4,500 babies are aborted. **Abortion** is defined as ending a pregnancy before the child is born; more specifically, direct (intentional) abortion is "any destruction of the product of human conception, whether before or after implantation in the womb."[5]

The Church has never wavered in her stance against abortion. One of the earliest Christian catechisms, the *Didache*, written before AD 100, states: "You shall not kill the embryo by abortion and shall not cause the newborn to perish" (quoted in *CCC*, 2271). More recently, Bl. Pope Paul VI stated explicitly

abortion The deliberate termination of a pregnancy by killing the unborn child.

NOTE TAKING

Finish the Sentences. Copy the following sentences in your notebook. As you read the section, fill in the missing words.

- Human life must be respected and protected absolutely from the moment of ___.
- Every human person, no matter the stage of his or her ___, has the right to life.
- The mind-set and language of abortion are part of a "culture of ___."
- The obligation to protect innocent life is derived from the ___ law.
- Abortion is never morally correct because killing an innocent human person is always an ___ evil.

that because the unique individuality of a human person is present at the moment of conception, abortion is condemned:

> From the time that the ovum is fertilized, a life is begun which is neither that of the father nor of the mother, it is rather the life of a new human being with his own growth. It would never be made human if it were not human already. . . . Divine law and natural reason, therefore, exclude all right to the direct killing of an innocent man. ("Declaration on Procured Abortion," 3, 14)

You likely cannot escape news about abortion. At your age, you may have a classmate or friend who has had an abortion or has considered having an abortion. It is important to know as much information about the recent history of abortion, especially in the United States, and the procedure for aborting children. First, consider these basic realities about abortion:

MAIN TYPES OF ABORTION

Suction aspiration is the abortion technique used in most first-trimester abortions. This technique inserts into the mother's womb a powerful suction tube with a sharp cutting edge. This device dismembers the body of the baby and tears the placenta from the uterine wall, sucking blood, amniotic fluid, placental tissue, and fetal parts into a collection bottle.[6]

Salt poisoning (saline amniocentesis) is often used to abort babies after sixteen weeks of pregnancy. A needle is inserted through the mother's abdomen to withdraw amniotic fluid and replace it with a solution of concentrated salt. The baby breathes in, swallows the salt, and dies, usually within an hour. The saline solution also causes painful burning and deterioration of the baby's skin. The mother goes into labor about thirty-three to thirty-five hours after instillation of the salt and delivers a dead, burned, shriveled baby.[7]

Human life begins from the time the ovum is fertilized. Further, genetic studies have shown that a new human being—genetically distinct from both mother and father—has begun the process of his or her growth at the moment of conception. This new human life demands protection, rights, and dignity. As the Vatican's *Declaration on Procured Abortion* emphatically states, "Any discrimination based on the various stages of life is no more justified than any other discrimination."[12]

This question thus emerges: how did the United States get into this position where so many innocent lives are legally murdered every year?

History of Abortion in the United States

You know that the abortion issue is a polarizing one in the United States. But did you realize that until 1965, *all* US states had laws *banning* abortion? It wasn't until the late 1960s that some states began loosening restrictions against surgical abortion. More laws restricting

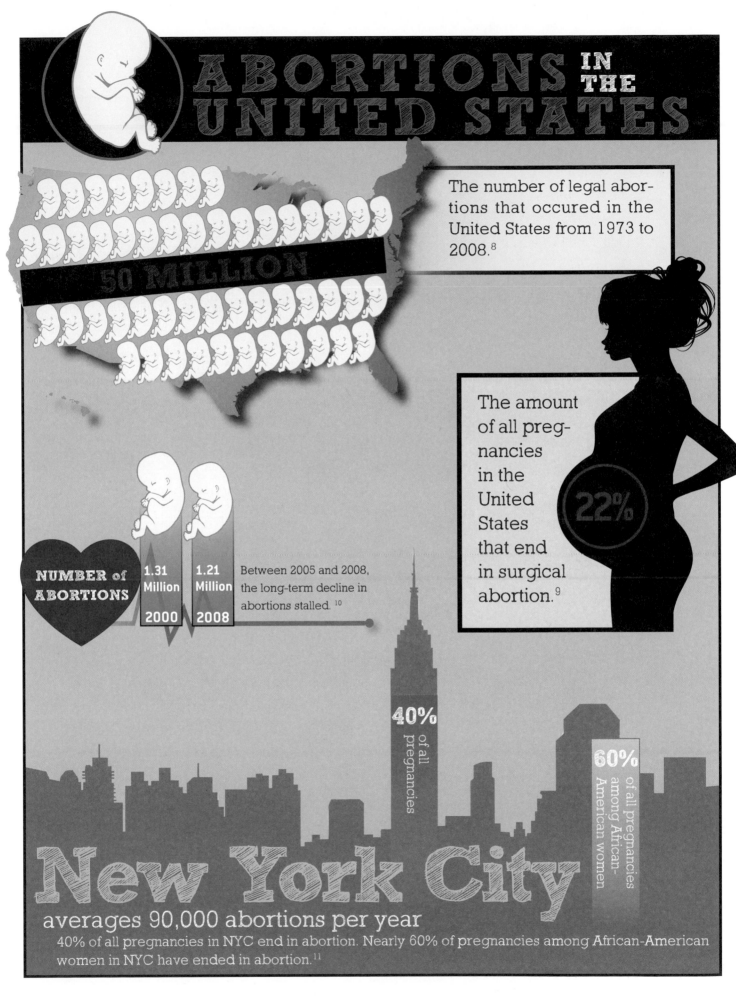

ABORTIONS IN THE UNITED STATES

50 MILLION

The number of legal abortions that occured in the United States from 1973 to 2008.[8]

The amount of all pregnancies in the United States that end in surgical abortion.[9]

22%

NUMBER of ABORTIONS

1.31 Million — 2000

1.21 Million — 2008

Between 2005 and 2008, the long-term decline in abortions stalled. [10]

40% of all pregnancies

60% of all pregnancies among African-American women

New York City

averages 90,000 abortions per year

40% of all pregnancies in NYC end in abortion. Nearly 60% of pregnancies among African-American women in NYC have ended in abortion.[11]

abortion were challenged, which led to the landmark Supreme Court decision, *Roe v. Wade,* in 1973. The court held that a woman's right to privacy includes her decision to have an abortion.

Norma McCorvey (on right), the plaintiff in the Roe v. Wade *lawsuit that legalized abortion, spoke out for the rights of the unborn in the office of US Representative Nancy Pelosi in 2009. She told Rep. Pelosi, "Roe versus Wade is a bad law and I'm sorry that I ever did it. But I've been healed and I'm a Catholic now, and I know my place in the pro-life movement."*

This case declared abortion a constitutional right in the United States, a country that had always prided itself on defending the weak. It is interesting to note that the original litigant in this famous case, Jane Roe—whose real name is Norma McCorvey—converted to Catholicism in 1998. She is now dedicating her life to reversing the infamous case that legalized abortion.[13]

Currently, abortion is still legal within the United States, with specific laws regulating it varying by state. Abortion policies in the United States are among the most permissive of any industrialized nation of the West.

Factors That Lead to Abortion

The mind-set and language that promote and praise unlimited freedom of choice, individualism that disregards responsibility to others, and a demand to an absolute right to privacy, is very present today. This worldview is supported by the news media, accepted in movie and television program plots, and sung about in popular music. All of this helps to make up a "culture of death" that does not guarantee life to those who most depend on others to protect them.

Related to these factors, disrespect for the sanctity of life leading to abortion can be traced to two major factors:[14]

1. Breakdown of the family. Recall the words of St. John Paul II in *Evangelium Vitae* that the family is the "sanctuary of life."[15] The family teaches fidelity, loyalty, and devotion to those who are young and old, disabled or sick; that is, to those who depend on others for their very existence.

Yet, contemporary society has undermined the family, changing traditional views on marriage and divorce. Today, marriage is often seen as optional for couples who live together, even for those who want to be parents. The legal system has also largely allowed people to divorce for virtually any reason, expanding the grounds for divorce far beyond the serious offenses of adultery, abuse, and desertion.

AN ARGUMENT AGAINST ABORTION THAT APPEALS TO REASON

Most people would agree that killing an innocent human life is a moral wrong. A trickier issue involves defining the meaning of human life. The Church teaches, and modern science agrees, that human life begins at the moment of conception. Would you be able to explain why this is true? Use the acronym SLED—size, level of development, environment, and degree of dependency—to help you make a good argument that an unborn baby (known scientifically as a zygote, blastocyst, embryo, and fetus) and a born baby are both human persons. The acronym can help you explain why.

S L E D

- *Size.* A small child is no less human than an adult. An extremely tall NBA player is no more human than someone of average height. No one would argue that harming a small child is less of a crime than harming a larger one; in fact, most would argue the opposite. That an unborn child is smaller than a born child has no bearing on his or her personhood.

- *Level of development.* An unborn child is certainly much less developed than a born baby. However, one's development does not determine one's personhood. For example, small children do not have fully developed reproductive systems. And a high school student is intellectually less developed than a college student. Does that make any of them "less" human? Of course not. Therefore, being less developed does not make an unborn baby less of a person.

- *Environment.* An unborn child is in a different environment than a born child. Nevertheless, *where* one is should not be the determining factor in *who* one is. Did you stop being you when you came to school this morning? What about when you walked from your bedroom to the kitchen? Then how does a journey of a few inches down the birth canal suddenly make an unborn baby human? Obviously, it does not. Therefore, environment has no bearing on an unborn baby's personhood.

- *Degree of dependency.* An unborn baby is undeniably dependent upon his or her mother. And yet, does being dependent upon someone or something make one less human? Even young children are completely dependent upon adults to survive. What about adults who are dependent upon medication or caregivers to live? No one would argue they are less human. Therefore, merely being dependent upon another does not make the unborn baby less of a person.

In short, the differences between an unborn infant and a born one are not morally relevant; they do not make the unborn less worthy of living than any other human.

Make a plan to share what you learned about the SLED acronym the next time you are questioned about the rights of an unborn child or the morality of abortion.

Commitment and responsibility are not as binding as they once were. As a result, the value of the family life erodes and those who need the protection of families suffer the most. (In the next chapter, you will study more closely the challenges families face in the modern world.)

2. Freedom as the absolute value. Many people in the fields of education, media, and politics preach the pursuit of individual happiness as the supreme right. Those who espouse a contrary point of view, emphasizing the value of fidelity to duty and service to others, often meet with ridicule.

The Church respects the exercise of freedom, especially in religious and moral matters, but teaches that the "exercise of freedom does not entail the putative right to say or do anything" (*CCC*, 1747).

Unchecked personal freedom leads to an excessive individualism that ignores other people, and especially those too weak or dependent to defend their own rights. Today's "me-first" culture has led to the idea that an unplanned baby somehow destroys individual freedom.

The result is that the "undesirable, unborn child" can be dispensed with before seeing the light of day.

Working to Eliminate Abortion

Proponents of legalized abortion often make the argument that making abortion illegal forces one's own personal beliefs on others. However, the obligation to protect innocent life is derived from natural law; even without the aid of Divine Revelation, one can see that taking the life of an innocent human being is morally wrong. The role of government is to protect human rights, especially the fundamental right to life. A tenet of democracy is that laws should protect the lives and rights of all people, especially the most defenseless.

The life of a defenseless child is more valuable than the opinion that human life is dispensable as an exercise of one's freedom.

Making abortion illegal through a constitutional amendment, backing efforts to restrict access to

The March for Life, held every January in Washington DC, to commemorate the legalization of abortion in the United States in 1973, regularly draws about 500,000 protestors.

abortions by eliminating government support of them, and voting for laws that provide morally acceptable alternatives to abortion will not prevent all abortions. However, such efforts would help to reduce the number of abortions being performed. This is an outcome worth fighting for, if it saves even one single human life.

Abortion laws as they stand today violate the natural law and the Fifth Commandment. Catholics are not bound to obey such laws, and must instead work to reform them. St. John Paul II wrote:

> Abortion [and euthanasia] are thus crimes which no human law can claim to legitimize. There is no obligation in conscience to obey such laws; instead there is a grave and clear obligation to oppose them by conscientious objection. (*Evangelium Vitae*, 73)

A proposal through the Health and Human Services Mandate to force insurance companies to cover birth control drugs that can cause abortions and sterilization as part of a national insurance plan brought about further protest by Catholics and others who support pro-life issues.

Difficult Circumstances Involving Abortion

Some try to argue that abortion is wrong, except for in certain cases such as rape or danger to the health of the mother. Although the circumstances surrounding a child conceived out of rape or incest are tragic and deplorable, the child himself or herself is no less of a person than a child conceived in the most ideal situation. The Church's stance against abortion, even in the unfortunate situation of rape, is not meant as an uncompassionate treatment of the woman who has experienced such violence, but instead a refusal to allow violence to be extended to another innocent victim—the unborn baby.

Rebecca Kiessling (center), an attorney and director of Save the 1, *a pro-life agency dedicated to the rights of children conceived in rape to be born, speaks to the Michigan legislature urging support of a citizen-proposed law prohibiting insurance coverage for abortion. Kiessling herself was conceived as a result of rape. Adopted at birth, she met her birth mother when she was eighteen years old. "She told me she would have aborted me if it had been legal then," Kiessling said.*

In regard to danger to the health of the mother, the cases in which a mother will die as a result of a pregnancy are extremely rare. The best example of a scenario in which the mother's life is at risk is an ectopic pregnancy, in which the fertilized egg implants in a woman's fallopian tube, instead of her uterus. In such a case, if the pregnancy continues, the baby will surely die, and the mother's life is at serious risk, too. Here, it is morally permissible to remove all or part of the fallopian tube, and the unintended consequence is that the child will pass away; however, this is morally much different than the direct killing of an innocent human life, because the termination of the pregnancy is a natural consequence of a procedure essential to saving the mother's life and not the direct intention of the procedure. The principle of double effect, explained below, provides further insight into this moral question.

PRINCIPLE OF DOUBLE EFFECT

The **principle of double effect** is a formula that aids in evaluating the morality of an act that causes an outcome one is normally obligated to avoid. Put another way, in some situations a good action may have two effects: one intended and good, the other unintended and bad. You can determine whether the unintended bad effect that results from the action is morally tolerable by considering the following questions:

1. Is the action either morally good or morally neutral?
2. Is the intention of the action the good effect and not the bad effect that results from it?
3. Does the good outcome outweigh the bad one?

If the answer to all three questions is yes, then it is permissible to proceed in the action.

The principle of double effect applies to situations like the example on page 79, in which a mother's life is in certain danger as a result of a pregnancy. Removing part or all of the fallopian tube with the implanted embryo is in and of itself a morally good act. The direct intention (saving the mother's life) is good, while the other effect (the death of the unborn life) is unintended, but rather a natural consequence of the action.

Exercise

Consider the following scenarios. For each, reflect on the three questions above.

1. To control costs, a company lays off a certain percentage of older workers.
2. To deter drug use and the possession of weapons, the school administration searches lockers without permission.
3. To beef up a college application, a student agrees to volunteer at a hospital once a week.

Finally, judge if the action in each scenario is moral or immoral. Write a short explanation for each scenario explaining your decision.

> **principle of double effect** A formula used for evaluating the permissibility of an act that is morally good when the act causes an effect one is normally obliged to avoid.

Offering Alternatives and Healing

Women who are contemplating an abortion and those who have had an abortion deserve compassion and care. The Church does not withhold her care for women in either situation.

For some girls or women facing an unplanned pregnancy, abortion may seem like the only solution. For teenage girls, pressure from a boyfriend or parents may exacerbate these feelings. For women living in poverty,

The Church invites those who are hurting due to participation in an abortion to bring their pain before the healing light of Christ.

the prospect of caring for a child—or another child—may be overwhelming. But the Church recognizes that even in the most difficult circumstances there are alternatives that support the unborn child's right to live. The Church also works to ensure that such alternatives are available and accessible. Through a variety of national Catholic organizations and ministries, teenage girls and women facing unplanned pregnancies can find material, emotional, and spiritual support, as well as access to medical care. In addition, many support services are provided at the parish or diocesan level.

The Church also offers compassion and care to women and men who have experienced the loss of a child through abortion. For example, Project Rachel, an organization founded in 1984 in the Archdiocese of Milwaukee, provides the one-on-one care of specially trained clergy, spiritual directors, and therapists to women and men who are experiencing emotional struggles after an abortion. Many also experience guilt and shame. Often these feelings are accompanied by grieving for the loss of the child. Project Rachel provides the opportunity to express and cope with these feelings, receive forgiveness, especially through the Sacrament of Penance and Reconciliation, and find peace.

For those seeking healing after an abortion, Project Rachel offers love and compassion and provides assistance in a nonjudgmental way. This is in keeping with the Church's view. While condemning the serious sin of abortion, the Church does not condemn or judge the woman or man who has participated in it. St. John Paul II expressed this position in these words to women who have had an abortion:

> The Church is aware of the many factors which may have influenced your decision, and she does not doubt that in many cases it was a painful and even shattering decision. The wound in your heart may not yet have healed. Certainly what happened was and remains terribly wrong. But do not give in to discouragement and do not lose hope. Try rather to understand what happened and face it honestly. If you have not already done so, give yourselves over with humility and trust to repentance. The Father of mercies is ready to give you his forgiveness and his peace in the Sacrament of Reconciliation. You will come to understand that nothing is definitively lost and you will also be able to ask forgiveness from your child, who is now living in the Lord. With the friendly and expert help and advice of other people, and as a result of your own painful experience, you can be among the most eloquent defenders of everyone's right to life. Through your commitment to life, whether by accepting the birth of other children or by welcoming and caring for those most in need of someone to be close to them, you will become promoters of a new way of looking at human life. (*Evangelium Vitae*, 99)

PROMOTING LIFE

Promote life by doing one of the following in the coming weeks:

- Pray daily for an end to abortion, for women contemplating an abortion, for doctors and nurses who face pressures to participate in abortions, for abortion providers, for legislators, for clergy, for those who work in the pro-life movement, and for those who do not realize how wrong abortion is.

- Help to collect a library of pamphlets, books, and DVDs for your school or parish. Include topics on abortion, adoption, Church doctrine, Project Rachel, and even factual information on Margaret Sanger and Planned Parenthood.

- Find out who the local abortionists are. Let them know your opposition to abortion with peaceful protest. Pray for them by name.

- Conduct fund-raising efforts for pro-life groups and groups that support pregnant women in crisis. You can organize a car wash, bake sale, raffle, or a penny drive, for example.

- Learn about the March for Life and the National Right to Life Conference, held in Washington, DC, every January and plan to participate in the next event. Or your own state may hold a similar event in January in which you can participate.

Check the United States Conference of Catholic Bishops Pro-Life Activities website for more ideas: www.usccb.org.

SECTION ASSESSMENT

NOTE TAKING
Use the sentences you completed for this section to answer the following questions.

1. When does human life—and thus the right to life—begin?
2. Why can't abortion ever be morally correct?

COMPREHENSION

3. What are two of the factors that can lead to a culture that supports abortion?
4. Explain the acronym "SLED."
5. How does this acronym help in the argument against abortion?

Other Beginning-of-Life Issues

Other beginning-of-life issues that must be considered in light of the Church's teaching are embryonic stem cell research and cloning and genetic manipulation.

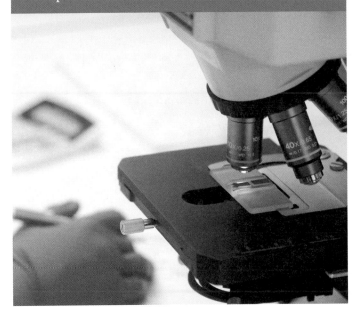

Abortion is not the only attack on the dignity of human persons at the beginning of life. The destruction of embryos and genetic manipulation also threaten life at its earliest stages.

In recent decades, rapid advances in medical science have given a special urgency in the public arena to the subject of stem cell research, both for its potential benefits to medical science and the moral and ethical dilemmas it presents, especially because of the harvesting of stems cells from living human embryos.

A stem cell is an unspecialized cell that has the potential to become one of many specific types of cells—a cell like itself or a more specialized cell; for example, a cell that can produce new white blood cells. Stem cells are a vital way for the body's cells to be replenished and offer hope for the cure of certain diseases.

Contrary to the belief of some, the Church does not oppose stem cell research. Many stem cells can be obtained without the loss of life—from adult tissue, the umbilical cord, the placenta. These are all known under the general term of "adult stem cells." However, another type of stem cell research destroys embryos in order to obtain stem cells: this is the kind seen as morally problematic, in that human lives are destroyed for the sake of research.

In a 2008 address, Pope Benedict XVI explained that the Church "appreciates and encourages the progress of the biomedical sciences which open up unprecedented therapeutic prospects."[16] However, though the purpose of this type of research might produce a good result, it does not justify the evil means of destroying

NOTE TAKING

Summarizing. Design a two-column chart like the one below for your notebook. As you read this section, list several important facts about each of these issues.

Embryonic Stem Cell Research	Cloning and Genetic Manipulation

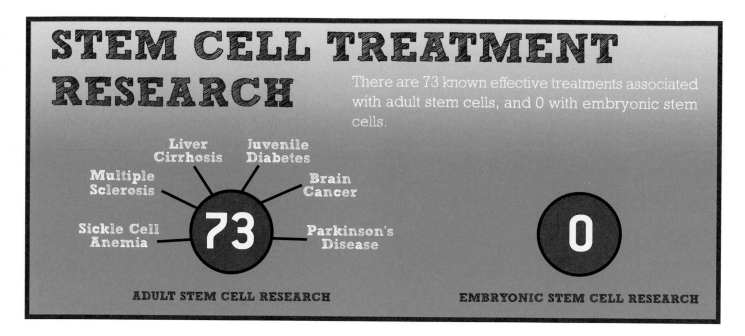

STEM CELL TREATMENT RESEARCH

There are 73 known effective treatments associated with adult stem cells, and 0 with embryonic stem cells.

Liver Cirrhosis
Juvenile Diabetes
Multiple Sclerosis
Brain Cancer
Sickle Cell Anemia
73
Parkinson's Disease

0

ADULT STEM CELL RESEARCH

EMBRYONIC STEM CELL RESEARCH

human life. Recall that it is a clear principle of Catholic morality that a good end or purpose does not justify an evil means to that end. Thus, it is evil to treat human lives as disposable commodities, as beings created in order to be killed for their cells.

The Church's consistent teaching opposes the direct destruction of human life from its earliest stages. For example, the Congregation for the Doctrine of the Faith's document *Dignitas Personae* ("On Certain Bioethical Questions") teaches:

> The body of a human being, from the very first stages of its existence, can never be reduced merely to a group of cells. The embryonic human body develops progressively according to a well-defined program with its proper finality, as is apparent in the birth of every baby. (*DP*, 4)

Just because an embryo is smaller and less developed than other persons does not make one less of a human. God said, "Before I formed you in the womb I knew you, before you were born I dedicated you" (Jer 1:5).

Results from Stem Cell Use

Interestingly, no cures have yet been attributed to embryonic stem cells; in contrast, more than seventy-three cures *are* attributed to adult stem cells,[17] in illnesses ranging from cancer, autoimmune diseases (including juvenile diabetes), liver disease, neural degenerative diseases (including spinal cord injury), as well as wounds and injuries.

Even though more significant advancements have been made using adult stem cells than embryonic ones, it must be noted that even if embryonic stem cell research became scientifically "successful," it does not change the fact that the process destroys innocent human lives, and is therefore an intrinsic evil. Although research to help cure diseases has the good intention of relieving human suffering, even the best intentions cannot justify intrinsically immoral means to achieve these ends. This point is made clear by the United States Conference of Catholic Bishops:

> We must help those who are suffering, but we may not use a good end to justify an evil means. Moreover, treatments that do not require destroying any human life are at least as promising—they are already healing some conditions, and are far closer to healing other

conditions than any approach using embryonic stem cells. The choice is not between science and ethics, but between science that is ethically responsible and science that is not. ("Stem Cell Research and Human Cloning: Questions and Answers")

There have been several recent occasions for obtaining licit stem cells, generally from the blood of the umbilical cord at the time of birth and from fetuses who have died of natural causes. With the permission of new mothers, a Catholic hospital in Tampa, Florida, has been collecting placentas for use in stem cell research.

Cloning and Genetic Manipulation

Related to embryonic stem cell research is the question of cloning and other genetic manipulation. Researchers have been "cloning" new embryos for the sole purpose of destroying them for scientific endeavors. The United States Conference of Catholic Bishops clearly warns that "human cloning is intrinsically evil because it reduces human procreation to a mere manufacturing

process, producing new human beings in the laboratory to predetermined specifications as though they were commodities."[18]

Looking back at the SLED argument on page 77, you will recall that a very small human life in embryonic form is still a *person*. Therefore, it cannot be used as a means to another's end, in this case scientific advancement. The Congregation for the Doctrine of the Faith exhorted:

> To create embryos with the intention of destroying them, even with the intention of helping the sick, is completely incompatible with human dignity, because it makes the existence of a human being at the embryonic stage nothing more than a means to be used and destroyed. It is *gravely immoral*. . . . (*Dignitas Personae*, 30)

Cloning has even been proposed for uses beyond the creation and destruction of embryos to the actual reproduction of humans. Although this has not yet happened, the Church is still firm in her opposition to such a proposition. A child has a right to be born from the mutual self-giving of a husband and wife; reproductive cloning opposes such a right.

Eventually, science may produce a child by cloning. Although the means to create the human would be intrinsically immoral, the "result" of such action—a human person—would still have inherent dignity. Compare this example to a child conceived through rape. The action (rape) is immoral and sinful; the child who results has no less personhood or dignity than one conceived in a loving marital relationship.

The cloning process of mammals first took place in 1996 in Scotland with the creation of a female sheep, named Dolly, through a process called nuclear transfer.

TAKE A STAND ON STEM CELL Research

Complete one or more of the following assignments.

1. Arrange a debate with classmates that focuses on the following questions:

   - Do you believe the government should promote research into high tech and expensive therapies that may be connected with for-profit companies and research institutions?

   - Should the government devote any of its resources to preventing disease? Explain.

   - How much input should the government take from the Church and other religious traditions related to the issue of stem cell research?

2. Locate *Donum Vitae* ("The Gift of Life") at www.vatican.va. Do one of the following:

   - Write a brief report on questions 2, 3, 4, 5, or 6 in Part 1.

   - Read the introductory section of Part 2 and the response to question 1. Then report on the answers given in questions 2, 3, 4, 5, or 6 in Part 2.

3. Research and report on some other aspect of the moral issues involved in embryonic stem cell research or the cloning of humans. Begin by browsing the USCCB website: www.usccb.org.

Cloning for "Superiority"

The intent of cloning is not just to create "any" human beings, but rather those with a particular genetic makeup. Subjecting a person to a predetermined genetic makeup imposes upon him a certain "biological slavery, from which it would be difficult to free himself."[19] In theory, reproductive cloning could be used to produce human beings with "superior" qualities or of a certain gender or even the exact genetic copy of another person. Such a perspective introduces a certain moral ambiguity as to what constitutes a "superior" human being and could lead to the notion that those who do not possess these particular qualities are inferior human beings.

Determining the genetic make-up of others is not the prerogative of human beings. Part of what makes humans unique, unrepeatable beings is the differences between them. At its core, reproductive cloning reduces the person to an object to be manipulated and controlled by another, even before he or she comes into existence; it is greatly contrary to the personalistic norm. The Congregation for the Doctrine of the Faith's *Dignitas Personae* ("On Certain Bioethical Questions") teaches further:

> The originality of every person is a consequence of the particular relationship that exists between God and a human being from the first moment of his existence and carries with it the obligation to respect the singularity and integrity of each person, even on the biological and genetic levels. (*DP*, 29)

In other words, God is the ultimate Creator of human life, life that is unique and unrepeatable. The most fitting place for such life to emerge is not in a laboratory, but rather in the love of husband and wife.

SECTION ASSESSMENT

NOTE TAKING

Use the summary items you listed for this section to answer the following questions.

1. Why is it morally problematic to use embryos for stem cell research?
2. Why are cloning and genetic manipulation morally problematic?

COMPREHENSION

3. What are stem cells?
4. Explain the difference between embryonic and adult stem cells.
5. Why is the attempt to clone humans morally wrong?

End-of-Life Concerns

MAIN IDEA

Every human life has dignity, regardless of the stage of life. This includes those suffering or dying, and even those sentenced to capital punishment.

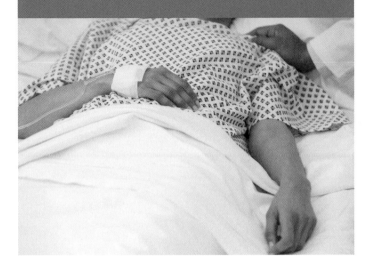

Euthanasia

Euthanasia literally means "easy death," and is defined as "any act or omission which, of itself or by intention, causes death in order to eliminate suffering" (*CCC*, 2277). Euthanasia can be voluntary or involuntary, in that one can choose it for oneself (voluntary) or someone else can choose it for the sick or dying person (involuntary). When it is voluntary, it is often referred to as assisted suicide or **physician-assisted suicide**.

> **euthanasia** Any act or omission which, of itself or by intention, causes death in order to eliminate suffering.
>
> **physician-assisted suicide** The process of ending one's own life with the help of a doctor rather than directly by the doctor's hand.

NOTE TAKING

Summarizing Main Ideas. Recreate a set of Note Taking points as listed below in your own notebook. As you read the following section, fill in the missing items.

I. Euthanasia
  A. Definition of euthanasia:
  B. Definition of the two types of euthanasia:
    1.
    2.
  C. Definition of physician-assisted suicide:
  D. Development of the Euthanasia Mentality
    1.
    2.
    3.
  E. Dignity of the Dying and Suffering
  F. Ordinary vs. Extraordinary Medical Treatment
    1. extraordinary medical treatment:
    2. ordinary medical treatment:
  G. Compassion for the Sick and Dying

II. Capital Punishment
  A. Four premises regarding the Church's Teaching on Self-Defense (summarize):
    1.
    2.
    3.
    4.
  B. Church Teaching on Capital Punishment

Human beings possess an inherent human dignity at all stages of life, right up until natural death. Offenses against human dignity that violate this principle are euthanasia and capital punishment. The Church speaks out against both moral issues, establishing clear principles for each.

Development of the Euthanasia Mentality

In more and more places around the world, there is a move to legalize physician-assisted suicide and euthanasia. In the United States, Oregon and Washington already permit physician-assisted suicide for those with terminal illnesses. Three reasons for this growing shift toward acceptance and legalization of euthanasia are:

1. *A cultural climate that sees no value in suffering.* When people abandon God, they often see life as simply the pursuit of pleasure. If pain enters the picture, and death looms on the horizon, then hastening death to be free from suffering seems like the best choice.

   Not all suffering is meaningless. When suffering is united to the Lord, especially in the last moments of life, the person can share in Christ's Passion. He or she can join Christ's sacrifice offered to the Father as an offering for his or her sins and for growth in holiness. A dying person should view impending death as a chance to say good-bye to loved ones and to prepare to meet the Lord Jesus.

   Offering our suffering to the Lord is heroic. However, the Church also recognizes that a person is not required to tolerate avoidable suffering. Therefore, Church teaching authorizes the use of painkilling drugs even if they may hasten death or cause unconsciousness. The intent in these situations is to relieve pain, not cause death.

2. *People who neglect God often think they have sole control over life and death.* Extreme individualism and the belief in an absolute right to freedom can lead people to believe they are the masters of their own life and death. For the elderly, being alone in times of serious illness and when approaching death can increase the temptation to take control over their own life and death through euthanasia.

Advances in medical science can also contribute to "playing God" in life-and-death situations.

3. *As an aging population puts pressure on a costly health care system, some see euthanasia and assisted suicide as "cost effective."* There are those who promote a "right to die" mentality, not out of compassion, but because they believe that keeping elderly people alive is too costly. Some who support assisted suicide and euthanasia do so to save money, believing that the terminally ill or elderly threaten the economic well-being of other members of society. Similarly, a contemporary preoccupation with efficiency may lead some people to judge the old and infirm as unproductive and therefore dispensable.

Dignity of the Dying and Suffering

Every human person is made in God's image and likeness and has inherent dignity; therefore, *every* person's life is worth living and worth protecting—whether the

Cardinal Joseph Bernardin said that euthanasia should be viewed as part of a consistent moral ethic of life he described as a "seamless garment."

person is healthy, sick, disabled, or dying. There is no arbitrary "range" of dignity that depends upon one's mental or physical state. Modern values sometimes run contrary to this notion, with emphasis placed on what one contributes to society—in other words, what someone *does*, rather than who someone *is*.

At the end of his life and during a difficult battle with pancreatic cancer, Cardinal Joseph Bernardin (1928–1996), no stranger to suffering, wrote to the US Supreme Court in a plea not to legalize physician-assisted suicide:

> I am at the end of my earthly life. There is much that I have contemplated these last few months of my illness, but as one who is dying I have especially come to appreciate the gift of life. . . . There can be no such thing as a "right to assisted suicide" because there can be no legal and moral order which tolerates the killing of innocent human life, even if the agent of death is self-administered. (*Chicago Tribune*, November 20, 1996)

Ordinary vs. Extraordinary Medical Treatment

No one is morally obliged to use every medical means available to prolong one's life. This decision involves family members and medical staff, besides the patient. It is morally permissible to refuse *extraordinary* medical treatment, especially those disproportionately burdensome to the quality of one's dying life. Extraordinary treatment is essentially that which attempts to do more than keep a patient comfortable and cared for in a basic manner; it includes experimental treatment and other means that can cause sickness and unnecessary affliction in one's dying days. For example, a patient may refuse chemotherapy in the last stages of a fight against cancer.

Not accepting extraordinary medical treatment is markedly different from euthanasia: the former is *accepting* death, whereas the latter is *causing* death.

In other words, a person is not required to do everything medically possible to stay alive, especially when the illness is painful and terminal. However, a person must always accept and allow *ordinary* medical treatment. Ordinary treatment includes standard medical care as well as food and water, even if the latter are administered artificially (such as through a feeding tube). Food and water are always considered ordinary medical treatment. Unfortunately, in every state, dying patients can refuse food and fluid (known medically as Patient Refusal of Nutrition and Hydration, or PRNH). Refusal of food and fluid is a form of euthanasia.

Compassion for the Sick and Dying

The *Catechism of the Catholic Church teaches*: "Those whose lives are diminished or weakened deserve special respect. Sick or handicapped persons should be helped to lead lives as normal as possible" (2276). Therefore, those who care for the sick and dying have a special obligation to treat them with compassion and charity. Although euthanasia and assisted suicide might appear compassionate, they involve a false mercy. As St. John Paul II explained:

> Even when not motivated by a selfish refusal to be burdened with the life of someone who is suffering, euthanasia must be called a false mercy, and indeed a disturbing "perversion" of mercy. True "compassion" leads to sharing another's pain; it does not kill the person whose suffering we cannot bear. Moreover, the act of euthanasia appears all the more perverse if it is carried out by those, like relatives, who are supposed to treat a family member with patience and love, or by those, such as doctors, who by virtue of their specific profession are

supposed to care for the sick person even in the most painful terminal stages.

The choice of euthanasia becomes more serious when it takes the form of a murder committed by others on a person who has in no way requested it and who has never consented to it. The height of arbitrariness and injustice is reached when certain people, such as physicians or legislators, arrogate to themselves the power to decide who ought to live and who ought to die. (*Evangelium Vitae*, § 56)

Euthanasia and assisted suicide are part of what St. John Paul II described as a "conspiracy against life." To combat this grave problem, society must guarantee the right of each person to be born as well as the right of each person to die a natural death. If society fails to protect a person's right to life when he or she is most vulnerable and helpless, then all human rights are gravely threatened.

Capital Punishment

Capital punishment is different from abortion and euthanasia in that it is not considered an intrinsic evil, because there are cases in which it can be morally permissible. As you will learn, however, in the modern world, the death penalty is more often than not an unnecessary offense against human life.

Self-Defense

The *Catechism of the Catholic Church* addresses the subject of the death penalty within the section on self-defense. To understand the connection, a few premises regarding self-defense must be understood:

- "Love of your own life" is an important tenet of morality; thus, respecting the dignity of the human person includes protecting one's own life.

- Recall that murder is defined as "the deliberate killing of an innocent human person." In this case, "innocent" does not mean a person who has never

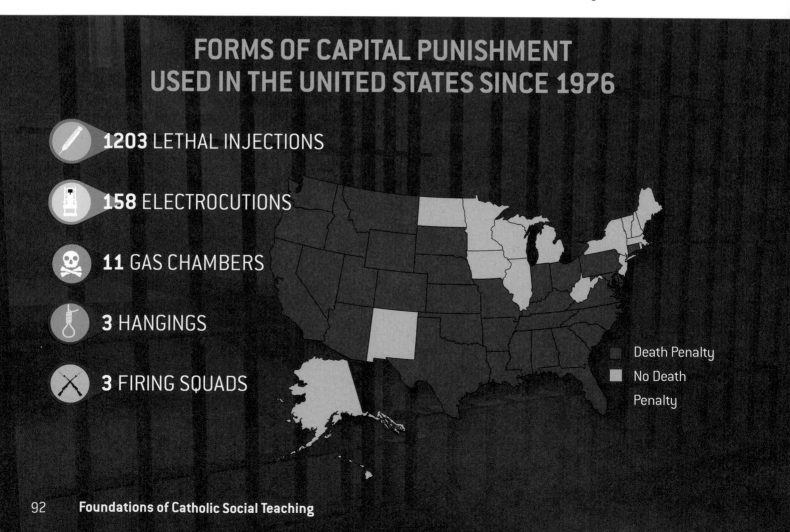

FORMS OF CAPITAL PUNISHMENT USED IN THE UNITED STATES SINCE 1976

1203 LETHAL INJECTIONS

158 ELECTROCUTIONS

11 GAS CHAMBERS

3 HANGINGS

3 FIRING SQUADS

Death Penalty

No Death Penalty

sinned or never done anything wrong. Rather, innocent in this case means a person who is not intending you harm at the particular moment. An unjust attacker is never "innocent" in this sense.

- Protecting one's own life or the life of another when it is within our means is a moral obligation. Therefore, taking the life of an aggressor when it is necessary to defend life does not render a person guilty of murder.

- Taking the life of another is only a last resort; if there are other means by which to stop the aggressor, they must be taken.

Church Teaching on Capital Punishment

These premises directly relate to the Church's teaching on the death penalty in that such legitimate defense is "not only a right but a grave duty" (*CCC*, 2265) of those in authority who are responsible for the lives of others. To protect the common good, legitimate public authority has the right to impose punishment in due proportion to the seriousness of the offense. According to St. Thomas Aquinas, criminals who are destructive of the community may be put to death. The *Catechism of the Catholic Church* confirms this teaching:

> The traditional teaching of the Church does not exclude recourse to the death penalty, if this is the only possible way of effectively defending human lives against the unjust aggressor. (*CCC*, 2267)

Thus, if the death penalty is the *only* way to stop an unjust aggressor and protect citizens' lives, legitimate authority has the prerogative to impose the death penalty.

The question today, however, is whether contemporary conditions warrant recourse to the death penalty. Church teaching holds that if nonlethal means are sufficient to defend and protect people's safety from the aggressor, public authority should limit itself to these means. Nonlethal means "are more in keeping with the

NO ONE Is Beyond REDEMPTION

Reform, deterrence, and retribution are the three traditional reasons for punishing someone. However, in the case of capital punishment, the reform of the criminal is impossible because a dead criminal cannot be reformed.

No one is beyond redemption. The New Testament has many stories of redemption in which sinners came to know the saving love of Jesus and transformed their lives. Read each of the following Scripture passages. Write a summary for each, explaining the message of forgiveness, redemption, and new life found in the passage.

- Luke 15:11–32
- Matthew 5:38–39
- Luke 6:35–37
- John 8:1–11
- Romans 12:14–19

concrete conditions of the common good and more in conformity with the dignity of the human person" (*CCC*, 2267). Today, in fact,

> as a consequence of the possibilities which the state has for effectively preventing crime, by rendering one who has committed an offense incapable of doing harm without definitively taking away from him the possibility of redeeming himself the cases in which the execution of the offender is an absolute necessity "are very rare, if not practically non-existent." (*Evangelium Vitae*, § 56, quoted in *CCC*, 2267)[20]

In the *Statement on Capital Punishment* (1980), the United States Conference of Catholic Bishops agrees that modern governments have many ways to control criminals so as to make the need for capital punishment unnecessary. They strongly urge Catholics and other American citizens to work to abolish the death penalty.

In urging the abolition of the death penalty, the bishops recognize that society must protect itself from criminals and that criminals deserve punishment. They are also aware that a majority of American citizens favor the death penalty, and are sensitive to the needs of the people involved in these crimes, both the victims and law enforcement personnel. Nevertheless, they reiterate the teaching of St. John Paul II that the circumstances in which the death penalty is necessary "are very rare, if not practically non-existent" (*Evangelium Vitae*, § 56, quoted in *CCC*, 2267).

SECTION ASSESSMENT

NOTE TAKING

Refer to the outline you constructed while reading this section to answer the following questions.

1. What are the two types of euthanasia?
2. Which type of euthanasia is often called "physician-assisted suicide"?
3. Regarding self-defense, and by extension capital punishment, what is the only circumstance in which it is morally permissible to take the life of the unjust aggressor?

COMPREHENSION

4. What is the difference between ordinary and extraordinary medical treatment?
5. What are the three traditional reasons for punishing criminals?

CRITICAL THINKING

6. Why is taking the life of someone who is sick or dying not true compassion?
7. How does the Church's teaching on self-defense relate to her teaching on capital punishment?
8. Explain why capital punishment is not an intrinsic evil.

Section Summaries

Focus Question

How do you witness to the dignity of every person?

Complete one of the following:

 Look up and write dictionary definitions for the following terms: murder, abortion, embryonic stem cell research, genetic manipulation, cloning, euthanasia, and capital punishment. How do these definitions compare to those introduced in this chapter?

 Carefully and prayerfully read the entirety of Psalm 139. Answer: What does this psalm have to do with the dignity of human life? What does it have to do with *your* life?

 Read paragraphs 2258 to 2283 in the *Catechism of the Catholic Church.* Write one paragraph that summarizes your reading.

INTRODUCTION (PAGES 69–72)
The Human Person

The basis of all of Catholic social teaching is the dignity of the human person—dignity rooted in being created in the image and likeness of God. As individuals and as a society we must treat every human life in a manner consistent with this reality.

 Share four examples of how the personalistic norm is ignored in today's society.

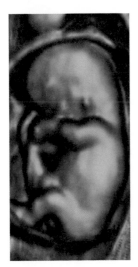

SECTION 1 (PAGES 73–82)
Abortion

Abortion, the direct killing of unborn humans, is the compelling social justice issue of the day. Abortion assaults human dignity and a person's worth as God's unique child, redeemed by Jesus Christ. Regardless of the motive, abortion is always morally wrong. Human life must be protected from the first moment of conception.

 Imagine that a close friend is contemplating getting an abortion. Write her a thoughtful, nonjudgmental letter, in which you try to dissuade her from making this decision. Be sure to let her know about alternatives available to her.

SECTION 2 (PAGES 83–88)
Other Beginning-of-Life Issues

Although the Church supports stem cell research using adult stem cells, she does not support the use of embryonic stem cells. Harvesting embryonic stem cells is an immoral practice because researchers must harvest stem cells from living human embryos, thus destroying innocent human life. Because human life must be protected from its earliest stages, cloning and other genetic manipulation is also morally impermissible.

 What would a world in which cloning and genetic manipulation were widespread look like? List at least four negative consequences of such a society.

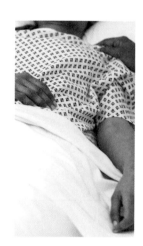

SECTION 3 (PAGES 89–94)
End-of-Life Concerns

The Church condemns euthanasia, which includes physician-assisted suicide. It is a violation of the Fifth Commandment and can never be justified. Euthanasia is a perversion of mercy: true compassion leads to sharing another's pain; it does not kill the person whose suffering we cannot bear. The Church has traditionally taught that capital punishment is permissible as a last resort for a society to defend itself against violent criminals. However, Church leaders teach that the circumstances in which the death penalty is necessary "are very rare, if not practically non-existent."

 Research nursing homes in your area. Call them and ask what type of volunteer activities are available for teenagers. Create a flier or social media announcement to promote these opportunities among your classmates. Look for ways that you can personally volunteer.

Chapter Assignments

Choose and complete at least one of the following three assignments to assess your understanding of the material in this chapter.

1. Papal Encyclical Summary

Read paragraphs 1 to 4 and 41 to 47 of *Evangelium Vitae* by St. John Paul II. For each paragraph, write a two- to three-sentence summary in your own words. You can access the encyclical at www.vatican.va.

2. Stages of Life Multimedia Presentation

Explain milestones of the life cycle of a very young human life—from the moment of conception to birth (be sure to use terms related to stages of development, such as *embryo* and *fetus*). Create a multimedia presentation with photos and captions for each stage.

Example:

Stages of Embryonic Development

- Day 1: Conception occurs when the father's sperm penetrates the mother's egg cell, forming a zygote. Genetic information from both parents interact to begin to create a new person. Cell division begins (the first cell divides into two, the two into four, etc.). The size of the embryo is no bigger than a grain of sugar.

- Days 5 to 9: Now known as a blastocyte, the tiny human attaches itself to the wall of the mother's uterus.

Continue in this format with the following entry dates: Days 10 to 14, 18, 20, 21 to 24, 28, 30, 35, 42 to 43, 45, and 9 Weeks, 11 Weeks, 16 Weeks, 18 Weeks, 5 Months, 7 Months, 9 Months.

3. Signs of Human Dignity

Imagine that you are part of a public relations firm and have been contacted by your diocese for help in educating the general population about the dignity of the human person and threats against this dignity. You have been asked to design three attractive billboards with slogans defending the sanctity of human life. They should be provocative, interesting, and inspiring, so as to encourage others to defend life and to learn more about attacks against it. Design and format your three billboards as posters. Before you begin, consider the following themes and the Scripture passages that follow. How can you include these themes in your presentation? How might you incorporate one or more of the Scripture passages in each billboard?

THEMES

God's law forbids the killing of innocent people.

God loves everyone, including those who commit crime.

Human life begins at the moment of conception.

God alone is in control of human life.

Christ Jesus is the Lord who conquered sin and death.

All people are made in God's image, and all deserve love and respect.

God is a just God who intervenes for the helpless.

SCRIPTURE

1 John 3:11–23

Psalm 139

Genesis 4:1–15

Proverbs 24:8–12

Psalm 72

John 1:1–5

As you prepare to create your billboards, ask yourself these questions:

- Who is my audience? Consider choosing an audience in particular need of hope or greater awareness about the dignity of human life. An audience might be teenagers, young parents, grade-school children, older adults, wealthy adults, and so on. Develop each billboard with your audience in mind.

- How will the message connect with the lives of its audience?

- What type of imagery or use of color will help promote the message?

- What key words about your topic need to be emphasized?

Faithful Disciple

Our Lady of Guadalupe

Sometimes it can be easy to forget that the greatest Christian saints had struggles to which the modern world can easily relate. Imagine the Blessed Virgin Mary as a young, unmarried peasant girl called by God's angel to have a child. Mary trusted in God's providence and gave her "yes" to his will.

It is no surprise, then, that Mary is known as the "patroness of the unborn," under the title of Our Lady of Guadalupe.

On December 9, 1531, Mary appeared to an Aztec man named Juan Diego, on Tepeyac Hill on the outskirts of what is today Mexico City. The Blessed Mother appeared as a young, pregnant native woman and spoke to Juan in his own language. Mary instructed Juan to go to the local bishop and ask him to build a shrine at Tepeyac in her name. The bishop was naturally skeptical. He told Juan to ask the Lady for a sign.

On December 12, Juan returned to the hill, where the Blessed Mother appeared to him again. She told Juan to go to the top of the hill

Our Lady of Guadalupe shrine

to gather roses. Juan followed her instructions, and although only cacti normally grew there, Juan found beautiful roses. He collected them in his *tilma*, or mantle, and brought them to the bishop.

The bishop was indeed surprised to see the roses. But what really moved him was the beautiful image of the Blessed Mother miraculously imprinted on the inside of Juan's mantle. The bishop acknowledged the miracle; he ordered a shrine dedicated to Mary to be built at Tepeyac Hill.

As word of the miracle spread, countless Aztecs converted to the Catholic faith. In a culture where human sacrifice was commonly practiced, the apparition of Mary as a young pregnant woman was fraught with meaning. Mary, who carried God himself in her womb, inspired a cultural conversion among the native peoples of Mexico.

Today the Basilica of Our Lady of Guadalupe is a major place of pilgrimage for Catholics in the Americas. The original tilma is still housed there. Our Lady of Guadalupe is the Patroness of the Americas and of the Unborn. She remains a beacon of a culture of life in a world that often exalts a culture of death.

Reading Comprehension

1. Where did Mary appear to Juan Diego?

2. How did the bishop come to accept Mary's message?

3. What was the effect of Mary's apparition on the people of Mexico?

Writing Task

- Our Lady of Guadalupe told St. Juan Diego:

  Am I not here, I, who am your Mother? Are you not under my shadow and protection? Am I not the source of your joy? Are you not in the hollow of my mantle, in the crossing of my arms? Do you need anything more? Let nothing else worry you, disturb you.

  Write a journal entry that responds to the following questions: What are some situations in your life that cause distress? How can you hand over your worry to God through the intercession of Mary?

Explaining the Faith

Are some human life issues more important than others?

Attitudes and practices related to care for human life should be *consistent* at all stages of life and in all circumstances. St. John Paul II commented:

> Where life is involved, the service of charity must be profoundly consistent. It cannot tolerate bias and discrimination, for human life is sacred and inviolable at every stage and in every situation; it is an indivisible good. We need then to "show care" for all life and for the life of everyone. (*Evangelium Vitae*, 87)

Attacks on the dignity of human life are interconnected and related. For example, both abortion and euthanasia are the killing of someone who is considered to be an inconvenience or unfit to live in society; both war (see Chapter 8) and capital punishment are sometimes seen as the only answer to maintain a peaceful society; and so forth. A society that sees death as an answer to its problems and inconveniences will allow this answer to permeate many different aspects of human relations.

Situations that take innocent lives will always have a priority, in that one's rights flow from the dignity of life itself. Certainly, there will be periods of time in which one human life issue will have a certain urgency about it. In the United States, for example, the sheer number of babies who die from abortion (over a million a year) puts this issue in a place of priority. Or another example: poverty will need to be addressed more pointedly during a time of economic recession or famine, simply because there will be more people in an impoverished state. That said, concentrating on poverty or homelessness should never be to the detriment of innocent human lives.

According to the United States Catholic Bishops, opposing abortion and euthanasia:

> does not excuse indifference to those who suffer from poverty, violence and injustice. Any politics of human life must work to resist the violence of war and the scandal of capital punishment. Any politics of human dignity must seriously address issues of racism, poverty, hunger, employment, education, housing and health care. ("Living the Gospel of Life," 23)

Yet, the US Catholic Bishops add:

> But being "right" in such matters can never excuse a wrong choice regarding direct attacks on innocent human life. Indeed, the failure to protect and defend life in its most vulnerable stages renders suspect any claims to the "rightness" of positions in other matters affecting the poorest and least powerful of the human community. ("Living the Gospel of Life," 23)

In other words, intentionally taking the life of an innocent person is *always* a moral evil. For example, encouraging a woman to have an abortion because having a child will put her into deeper poverty is still an intrinsic evil. A "consistent life ethic" does not allow for an "either/or" approach, but rather a "both/and" approach to addressing life issues. That means that in the previous example, the goal should be to save the unborn life *and* help the woman rise out of poverty.

 ## Further Research

- Read paragraph 87 from St. John Paul II's encyclical *Evangelium Vitae*, which you can access at www.vatican.va. Write a one-paragraph response to the following question: How can you "honor the body of Christ" *consistently* with those whom you encounter in life?

Prayer
Prayer for the Unborn

Lord Jesus,
You who faithfully visit and fulfill with your
    Presence
the Church and the history of all;
You who in the miraculous Sacrament of your
    Body and Blood
render us participants in Divine Life
and allow us a foretaste of the joy of eternal
    life;
We adore and bless you.

Prostrated before you, source and lover of
    Life,
truly present and alive among us, we beg you.

Reawaken in us respect for every unborn life,
make us capable of seeing in the fruit of the
    maternal womb
the miraculous work of the Creator,
open our hearts to generously welcoming
    every child
that comes into life.

Bless all families,
sanctify the union of spouses,
render fruitful their love.

Accompany the choices of legislative
    assemblies
with the light of your Spirit,
so that peoples and nations may recognize
    and respect
the sacred nature of life, of every human life.

Guide the work of scientists and doctors,
so that all progress contributes to the integral
    well-being of the person,
and no one endures suppression or injustice.

Give creative charity to administrators and
    economists,
so they may realize and promote sufficient
    conditions
so that young families can serenely embrace
the birth of new children.

Console the married couples who suffer
because they are unable to have children
and in Your goodness provide for them.

Teach us all to care for orphaned or aban-
    doned children,
so they may experience the warmth of your
    Charity,
the consolation of your divine heart.

Together with Mary, your Mother, the great
    believer,
in whose womb you took on our human
    nature,
we wait to receive from you, our Only True
    Good and Savior,
the strength to love and serve life,
in anticipation of living forever in you,
in communion with the Blessed Trinity.
Amen.

—Pope Benedict XVI

4

REWARDS AND CHALLENGES OF FAMILY LIFE

A COMPLICATED
SURROGACY

A couple in Connecticut reportedly paid Crystal Kelley $22,000 to be a surrogate for their baby. An embryo created in a laboratory from the genetic material of the husband and an anonymous egg donor was placed inside Crystal Kelley. When she delivered the baby, she would be legally required to hand over the baby to the paying parents.

The situation became complicated when ultrasounds showed the little girl Crystal was carrying had a cleft palate, a brain cyst, a heart abnormality, and other serious medical conditions. The couple who hired her insisted that she get an abortion. They even offered her $10,000 to do so. Crystal refused to have an abortion.

Crystal fled to Michigan, where state law gave her rights as the child's mother. She eventually gave birth to the baby, who was indeed born with serious medical issues. There were legal complications regarding who the actual parents of this baby were. Eventually, however, the biological parents relinquished their legal rights, and another couple adopted the baby.

The biological parents' offer of $10,000 to abort the baby because of medical problems and the surrogate mother's defense of the child rightly provoke strong emotions. However, the moral dilemma at the surface of this situation belies a deeper issue: that is, surrogacy itself.

Despite the good intentions behind surrogacy and other artificial means of conception, the methods remain morally flawed because they separate procreation from its rightful context: the loving sexual union of a husband and wife.

105

FOCUS QUESTION

How can you live a LIFE OF CHASTITY that serves the family AS THE FOUNDATION OF SOCIETY?

INTRODUCTION
Community and Family

Have you ever wondered what it would be like to live on your own, without a family? In what ways would your life be different?

The second theme from the USCCB document *Sharing Catholic Social Teaching* is the "call to family, community, and participation." Like the first theme, this one is centered on human dignity—in this case, the dignity of social groups and the individuals who are a part of them.

Every day you encounter various social groups: your family, your school, your parish community, your neighborhood, your city, your state, and so forth. The ideal of these communities is to form and foster the individual dignity of every member. A paraphrase of a famous saying is that "no person is an island."[1] That is to say, no person is ever truly isolated from others. Even the person called to be a hermit, away from society, is still in communion with the people of God through prayer.

However, being a part of a community does not negate one's individuality; instead, it should aim to support and uphold the dignity of individual human persons. Pope Benedict XVI made this very clear in his encyclical *Caritas in Veritate*, in which he said that the human person is actually defined by his relations with others. And "the more authentically he or she lives these relations, the more his or her own personal

NOTE TAKING

Naming and Classifying Characteristics. Create a table like the one below. In the first column, list the characteristics of marriage described in this section. In the second column, write a description of each characteristic. The first has been completed for you.

Characteristic	Description
Totality	man and woman give a complete gift of self

identity matures."[2] It is not by being alone that one's worth is established, but rather by placing oneself "in relation with others and with God."[3]

God is not an isolated being. The Blessed Trinity is a communion of Persons: "God has revealed his innermost secret: God himself is an eternal exchange of love, Father, Son and Holy Spirit" (*CCC*, 221). Your social nature is rooted in your being made in God's image and likeness. You are called to embody this Trinitarian self-giving love. Such a reality points you toward your ultimate communion with this eternal exchange of divine love—the Blessed Trinity—in Heaven.

Family: The Foundation of Society

The family is the first social group naturally possible. Every human being comes from two other human beings. Even a child who does not know his or her parents or whose family is broken, is still inherently part of a family. And so, calling the family "the original

The Holy Family

> **domestic church** A name for the Christian family. In the family, parents and children exercise their priesthood of the baptized by worshiping God, receiving the sacraments, and witnessing to Christ and the Church by living as faithful disciples.

cell of social life" (*CCC*, 2207) indicates that just as any living thing is made up of many cells, so too is any society built from families.

St. John Paul II said that the family is "the cradle of life and love, the place in which the individual 'is born' and 'grows'. . . . [It is] the primary place of 'humanization' for the person and society."[4] On a basic level, the family is a "privileged community" (*CCC*, 2206), where one's initiation into life in society takes place. For example:

- You learn morals and what it truly means to be human in a family.
- You develop your potential within a family.
- You become aware of your dignity within a family.
- In a family, you prepare for your unique and individual destiny.[5]

Therefore, a weakening or disintegration of the family leads to the weakening or disintegration of human society. Even more, you can learn through Revelation that the family life images the Blessed Trinity: it is a sign and image of the communion of the Father and the Son in the Holy Spirit. The family is the **domestic church**, which means it is truly the Church, the Body of Christ, lived out within the home.

Jesus himself was part of a human family. This illustrates how consequential the family is even to the plan of Salvation. Bl. Pope Paul VI explained the lessons to be learned from the Holy Family:

> May Nazareth remind us what the family is, what the communion of love is, its stark and simple beauty, its sacred and inviolable character; may it help us to see how sweet and

Holy Family Reflection

Imagine what the day-to-day family life would have looked like for Mary and Joseph and Jesus. What would have been their struggles? Their joys?

Compose a prayer that asks for the intercession of the Holy Family for your *own* family. Feel free to be specific in your requests.

irreplaceable education in the family is; may it teach us its natural function in the social order. (*Compendium of the Social Doctrine of the Church*, footnote 461, quoting Pope Paul VI)

Christian families look to the Holy Family as an example of how to love one another in ways that reflect the love of God.

Marriage: The Foundation of the Family

Family life begins with the marriage of a man and a woman. This teaching is rooted in the first book of the Bible when God declared that "it is not good for man to be alone" (Gn 2:18). And thus, God gave Eve to Adam: this primordial couple is the first communion of persons. The communion of man and woman gives rise to the community of the family. And therefore, the nature of the marital relationship is crucial to the study of the family.

Marriage is an objective reality that man did not create: it is a gift of God to humanity. In an age when votes are taken and laws written to "redefine" marriage, remember this central teaching that marriage was established by God and written into the nature of man and woman. "God himself is the author of matrimony,

endowed as it is with various benefits and purposes."[6] Some of the specific characteristics of marriage and the nature of marriage are shared the following sections.

Characteristics of Marriage

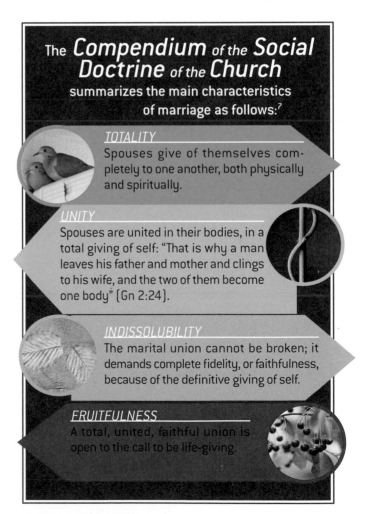

The ***Compendium*** *of the* **Social Doctrine** *of the* **Church** summarizes the main characteristics of marriage as follows:[7]

TOTALITY
Spouses give of themselves completely to one another, both physically and spiritually.

UNITY
Spouses are united in their bodies, in a total giving of self: "That is why a man leaves his father and mother and clings to his wife, and the two of them become one body" (Gn 2:24).

INDISSOLUBILITY
The marital union cannot be broken; it demands complete fidelity, or faithfulness, because of the definitive giving of self.

FRUITFULNESS
A total, united, faithful union is open to the call to be life-giving.

Marriage is ultimately ordered to:

1. the good of the spouses (**fidelity**) and

2. the procreation (**fecundity**) and education of children.

Therefore, the love between a husband and wife must always follow this ordering of marriage, in that it is ordered to the good of the other spouse and is open to life.

Also important to the understanding of marriage is that Christ raised marriage to the level of a *sacrament* and that the union of the husband and wife's souls mirrors the union of Christ, the Bridegroom, and the Church, his bride.

Complementarity of the Sexes

An integral component of the nature of marriage is the complementarity of the sexes. Men and women, because they are human persons, are equal in dignity. That reality is undeniable. However, within their

> **fidelity** Faithfulness. In relation to marriage, fidelity refers to one of the purposes of marriage. Both spouses give of themselves definitively and totally to one another. They are no longer two; from now on they form one flesh. The covenant they freely contracted imposes on the spouses the obligation to preserve it as unique and indissoluble (*CCC*, 2364).

> **fecundity** Fruitfulness. In relation to marriage, fecundity refers to procreation and education of children as one of the purposes of marriage.

equality, men and women are different. This is seen on a basic physical level, but it also affects one's psychology and spirituality. These differences, instead of giving rise to conflict, can serve mutual self-giving: men and women's differences can, indeed, complement one another.

The *Catechism of the Catholic Church* explains that differences and complementarity between males and females are physical, moral, and spiritual and "are oriented toward the goods of marriage and the flourishing of family life" (*CCC*, 2333).

SEEKING A VIRTUOUS FRIENDSHIP

Who doesn't need and want a friend? The Book of Sirach described a faithful friend as "a sturdy shelter; he who finds one finds a treasure" (Sir 6:14). The classic philosopher Aristotle defined three "types" of friendships in his work *Nicomachean Ethics*: the first is based on utility, the second on pleasure, and the third on virtue.

You can probably identify these types of friends in your own life. In a *friendship of utility* the friendship serves a need for one or both people. The friendship ends when the need no longer exists. For example, perhaps you are casual friends with your hairdresser and you have good conversations during your appointments; however, if you find a better hairdresser more suitable to your needs, that friendship will end.

In a *friendship of pleasure* individuals are drawn to one another based on the pleasure they derive from the friendship, such as because of the friend's personality, looks, and so forth. This type of friendship involves friends who entertain you, with whom you have a good time. Again, these friendships come and go, based on your desires of the moment.

In a *friendship of virtue*, both people value the other's virtue and encourage one another to strive for virtuousness. Aristotle held this to be the highest form of friendship. These are the friends who bring out virtue in you. In other words, they help you become a better person. In turn, you also help them in this pursuit. Perhaps this is the type of friendship the author of Sirach had in mind. To continue the quotation from Sirach:

> A faithful friend is beyond price, no sum can balance his worth. A faithful friend is a life-saving remedy, such as he who fears God finds; for he who fears God behaves accordingly, and his friend will be like himself. (Sir 6:15)

Christian tradition has always upheld the beauty and necessity of true friendships, the "virtuous" kinds of friendships that Aristotle hailed. There have been many virtuous friendships among the saints—between, for example, St. Ignatius of Loyola and St. Francis Xavier, St. Rose of Lima and St. Martin de Porres, St. John of the Cross and St. Teresa of Avila, and St. Francis of Assisi and St. Clare of Assisi.

JOURNAL QUESTIONS

1. Reflect on friendships in your own life. Which would you describe as virtuous friendships? Why?

2. How can you be a virtuous friend to others?

SECTION ASSESSMENT

NOTE TAKING

Use your Note Taking chart to answer the following questions:

1. Name and describe four characteristics of marriage.

2. How do these characteristics distinguish marriage from other relationships?

VOCABULARY

3. Define *domestic church*.

FILL IN THE BLANK

4. An integral component of the nature of marriage is the _____ of the sexes.

5. Even though you are social, this social nature does not negate your _____.

COMPREHENSION

6. What is the "original cell" of social life? How so?

SECTION 1

Understanding the Rewards and Challenges of Chaste Living

MAIN IDEA
Chastity is essential to our sexual integrity and should guide us in all our relationships and all our actions. Sins against chastity harm the individual and society.

The Sixth Commandment, "You shall not commit adultery," and the Ninth Commandment, "You shall not covet your neighbor's wife," go beyond merely being faithful to one's spouse, although that is certainly an important part of each commandment. As Jesus exhorted, "Everyone who looks at a woman with lust has already committed adultery with her in his heart" (Mt 5:28). What this indicates is that living a life of **chastity** is much more than just fulfilling the minimum of the commandments; rather, it is a lifestyle of freedom that involves the entire person, at every stage of his or her life.

Chaste people are not uncomfortable with the gift of sexuality. In fact, they are very aware of the value of the gift of sexuality and honor it in all aspects of their lives—in their speech, in the way they dress, and in their thoughts and actions. They also respect the gift of sexuality in others, and do not treat others in ways

> **chastity** The moral virtue which provides for the successful integration of sexuality within one's whole identity, leading to the inner unity of the physical and spiritual being (*CCC*, 2337).

NOTE TAKING

Categorizing Concepts. Create a table like the one below. List the sins against chastity noted in this section. Tell how each hurts the individual and how it harms others or society.

Sin against Chastity	Effect on Individual	Effect on Others or Society
Adultery	Damages the person's marriage, perhaps permanently	

that demean their sexuality. Chaste living is a great challenge. It is regularly disparaged in music lyrics and television plots, and by peers and even adults in authority. Chastity is often portrayed as an impossibly difficult way to live.

The truth is that living a chaste life is an important basis for establishing healthy relationships built on mutual respect and a genuine interest in the good of the other person. The negative cultural reality makes it an imperative to recognize the immorality of acts that violate the dignity of sexuality, and to understand the ways they can harm you as an individual and the society you live in. These are addressed in the following sections.

Adultery

One of the starting points of chastity is a proper understanding of conjugal love, or the sexual act in marriage. As previously mentioned, marriage is aimed both at fidelity (faithfulness) and fecundity (fruitfulness). The sexual act in marriage has two main purposes:

- to unify a man and woman (union) and
- to bring forth life (procreation).

But the self-gift of marriage goes beyond just physicality and addresses the total person. St. John Paul II explains:

Sexuality, by means of which man and woman give themselves to one another through the acts which are proper and exclusive to spouses, is not something simply biological, but concerns the innermost being of the human person as such. It is realized in a truly human way only if it is an integral part of the love by which a man and woman commit themselves totally to one another until death. (*Familiaris Consortio*, 11)

Because marriage involves the *total* person, the exclusivity of the marital covenant is integral to its nature. **Adultery** betrays this exclusivity and the lifelong fidelity between a man and a woman that marriage requires. It is a sin against the Sixth Commandment and is inherently a lie in the language of the body. Once you have given your entire self to someone in marriage, you cannot give yourself to someone else.

It is easy to recognize the pain and difficulty such extramarital relationships cause, especially to the family. Adultery undermines marriage by breaking the covenant on which it is based. It also harms "the welfare of children who need their parents' stable union" (*CCC*, 2381).

Fornication

Sex is more than merely a biological act, but rather involves the innermost being of the person. Therefore, **fornication**, or sex outside of marriage, in which the total gift of self—emotional, physical, and spiritual—has not been made, violates the nature of the gift of sexuality and the sexual act. Like adultery, fornication

> **adultery** Marital infidelity, or sexual relations between two persons, at least one of whom is married to another (*CCC*, Glossary).
>
> **fornication** Sexual intercourse between an unmarried man and an unmarried woman (*CCC*, Glossary).

is gravely wrong and is a sin against the Sixth Commandment. It too is a lie in the language of the body. Fornication asks the body to make promises that cannot be kept. Even the souls of couples engaged to be married are *not* united, so sexual relations in that case, before the marriage vows, would be a lie.

Along with the spiritual and emotional harm fornication can cause to the individuals engaged in it, sex outside of marriage can also lead to negative social consequences, including the spread of disease. Also, children born outside of marriage are often deprived of the material and emotional support parents are called to provide. The birth of children from the union of a couple in a lifelong commitment of marriage serves the good of both the children themselves and society.

Masturbation

Because masturbation is understood as "the deliberate stimulation of genital organs in order to derive sexual pleasure" (*CCC*, 2352) and the purpose of one's sexual faculties is for a total self-gift to another, masturbation is inherently opposed to the nature of human sexuality. Masturbation is an intrinsically disordered use of one's sexuality because any use of the sexual faculty other than within the conjugal union is against the purpose of marriage.

Although masturbation may seem like an act of the individual that does not affect others, it does in fact have a bearing on one's relationships with others. It trains the person engaging in such an act to use his or her sexuality selfishly. Instead of approaching the sexual act as a selfless gift to another, it becomes only a means for one's own temporary pleasure. This attitude flows into social relationships, such as the way one treats a spouse.

As with every moral or immoral act, a person's personal culpability (guiltiness) can be lessened or increased because of the circumstances surrounding the act. In the case of masturbation, certain factors may lessen one's guilt, such as "immaturity, force of

> **rape** The forcible violation of the sexual intimacy of another person (*CCC*, 2356).
>
> **prostitution** The act of providing sexual services in exchange for money or other material gain.

acquired habit, conditions of anxiety or other psychological or social factors" (*CCC*, 2352). However, diminished culpability still does not diminish the intrinsic wrong of the act.

Rape

Rape, the sexual assault of another person, is quite obviously opposed to God's plan for the gift of sexuality. Rape is a profound violation of justice and charity and brings deep, and often lasting, wounds to its victims. It "deeply wounds the respect, freedom, and physical and moral integrity to which every person has a right" (*CCC*, 2356).

Prostitution

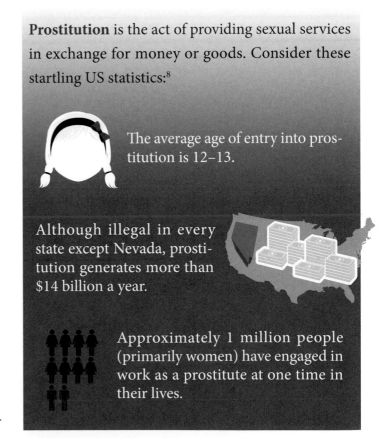

Prostitution is the act of providing sexual services in exchange for money or goods. Consider these startling US statistics:[8]

The average age of entry into prostitution is 12–13.

Although illegal in every state except Nevada, prostitution generates more than $14 billion a year.

Approximately 1 million people (primarily women) have engaged in work as a prostitute at one time in their lives.

Prostitution reduces sexuality to a commodity to be traded rather than an act of self-giving love. It diminishes the value of the human person to that of an object that gives or takes sexual pleasure. It is opposed to every purpose of human sexuality.

Prostitution often leads to other social sins, such as human trafficking (often of children). Further, prostitutes (both male and female) are often the victims of abuse and are routinely exposed to disease. The social causes of prostitution often are rooted in impoverishment or addiction. The *Catechism of the Catholic Church* calls prostitution a "social scourge," noting that the involvement of children and adolescents is particularly scandalous (*CCC*, 2355).

Pornography

Pornography is the depiction of sexual acts or nudity with the purpose of stimulating and gratifying lustful desires. Pornography is another sinful action that perverts the conjugal act. It reduces people to mere objects and promotes a distorted and selfish view of sexuality. Pornography strongly denies the personalistic norm and "does grave injury to the dignity of its participants (actors, vendors, the public), since each one becomes an object of base pleasure and illicit profit for others. It immerses all who are involved in the illusion of a fantasy world" (*CCC*, 2354).

In other words, pornography hurts all those involved:

- It harms the viewer by training the person to use others for selfish gratification. Consequently, it can cause great division and hurt in marriages and even future marriages.

- It hurts the persons being portrayed—even if willingly—in that they renounce their true personhood to be treated as objects.

Pornography is a widespread, multibillion-dollar industry in the United States. Many are addicted to it and enslaved by it. Yet, the grace of Christ poured out in the sacraments, especially the Sacraments of Penance and Holy Eucharist, can bring freedom from even the most difficult addictions.

> **pornography** The written or visual depiction of sexual acts or nudity with the purpose of stimulating and gratifying lustful desires. Pornography debases human dignity by turning people into objects to be used for selfish gratification.

SECTION ASSESSMENT

 NOTE TAKING

Use the chart you created to answer the following questions.

1. How do sins against living chastely harm the person committing them?

2. In what ways do individual sins against chastity have a wider impact, on others and on society?

 VOCABULARY

3. Define *chastity*.

 COMPREHENSION

4. What does it mean to say that chaste people are deeply aware of, and value, the gift of their sexuality?

Sins against the Nature of Conjugal Love

Continuing the examination of sin and social injustices that strike at the root of conjugal love this section examines how the homosexual act, contraception, and artificial means of conception are inconsistent with the nature of conjugal love and the call of spouses to be cooperators with God in creating new life.

Homosexual Acts

As you have already learned, the sexual act has two main purposes: a deepening of the union between spouses and the bearing of life. Any act that is opposed to either purpose is disordered and morally wrong. Therefore, homosexual acts are intrinsically wrong. As the *Catechism of the Catholic Church* states, "They are contrary to the natural law. They close the sexual act to the gift of life. They do not proceed from a genuine affective and sexual complementarity. Under no circumstances can they be approved" (*CCC*, 2357).

That said, there is an important distinction between *persons who experience same-sex attraction* and *the homosexual act itself.* The exact origin of the

NOTE TAKING

Summarizing Key References. Create a chart like the following. Summarize Church teaching on the issues listed. For each, cite a paragraph from the *Catechism of the Catholic Church* or another Church document referenced in this section.

Issue	Church Teaching Summary	Document Paragraph
The immorality of homosexual acts	Under no circumstance are they morally permissible.	*CCC*, 2357
How persons with same-sex attractions should be treated	They should be treated with respect and compassion.	*CCC*, 2358
How persons with same-sex attraction are to live		
Teaching regarding artificial contraception		
What couples "say" to each other through artificial contraception		
Regarding artificial methods of conception		

homosexual orientation is largely unknown; regardless, many persons with such tendencies do not choose these attractions. Thus, merely having a homosexual attraction is not morally wrong. However, *acting* upon such tendencies—the homosexual act—is always morally wrong.

Like everyone, persons with homosexual tendencies are called to a life of chastity, which in their case includes a life of abstinence from homosexual acts. People with a homosexual orientation or tendencies are called to be saints and live a full, Christian life while participating as a valued member of the Church. This involves bearing their particular cross lovingly within society.

At first glance, this may seem unfair; however, many people have to endure emotional or physical struggles in their lives and crosses that are not their fault, but still must be met with heroic virtue (for example, persons born into poverty, or those who develop a physical disability; the list is endless). In striving to bear one's difficult circumstances, Christ's grace can be a source of strength, for Christ promises, "I will not leave you orphans" (Jn 14:18) and "my grace is sufficient for you" (2 Cor 12:9). The *Catechism of the Catholic Church* explains how this grace can strengthen those with same-sex attraction:

> Homosexual persons are called to chastity. By the virtues of self-mastery that teach them inner freedom, at times by the support of disinterested friendship, by prayer and sacramental grace, they can and should gradually and resolutely approach Christian perfection. (*CCC,* 2359)

Persons with same-sex attraction are to unite their sacrifices to Christ's Cross, and—like all persons—practice the virtue of chastity in their state of life. It's important to note that just as the Church's teaching on homosexuality is clear, the Church is also clear about how persons with same-sex attractions are to be treated:

> They must be accepted with respect, compassion, and sensitivity. Every sign of unjust discrimination in their regard should be avoided. (*CCC,* 2358)

Artificial Contraception

When God created the first man and woman, the very first words he spoke to them were, "Be fertile and multiply; fill the earth and subdue it" (Gn 1:28). The call to bear children and welcome them as a blessing is echoed throughout Scripture. For example, Psalm 127 proclaims: "Children too are a gift from the Lord, the fruit of the womb, a reward" (Ps 127:3).

Throughout the centuries, the Catholic Church has been clear that the call to "be fertile and multiply" is an integral part of the marriage covenant. Parents truly are cooperators with God in the creation of new life. A child springs forth from the mutual self-gift of the parents: the unitive and procreative elements of conjugal love are inherently linked.

Artificial contraception is designed to deny the procreative dimension of the sexual union of spouses. In fact, break down the word to "contra" and "conception" and you can quickly understand it to mean "against conception," as in "against conception of human life." Taking away one of the purposes of sex results in adverse effects for the individual, the couple, and society as a whole.

Bl. Pope Paul VI reaffirmed the Church's teaching against artificial contraception in his landmark encyclical, *Humanae Vitae*. He wrote:

> **artificial contraception** The use of mechanical, chemical, or medical means to prevent conception from taking place as a result of sexual intercourse (*CCC,* Glossary).

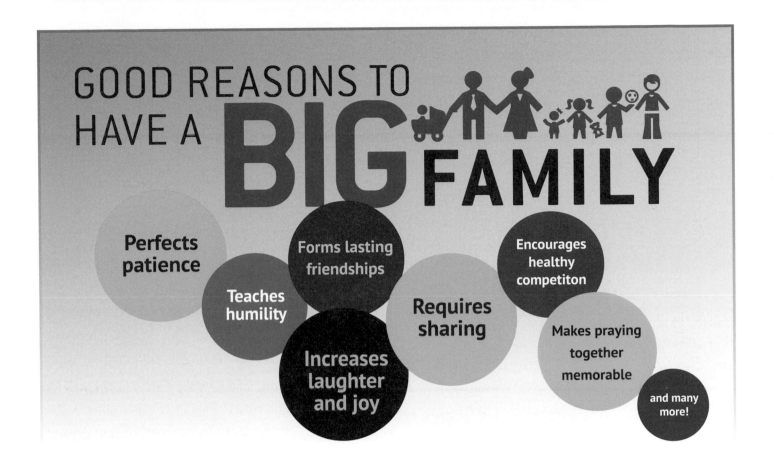

GOOD REASONS TO HAVE A BIG FAMILY

- Perfects patience
- Teaches humility
- Forms lasting friendships
- Increases laughter and joy
- Requires sharing
- Encourages healthy competiton
- Makes praying together memorable
- and many more!

By safeguarding both these essential aspects, the unitive and the procreative, the conjugal act preserves in its fullness the sense of true mutual love and its orientation toward man's exalted vocation to parenthood. (*HV*, 12)

The Church has consistently taught that any act that purposefully rejects procreation is intrinsically wrong. This is not meant to be a condemnation, but rather an invitation to see the great beauty and blessing of life and its inherent connection to marriage. Though most couples would not intend this, in contracepting, they are lying to each other with their bodies and changing the language of sex, as St. John Paul II explained in *Familiaris Consortio*:

> Thus the innate language that expresses the total reciprocal self-giving of husband and wife is overlaid, through contraception, by an objectively contradictory language, namely, that of not giving oneself totally to the other. This leads not only to a positive refusal to be open to life but also to a falsification of the inner truth of conjugal love, which is called upon to give itself in personal totality. (*FC*, 32)

The Church's teaching against contraception does not mean that every married couple is morally required to have as many children as humanly possible. The Church is very clear about responsible parenthood, which often includes the regulation of procreation. For just and grave reasons (such as those "arising from the physical or psychological condition of husband or wife, or from external circumstances"[9]) a husband and wife may choose to space out the births of their children. However, they still have a "duty to make certain that their desire is not motivated by selfishness but is in conformity with the generosity appropriate to responsible parenthood" (*CCC*, 2368).

The spacing out of births can be done through "periodic continence," or what is more widely known as Natural Family Planning (NFP). In this process, a couple watches the signs of a woman's body and refrains from the sexual act during the time in the month in which she is fertile. This is vastly different from using contraception, because the couple is not changing what the conjugal act is, but rather merely choosing abstinence during certain periods of the month. Even during these infertile periods, the act of sexual intercourse is still procreative, because the couple has not done anything to *change* it.

Artificial Means of Conception

A great cross many married persons have to endure is that of infertility. This struggle is clearly seen in Scripture: Abraham asks God, "Oh Lord God, what good will your gifts be, if I keep on being childless . . . ?" (Gn 15:2). And Rachel says to her husband, Jacob, "Give me children, or I shall die!" (Gn 30:1).

Like many other women in Scripture, Elizabeth had also given up hope for bearing a child. She was elderly when she gave birth to John the Baptist. See Luke 1:5–25.

> **in vitro fertilization** The fertilization of a woman's ovum (egg) with a man's sperm through a clinical procedure, then implanting the fertilized egg in the woman's uterus. In vitro fertilization violates the dignity of procreation.
>
> **artificial insemination** A fertility technique in which a man's sperm and a woman's egg are united through clinical means—most commonly by injecting sperm into a woman's cervical canal.
>
> **surrogate motherhood** A medical process in which a woman becomes pregnant through artificial means and carries the child for someone else. The procedure separates intercourse from the act of procreation and is morally wrong.

In today's world, there are medical means to overcome struggles with infertility. Those that do not change the nature or the object of sexual intercourse are consistent with God's law and Church teaching and permissible. Conversely, any type of artificial fertilization or insemination is intrinsically immoral. The dignity of sexuality requires that children be conceived naturally, through the loving union of spouses in sexual intercourse, and not through artificial means. Therefore, **in vitro fertilization**, in which the mother's egg and the man's sperm are joined in a laboratory and implanted in the mother's womb, is morally wrong Similarly, **artificial insemination**, a fertility technique in which a man's sperm is artificially implanted in the mother's womb, and **surrogate motherhood**—placing a fertilized ovum in another woman's womb and letting the baby grow inside her, to be delivered for the biological parents—also are morally wrong. Like in vitro fertilization, these artificial means of conception separate the conception of a child from the loving union of the married couple (see *CCC*, 2377).

In addition to the moral obstacles to artificial methods of conception is the reality that often the methods produce multiple embryos, or embryos that cannot be viably implanted in the woman's womb, and which are therefore destroyed. Thus, in addition to violating the dignity of our gift of sexuality, these practices often also violate the Fifth Commandment.

The Church's rejection of artificial reproductive methods does not imply a lack of understanding or compassion for those who suffer the emotional pain of infertility. Yet, the Church emphasizes that a child is not something *owed* to a couple, but rather a *gift*, the greatest gift of marriage, and calls couples bearing this particular cross to imitate Christ in accepting his Cross, and to live their married life within society in a life-giving manner, such as "adopting abandoned children or performing demanding services for others" (*CCC*, 2379).

SECTION ASSESSMENT

NOTE TAKING

Using the notes you created for this section, summarize the Church's teaching on:

1. homosexual acts
2. artificial contraception
3. artificial means of conception

COMPREHENSION

4. Why is the homosexual act immoral?
5. How are artificial means of conception inconsistent with spouses' call to be cooperators with God in creating new life?
6. What is periodic continence (Natural Family Planning)?

REFLECTION

7. Write a short prayer for someone you may know who is experiencing one of the crosses described in this section.

SECTION 3

Attacks against the Dignity of Marriage

MAIN IDEA

God instituted the nature of marriage; it cannot be altered by societal trends. The acceptance of both cohabitation and same-sex unions undermines the dignity of marriage and harms society.

The two previous sections in this chapter looked at sins against chastity and the nature of conjugal love, and thus, against the nature of marriage. This section addresses two issues that more specifically deal with marriage's status within society—namely, cohabitation and same-sex unions.

Cohabitation

In the modern world, **cohabitation** (also known as "free unions" or "*de facto* unions" or simply "living together") has become commonplace. In fact, almost 60 percent of all marriages are preceded by cohabitation. And yet, think about these other statistics:

- Fewer than half of cohabitation unions result in marriage.

- Marriage preceded by cohabitation is 46 percent more likely to end in divorce than marriage in which the couple did not cohabit.

- Forty percent of cohabiting households include children. After five years, one-half of these couples will have broken up, compared to 15 percent of married parents.[10]

> **cohabitation** Living together in a sexual relationship without the lifelong commitment of a sacramental marriage.

NOTE TAKING

Concept Web. As you read this section, make a concept web like the one below. Summarize how each of the issues discussed challenges the establishment of marriage in society.

A couple who lives together as if they were married, without the commitment of a sacramental marriage, commits a sin against the dignity of marriage. Cohabitation leads to a relativistic view of the family—one based on a person's whims and desires, instead of on the natural law and Divine Revelation.

There are many reasons why couples cohabit, such as financial pressures (or for financial conveniences) or a desire to ensure the soundness of the relationship ahead of marriage. Yet no matter the reason, living as a married couple and sharing in the pleasure of sex without the commitment of marriage is never the right choice. Along with the spiritual consequences for the couple, there are also practical consequences to them and to society. For the couple, the lack of a permanent commitment means it is easy to abandon the relationship in the face of hardship. When the couple's (or one individual's) children live with them, the children are vulnerable to the impermanence of the relationship and are deprived of the example of committed marital love. For society, cohabitation leads to further breakdown of the family structure.

"Marriage is not a simple agreement to live together, but a relationship with a social dimension that is unique with regard to all other relationships, since the *family* . . . is the principal instrument for making each person grow in an integral manner and integrating him positively into social life."[11]

Same-Sex Unions

In recent years, there have been strong legal and media efforts in the United States and in countries around the world to allow persons of the same sex to "marry" each other. At very first glance, allowing such unions may seem like an act of compassion or a matter of civil rights. However, upon further reflection, you can see that putting such unions on the same level as marriage changes society's perception of a truth—that of marriage—which, in reality, is unchangeable.

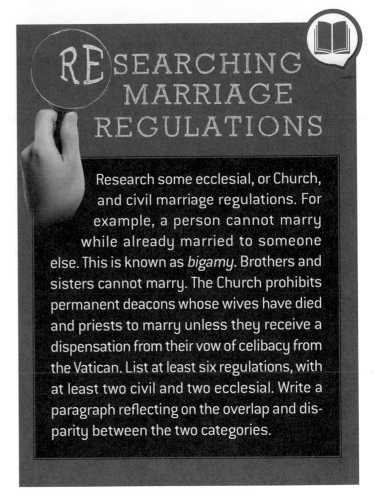

RESEARCHING MARRIAGE REGULATIONS

Research some ecclesial, or Church, and civil marriage regulations. For example, a person cannot marry while already married to someone else. This is known as *bigamy*. Brothers and sisters cannot marry. The Church prohibits permanent deacons whose wives have died and priests to marry unless they receive a dispensation from their vow of celibacy from the Vatican. List at least six regulations, with at least two civil and two ecclesial. Write a paragraph reflecting on the overlap and disparity between the two categories.

Marriage is more than just a public declaration of your love for someone. You are called to love *everyone*, but you do not have a right to marry *anyone*. Throughout human history, including the present, societies put restrictions on whom one can marry. Examples include laws against marrying one's close relative, or against marrying more than one person, or marrying an underage child. This is because society recognizes that certain unions are not good for individuals or for society. In other words, restrictions placed on marriage are for the common good.

Many people argue that since artificial means of conception have become more medically advanced and more widely available, in some ways the procreative outcome for marriage has become less necessary in our modern world. However, the nature of the gift of sexuality clearly contradicts this view. Procreation is brought about through the complementarity of men and women, and is a goal of the Sacrament of

Learning *more about* Marriage

How much do you know about marriage and caring for children? Meet with a couple that has been married at least ten years and are also parents. (It's okay to interview your own parents.) Interview them to learn more about their lives and how they live their marriage vocation. Following your interview, write a one-page report that summarizes what you learned about marriage from the couple, what new insights you gained, and how what you learned is helpful to you in thinking about the possibility of your own marriage in the future.

Some questions you can ask:

- How long have you been married?
- What was your first year of marriage like?
- What was marriage like after three years? Five years?
- How do you resolve disagreements?
- Do you find finances to be a source of stress?
- What are two techniques you find most effective in disciplining your children?
- What is the hardest part of raising a child?
- How important is faith to your marriage?
- How has the faith of each spouse changed over the years?
- How does faith play a role in your raising of children?
- How does faith play a role in family decisions?
- What advice would you give to someone today regarding marriage in the following areas?
    - How to prepare for marriage
    - What to expect in marriage
    - How to succeed in marriage
- Would you recommend marriage to others? Why?

Matrimony. Because the homosexual act cannot bring forth new life, it is not in accord with the nature of marriage.

In addition to the absence of procreative potential, same-sex unions also deny the necessary complementarity of man and woman. St. John Paul II explained:

> Another obstacle is the absence of the conditions for the interpersonal complementarity between male and female willed by the Creator at both the physical-biological and eminently psychological levels. It is only in the union of two sexually different persons that the individual can achieve perfection in a synthesis of unity and mutual psychophysical completion. (*Compendium of the Social Doctrine of the Church*, 228, quoting St. John Paul II)

In its defense of marriage as a sacramental bond between a baptized man and a baptized woman, the Church does not imply condemnation for persons struggling with homosexuality. They are not "lesser" citizens by any means. However, *no one* has the natural right to marry anyone they wish. Because marriage and the family is the building block of society, society has the obligation to preserve the truth of this institution. This obligation begins with the witness of Catholic marriages to the genuine meaning of their existence.

Instead of just talking about the moral wrongness of same-sex unions, Catholic men and women called to the vocation of marriage must *live* it in such a way as to witness to the world the truth of this God-instituted reality. Spouses are called to be signs and instruments of Christ's love in the world and to witness to the religious meaning of marriage.

SECTION ASSESSMENT

NOTE TAKING
Use the concept web you created for this section to complete the following items.

1. Name and explain at least two ways cohabitation undermines marriage.
2. Name and explain at least two ways same-sex unions undermine marriage.

COMPREHENSION

3. What are some of the negative consequences of cohabitation for the couple and for children living with them?
4. What are some examples of current or historical civil laws regulating whom a person can marry?

REFLECTION

5. How can Catholic men and women best represent the vocation of marriage to society? Write a two- to three-paragraph response sharing your ideas.

Section Summaries

Focus Question

How can you live a life of chastity that serves the family as the foundation of society?

Complete one of the following:

 Read and summarize paragraphs 2331–2345 in the *Catechism of the Catholic Church*. These paragraphs cover issues related to the Sixth Commandment, including the origins of marriage and the vocation to chastity.

 Share an effective strategy for explaining the importance of chastity to middle school students. Be sure to keep your terms and instructions age-appropriate.

 Imagine yourself in fifteen years. Write a letter to your future spouse telling how you lived chastely in preparation for marriage and family life. *Optional*: If you are considering the priesthood or religious life, write the same type of letter to your bishop or religious superior.

INTRODUCTION (PAGES 107–112)

Community and Family

Belonging to a community is essential to your well-being. The family is the foundational community. Marriage is the building block for family life. The characteristics of marriage are *totality, unity, indissolubility, and fruitfulness.*

 St. John Paul II wrote, "As the family goes, so goes the nation, and so goes the whole world in which we live."[12] List three reasons why this is true.

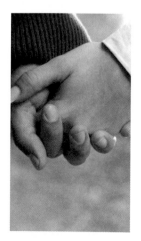

SECTION 1 (PAGES 113–116)

Understanding the Rewards and Challenges of Chaste Living

You are called to live a chaste life in all your relationships and actions. Sins against chastity include adultery, fornication, masturbation, rape, prostitution, and pornography. These sins bring harm to the individual as well as to society.

 Research the issue of human trafficking on the US Conference of Catholic Bishops website (www.usccb.org). Write a short advertisement with an appropriate marketing slogan that promotes awareness of this issue.

SECTION 2 (PAGES 117–121)

Sins against the Nature of Conjugal Love

Contraception, the homosexual act, and artificial means of conception, such as vitro fertilization, undermine the dignity of the sexual union of spouses and take away spouses' call to share in God's work in creating new life.

 Other than following Church teaching, what do you think would be some advantages to a couple using Natural Family Planning? List at least three advantages.

SECTION 3 (PAGES 122–125)

Attacks against the Dignity of Marriage

The dignity and value of marriage has been undermined by the widespread acceptance of cohabitation and same-sex unions. Church teaching emphasizes the immorality of these acts and the essential role of the marriage covenant in society.

 Write a letter or an e-mail to a local or national political representative that explains the importance of marriage as a lifelong, life-giving commitment, which is made for a man and a woman.

Chapter Assignments

Choose and complete at least one of the following three assignments to assess your understanding of the material in this chapter.

1. Examining Primary Sources: *Familiaris Consortio*

 Read the following paragraphs from *Familiaris Consortio* by St. John Paul II: 1, 3, 6, 8, 11, 13–15. You can access the encyclical at www.vatican.va. Write a two- to three-sentence summary of each paragraph in your own words. Create a pamphlet, short video, multimedia presentation or use another media format to share this information creatively.

2. Recognizing Challenges to the Rights of the Family

 Locate the *Charter of the Rights of the Family*, presented by St. John Paul II at the request of the Synod of Bishops, at the Vatican website (www.vatican.va). List six of the rights of families identified in the charter. Then choose two of the rights and, for each, share an example from current events showing how the right is being challenged in today's world.

3. A Mock E-mail Exchange on Cohabitation or Same-Sex Unions

 Choose to research Church teaching on *either* cohabitation or same-sex unions. Information can be found on the US Bishops' website, www.usccb.org.

Then, pretend you are e-mailing a friend who is "for" one of these issues. Explain the Church's teaching clearly over a series of two or three e-mails. For each e-mail you send, also create an e-mail response from your friend, presenting a contrary perspective. Conclude the exchange with an e-mail in which you summarize the truth of the Church's teaching regarding marriage.

Faithful Disciples

Bl. Louis and Zélie Martin

As the domestic church, the family is the setting in which saints are made. For one of the greatest saints of modern times, St. Thérèse of Lisieux, this reality is certainly true. St. Thérèse was born in 1873, one of nine children born to Louis and Zélie Martin.

Louis Martin

Zélie Martin

Before marriage, Zélie (born Marie-Azélie Guerin) had wanted to enter religious life, but eventually discerned that it was not her calling. She took up the trade of lace-making, in which she was highly skilled. Following a similar path, Louis had intended to become a monk, but he too discerned that it was not the Lord's calling for him. He became a talented watchmaker.

Zélie and Louis were both working in Alençon, France, when one day they passed each other by on a bridge. It is said that Zélie heard an internal voice that said, "This is he whom I have prepared for you." They met not long after, and were married three months later, in 1858.

Both Zélie and Louis wanted to live a life dedicated to the Lord. Their family motto was "serve God first." Their marriage faced many hardships. Of their nine children, only five survived past early childhood. Yet they continually turned to God through their sufferings. Their faith did not waver, but rather became stronger.

In 1877, after only fifteen years of marriage, Zélie succumbed to breast cancer. Thérèse, the youngest daughter, was only four years old at the time of her mother's death. Louis moved the family to Lisieux, France, to be closer to his brother and his family. Louis himself battled sickness for many years, until his death in 1894.

The Martins' devotion bore fruit in their children's lives. Although neither Zélie nor Louis was called to religious life, their five daughters all entered religious life with the Carmelites. Thérèse, also known as the "Little Flower," was declared a saint and a doctor of the Church. But the Martins are not honored simply because their children entered religious life. Rather, the Church honors them for their unwavering faith in God and faithfulness to his will, most especially in living out their marriage vocation and caring for their children and instilling in them a deep faith in God.

There have been plenty of married saints, but Louis and Zélie are the first married couple to be beatified together. St. Thérèse said in a letter, "God gave me a father and a mother who were more worthy of heaven than of earth."

At their beatification, Cardinal José Saraiva Martins, the Prefect of the Congregation for the Causes of Saints, said "Louis and Zélie understood that they could become holy not in spite of marriage, but through, in, and by marriage, and that their becoming a couple was the beginning of an ascent together."

Reading Comprehension

1. Why does the Church honor Zélie and Louis Martin?

2. What was the Martins' response to the trials they faced as a married couple?

Writing Task

- At the beatification of Bl. Louis and Zélie, Cardinal José Saraiva Martins, at the time the Prefect of the Congregation for the Causes of Saints, said of their story:

> My heart is full of gratitude to God for this exemplary witness of conjugal love .... I thought of *my* father and mother, and now I invite you to think of your parents that together we may thank God for having created and made us Christians through the conjugal love of our parents. The gift of life is a marvelous thing, but even more wonderful for us is that our parents led us to the Church which alone is capable of making us Christians. For no one becomes a Christian by oneself.

Write your response to the following:

1. What does it mean to say, "no one becomes a Christian by oneself"?

2. Have your parents helped you along the Christian path? If so, how?

3. If you are called to be a mother or father in the future, what are some ways in which you could help raise saints?

Explaining the Faith

How is Natural Family Planning morally different from artificial contraception?

Spacing out the birth of children may be a responsible and appropriate choice. However, even right intentions do not justify immoral means for achieving them. For example, you may wish that your elderly, very sick grandmother passes away so that she is no longer suffering, but intentionally ending her life is radically different than supporting and loving her as she dies naturally. Similar to this, there are both moral and immoral means for postponing a pregnancy. But what makes artificial contraception morally wrong? Is it simply because it is "artificial"? After all, there are many artificial things one can do to his or her body that are not morally problematic, such as wearing contact lenses or having a prosthetic leg. Yet in these cases, the artificial things *help* a person perform a natural function, namely seeing or walking. Conversely, artificial contraception impedes a natural function. Thus, it is more than merely artificial: it is *unnatural*. One could even argue that is *anti-natural*; that is, against the natural reality of the sexual act. Contraception interferes with the natural process of conception that results from sexual intercourse. Therefore, even if the intention and outcome are the same—namely, postponing pregnancy—achieving the outcome through natural means, without interfering with the natural process of conception, is what separates the morality of Natural Family Planning from the morally wrong choice of artificial contraception.

 Further Research

- Read section 32 of St. John Paul II's *Familiaris Consortio*. (You can find it at www.vatican.va.) Answer the following question: What happens when couples who use artificial contraception separate the two meanings of sex that God has inscribed on the human person?

Prayer
Prayer for Families

Lord, from you every family in heaven and on earth takes it name. Father, you are Love and Life.

Through your Son, Jesus Christ, born of woman, and through the Holy Spirit, the fountain of divine charity, grant that every family on earth may become for each successive generation a true shrine of life and love.

Grant that your grace may guide the thoughts and actions of husbands and wives for the good of their families and of all the families of the world.

Grant that the young may find in the family solid support for their human dignity and for their growth in truth and love.

Grant that love, strengthened by the grace of the Sacrament of Marriage, may prove mightier than all the weaknesses and trials through which our families sometimes pass.

Through the intercession of the Holy Family of Nazareth, grant that the Church may fruitfully carry out her worldwide mission in the family and through the family.

We ask this of you, who are Life, Truth, and Love with the Son and the Holy Spirit. Amen.[13]

—St. John Paul II

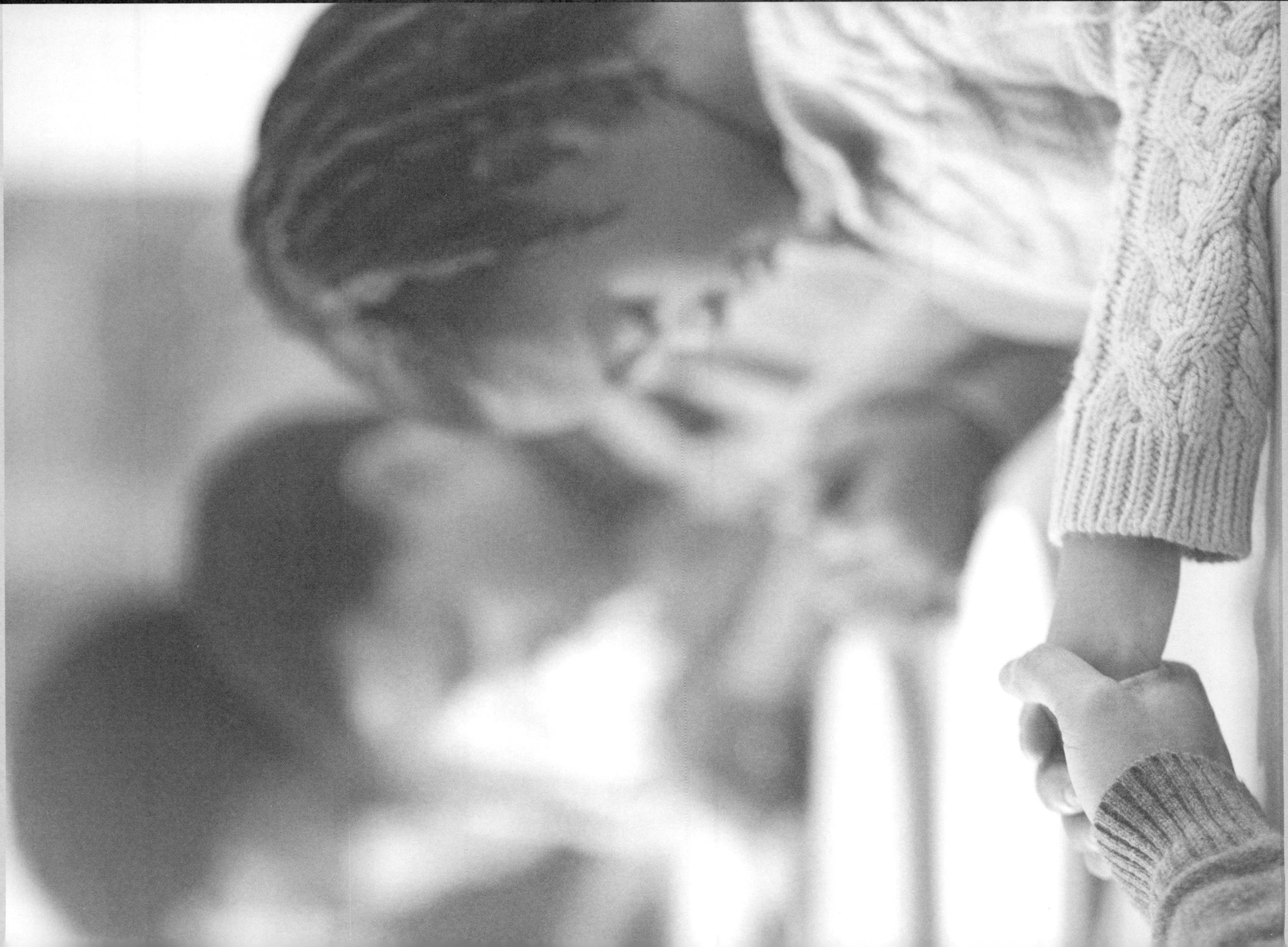

RIGHTS AND RESPONSIBILITIES

HEALTH and HUMAN SERVICES
MANDATE

In 2012, the United States Department of Health and Human Services (HHS) released a mandate requiring all health insurance plans to cover sterilizations and contraceptives, even those that induce an early abortion by preventing a human life in its earliest of stages from implanting in the womb.

The mandate included a "religious exemption," but it was so narrowly defined that virtually all Catholic and Christian organizations—such as hospitals, universities, and charitable associations—would not fit the parameters. Also, there were no provisions for companies in the for-profit category in which the owners or employees objected to their health insurance money going toward such services.

The United States Conference of Catholic Bishops rallied to fight the mandate; they called it "an unprecedented . . . violation of religious liberty by the federal government." Joining them were clergy from other faith denominations who saw any restriction on conscience as an attack on religious freedom.

Many Catholic and Christian universities, other religious institutions, and even for-profit businesses like Hobby Lobby filed lawsuits against the federal government in this matter (Hobby Lobby won a 5–4 Supreme Court decision in its favor in 2014). The case led to an ongoing effort by the USCCB to fight against this and other government mandates that threaten the First Amendment right to religious liberty.

FOCUS QUESTION

What are all people's **FUNDAMENTAL HUMAN RIGHTS,** and what are the **RESPONSIBILITIES** that go with them?

Chapter Overview

Introduction Basic Human Rights

Section 1 Responsibilities in Civil Society

Section 2 The Government and Human Rights

Section 3 Catholic Understanding of Government

Section 4 Politics and Conscience

INTRODUCTION
Basic Human Rights

MAIN IDEA
God bestows basic human rights—that is, the fundamental rights required for living with dignity. The most basic of all rights is the right to life. Corresponding to all rights are duties and responsibilities.

The Catholic social teaching principle known as "rights and responsibilities" refers to the fact that every person has individual human rights, but correspondingly each person also has responsibilities toward both society and oneself. When either of these is emphasized at the expense of the other, problems can arise.

When people focus only on what they are owed (looking only at their "rights"), instead of what they owe others or society, they can develop a sense of entitlement. Conversely, ignoring people's rights and focusing only on their "responsibilities" often leads to a denial of people's dignity. The Catholic social teaching principle of rights and responsibilities emphasizes a both/and approach—that is, that all people have God-given human rights, and all people have duties to others and to society.

Fundamental Human Rights

All human rights are based on your fundamental dignity as a human being. True rights are not derived from society or from a consensus, but rather they are inherently part of your dignity as being made in God's image and likeness. They are written into the natural law, inherent to the intellectual and free nature of human beings. Therefore, all basic human rights are:

- *Universal.* Human rights are present in each person, regardless of time or location. No matter the continent or culture or time period, human rights remain the same.

- *Inviolable.* Human rights must not be assaulted or violated because they are inherent in the human person and come directly from God. This doesn't mean that rights are *never* assaulted or violated—this happens all too often—but rather that these

NOTE TAKING

Summarizing Concepts and Finding Examples. Make a chart like the one below. In the first column, list a fundamental human right mentioned in this section. In the second column, summarize the right in your own words. In the third column, share an example of a way this right is violated. The first one has been done for you.

Right	Summary	Example
Right to Life	Everyone has a right to live and to have the basic necessities needed for life.	A family living in poverty

violations cannot truly eliminate or harm the right, because they are essential to one's personhood.

- *Inalienable.* Human rights cannot be taken away because they are inherent and beyond challenge. No one has authority to remove these rights because they come from God. Even if there was a society in which it appeared all human rights were taken away, they would still remain.

St. John XXIII enumerated some of the most fundamental human rights in his encyclical, *Pacem in Terris* ("Peace on Earth") outlined in the infographic below.

FUNDAMENTAL HUMAN RIGHTS

according to St. John XXIII

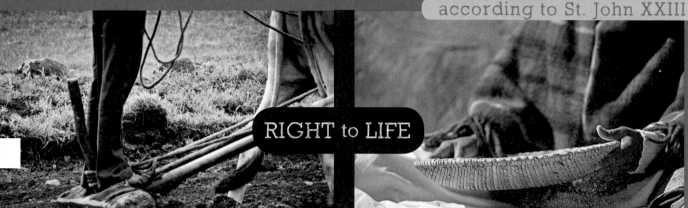

RIGHT to LIFE

We see that every man has the right to life, to bodily integrity, and to the means which are suitable for the proper development of life; these are primarily food, clothing, shelter, rest, medical care, and finally the necessary social services. Therefore a human being also has the right to security in cases of sickness, inability to work, widowhood, old age, unemployment, or in any other case in which he is deprived of the means of subsistence through no fault of his own. (§11)

MORAL and CULTURAL RIGHTS

By the natural law every human being has the right to receive respect for his person, his good reputation, freedom in searching for truth and in expressing and communicating his opinions, and pursuit of art, within the limits laid down by the moral order and the common good; and he has the right to be informed truthfully about public events. (§12)

The natural law also gives man the right to share in the benefits of culture, and therefore the right to a basic education. (§13)

RIGHT to WORSHIP GOD

The first three of the Ten Commandments guarantee that humans can maintain a relationship with God, to be able to freely worship him. This too must be listed among the rights of a human being: the freedom to honor God according to the sincere dictates of his own conscience, and therefore the right to practice his religion privately and publicly. (§14)

RIGHT to CHOOSE FREELY ONE'S STATE of LIFE

Human beings have the right to choose freely the state of life which they prefer, and therefore the right to set up a family, with equal rights and duties for a man and woman, and also the right to follow a vocation to the priesthood or religious life. (§15)

The family, grounded on marriage freely contracted, monogamous and indissoluble, is and must be considered the first and essential cell of human society. From this it follows that most careful provision must be made for the family both in economic and social matters as well as in those which are of a cultural and moral nature, all of which look to the strengthening of the family and helping it carry out its function. (§16)

Parents, however, have a prior right in the support and education of their children. (§17)

ECONOMIC RIGHTS

If we turn our attention to the economic sphere, it is clear that people have a right by the natural law not only to opportunities to work, but also the right to go about work without coercion. (§18)

The right to private property, even of productive goods, also derives from the nature of man. (§21)

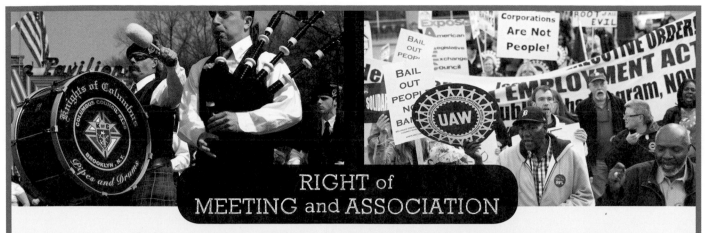

RIGHT of MEETING and ASSOCIATION

From the fact that human beings are by nature social, there arises the right of assembly and association. (§23)

RIGHT to EMIGRATE and IMMIGRATE

Every human being has the right to freedom of movement and of residence within the confines of his own country; and, when there are just reasons for it, the right to emigrate to other countries and take up residence there. (§25)

POLITICAL RIGHTS

The dignity of the human person involves the right to take an active part in public affairs and to contribute one's part to the common good of the citizens. (§26)

Certain responsibilities of individuals and society undergird the rights named by St. John XXIII and all other human rights. The first of these is the responsibility to protect these rights, because all are vital to the dignity of the human person and thus the common good. Further responsibilities are associated with each specific right. For example:

- The right to life for all humans requires the responsibility to take care of, and preserve, one's own life.

- The right to a decent standard of living is associated with living a responsible lifestyle.

- The right to seek out the truth calls for the corresponding responsibility to search for truth and is a demand of the Eighth Commandment. To live in the truth means to believe in Jesus Christ who is Truth Incarnate.

To claim one's rights while ignoring one's responsibilities diminishes the dignity of humans. You also have the duty to respect other people's rights.

The Source of Human Rights

Essential to all human rights is the right to religious freedom, that is, according to St. John Paul II, "the right to live in the truth of one's faith and in conformity with one's transcendent dignity as a person."[1]

As Karol Jozef Wojtyla, growing up in Poland during the rise of Nazism and later serving as Archbishop of Kraków during a period of communist tyranny, St. John Paul II experienced firsthand the suppression of religious freedom and its consequences. He clearly understood the Church's teaching that religious freedom is the source of all human rights. A person who respects, honors, and worships God, who is author of life, is able to naturally arrive at an understanding of the other basic human rights, including those addressed by St. John XXIII.

This chapter will examine rights and responsibilities primarily within civil society, including what you expect from, and what you are responsible for, in government. Rights and responsibilities associated with economic society will be addressed in Chapter 7.

SECTION ASSESSMENT

NOTE TAKING

Use the notes you created to match the rights listed in the left column with the example in the right column.

1. Right to Life
2. Moral and Cultural Rights
3. Right to Worship God
4. Right to Choose Freely One's State in Life
5. Economic Rights
6. Right of Meeting and Association
7. Right to Emigrate and Immigrate
8. Political Rights

A. freedom of movement
B. has origins in our social nature
C. freedom of expression
D. able to own private property
E. freedom to publicly pray
F. able to contribute to public life
G. basic necessities, like food and water
H. vocational choice

COMPREHENSION

9. What constitutes a human right?
10. Why are rights inalienable?
11. What is the most fundamental of all rights?
12. What did St. John Paul II teach was the source of all rights?

REFLECTION

13. What human rights do you think are most abused in today's society?

SECTION 1
Responsibilities in Civil Society

MAIN IDEA
The principle of subsidiarity establishes a hierarchy of functions and responsibilities.

You live in a **civil society**. You expect your government to defend your nation against attacks by enemies, your local police and fire agencies to be there for you when there is an emergency, and your city or town to provide essential services such as trash collection and snow plowing. In turn, you are expected to participate in civil society in many different ways, such as by voting in local and national elections, joining neighborhood associations, school boards, business clubs, and so forth.

Civil society is the blanket term for all social communities outside the family and Church. To better understand how civil society operates, it is important to understand how its tasks are to be performed in a hierarchical structure defined around the principle of subsidiarity. As you learned in Chapter 2, this principle teaches that the promotion of justice and the common good is best achieved at the most immediate level, beginning with the foundational society, the family, and working its way up to larger groups from the local to national level.

This section examines how the principle of subsidiarity can help you evaluate how you can naturally integrate your participation in family life and the Church with your participation in civil society.

> **civil society** The sum of relationships and resources, cultural and associative, that are relatively independent from the political sphere and the economic sector.

NOTE TAKING

Understanding the Main Concept. Copy the following scenarios into your notes. After you have a grasp on the principle of subsidiarity, write whether that principle is being violated in each scenario.

1. The federal government legislates the speed limit for interstate highways.

2. The state government passes a law dictating which books must be read in senior high school English classes for each school district.

3. The United States Congress passes an environmental law that limits the amount of carbon emissions Midwest factories may release into the atmosphere.

Subsidiarity: A Hierarchy of Responsibility in Civil Society

Your responsibility to care for your God-given rights begins with individual responsibility. The principle of subsidiarity establishes a hierarchy of functions and responsibilities. It means that the individual and the social group closest to the individual must take care of his or her needs. The social group closest to the individual is the family.

In other words, responsibility for your needs should be taken up at the "lowest" level possible. The logic behind this concept is straight-forward: big, remote social entities do not do as good a job of meeting the rights of an individual as do smaller entities that are "closer" in knowledge and proximity to the person. Correspondingly, the social entity closest to the individual has the greatest connection in sharing the same rights and responsibilities. For example,

parents have more to gain by making sure their children are fed, clothed, educated, free to follow their own vocation, and the like, than a government agency does. Parents know and love their children and have an intimate relationship with them. Larger entities that might also be able to offer the basic necessities (food, shelter, clothing) do not.

Like everything else in Catholic social doctrine, this always relates back to the dignity of the human person. The *Compendium of the Social Doctrine of the Church* explains that "the principle of subsidiarity protects people from abuses by higher-level social authority and calls on these same authorities to help individuals and intermediate groups to fulfill their duties" (*CSDC*, §187).

In *Quadragesimo Anno* ("On the Fortieth Anniversary" of *Rerum Novarum*) Pope Pius XI described contradicting the principle of subsidiarity as a "grave evil." This is primarily because giving the responsibility to take care of the human person to an entity far removed from his or her personal situation often leads to a denial of the person's dignity, because his or her rights are not met in a manner best suited to the circumstances. In such situation, the human person becomes merely a "number" of a whole and is not treated with the individuality he deserves. Pope Pius XI explained it this way:

> Just as it is gravely wrong to take from individuals what they can accomplish by their own initiative and industry and give it to the community, so also it is an injustice and at the same time a grave evil and disturbance of right order to assign to a greater and higher association what lesser and subordinate organizations can do. For every social activity ought of its very nature to furnish help to the members of the body social, and never destroy and absorb them. (*QA*, § 79)

Under the principle of subsidiarity, people should take responsibility to provide for their own welfare, given the situation they are dealing with. It is wrong for the government to take over what families or voluntary organizations can do for themselves. For example, it is wise for school board representatives to be elected by the local community rather than appointed by the federal government. The government should only be involved when the needs of people cannot be met at a more local level.

The principle of subsidiarity discourages attempts to maximize or centralize the power of the state at the expense of local institutions. The principle of subsidiarity wisely supports the sharing of power and authority on the grassroots level. It prefers local control over central decision-making. The sign of a just government is one that frees people to exercise their own responsibility. A just government is one that is small enough not to intrude unnecessarily into people's lives, yet is large enough to promote the common good and guarantee basic human rights.

How the Principle of Subsidiarity Works

The principle of subsidiarity implies the existence of a variety of associations and institutions below the level of the central government. Examples include neighborhood associations, school boards, zoning

Sometimes it is impossible for people to obtain justice on the local level because of ingrained prejudice or local customs and laws. A good historical example took place in states that set up "separate but equal" schools for African Americans beginning in the 1890s. Unfortunately, the schools were not equal. So ingrained was discrimination against African Americans that the federal government had to get involved to ensure the basic human rights of citizens of all states. Civil rights laws on the national level were (and are) necessary to guarantee that basic human rights are respected in all states of the union. In this example, and others like it, the proper application of the principle of subsidiarity allows the large governmental unit to step in and take action when necessary. The federal government is often the only agency that can effectively achieve a desired goal. Sometimes only at this level can the common good of all citizens be guaranteed.

commissions, city councils, and political action committees. Some of these associations or institutions are responsible for making decisions that affect individual citizens. For example, the city council may pass a curfew law after consulting citizen groups, with the goal of protecting citizens and bringing law and order to the community. Other associations have the purpose of influencing how decisions are made at higher levels of government. For example, the National Right to Life Association lobbies legislators to pass pro-life amendments. Or, labor unions lend financial support to legislators who support raising the minimum wage.

You may have noticed that the definition of subsidiarity comprises both "negative" and "positive" obligations. On the negative side, larger societies should not interfere with smaller societies; on the positive side, they also have an obligation to help these smaller societies develop and grow. "On the basis of this principle, all societies of a superior order must adopt attitudes of help ("*subsidium*")—therefore of support, promotion, development—with respect to lower-order societies."[2]

The principle of subsidiarity is not meant to maintain a status quo that denies individuals their rights. It can never be an excuse for selfishness, ignoring the common good, or preventing human solidarity. It should not be used as an excuse to support governmental policies that work against the poorest of society. It cannot be used to silence those whose voices have difficulty getting heard.

SECTION ASSESSMENT

NOTE TAKING

Review the scenarios you commented on from your Note Taking assignment to complete the following task.

1. Explain whether the principle of subsidiarity is being violated in the following scenario: Your school administration passed a rule that student athletes must have a 2.0 grade point average to participate in sports; the state requirement is a 1.5 grade point average (on a 4.0 scale).

VOCABULARY

2. Define *civil society*.

3. Write a definition of subsidiarity in your own words. Include your own example.

FILL IN THE BLANK

4. The principle of subsidiarity encourages the _____ of power and authority on a grassroots level.

CRITICAL THINKING

5. What would be a situation in which it would be just for the larger community (such as the federal government) to be involved in a local matter?

The Government and Human Rights

Vital to a just civil society is the political society or government. The government is the body of **civil authority** that keeps order in civil society and administers its laws. As with the objective of civil society, government exists primarily to promote the welfare of individuals. One of its purposes is to apply the principle of subsidiarity. Pope Pius XI stated: "The supreme authority of the State ought, therefore, to let subordinate groups handle matters and concerns of lesser importance which would otherwise dissipate its efforts greatly."[3]

Humans as the Foundation and Purpose of Government

The goal of government is the growth and development of the human person. Governments only exist to serve their people. Though human beings are inherently social, each person also has a unique individuality that can never be denied. A task of government is to support the individuality of its citizens. Recall that the common good is only obtained when the needs of individuals are met.

This means that the first priority of government must be the promotion of human rights. Humans have intrinsic rights, as described on pages 138–140. The government has a responsibility to uphold these rights. And, this responsibility should be undertaken as more than just a duty, but rather as a "civil friendship,"[4] based on the virtue of charity. These actions are always aimed at justice.

> **civil authority** Leaders of public groups—particularly government leaders—or institutions that make laws.

NOTE TAKING

Fill in the Blanks. Copy each sentence listed below in your notebook. As you read the section, complete the sentence with the word(s) that make it complete.

- Governments only exist to ___ people.
- The government does not give rights, but rather it ___ them.
- Authority is legitimate when it seeks the ___ good.
- The ___ ___ requires you to respect legitimate authorities in civil society.
- ___ ___ means that you have a duty to follow human laws when they agree with divine laws.

The first column in the chart below emphasizes some key, specific responsibilities of the government to its people. The second column names corresponding responsibilities of individual citizens. All of these actions support basic human rights.

Responsibilities of Government	Responsibilities of Individuals
1. Guarantee the conditions that allow associations and individuals to obtain their due, according to their vocation and nature.	Help shape a just, loving society that promotes love of God and neighbor. Minimally, be on the alert to root out any laws or practices that cause sin or undermine human dignity.
2. Root out any form of social, religious, cultural, racial, economic, ethnic, or gender discrimination that denies people their fundamental human rights.	Take special vigilance to see that those with most need are cared for in society. Support causes, laws, and institutions that guarantee the rights of the poor.
3. Guarantee the most basic right of all, the right to life. Outlaw crimes against life like direct abortion, murder, euthanasia, assisted suicide, and fetal experimentation.	Treat each person as another self. Exercise the virtue of solidarity by viewing others as members of one family of God.
4. Create a climate where people can participate and contribute to the common good. Foster honest, just, and open communication based on truth, freedom, justice, and solidarity.	Exercise one's right to participate in society. Everyone has a duty to engage in voluntary and generous social interchange according to one's position, role, talents, and interests. Minimally, one must meet family and work obligations, contribute to the Church community, and be involved in public affairs.
5. Ensure that those who hold public authority always promote the common good, recognize the sovereignty of the law, and promote the principle of subsidiarity and the practice of limited government	Respect those who have legitimate positions of authority and obey established laws. Protest, even through civil disobedience, unjust laws that undermine human dignity.

This is not an exhaustive list of responsibilities of society and corresponding responsibilities of individuals. However, it does highlight many key responsibilities both societies and individuals have that flow from their social nature.

The Role of Authority

The Fourth Commandment—"Honor your father and your mother"—also applies to legitimate authorities in civil society. This includes people such as teachers, coaches, and police officers. It also includes political authorities and the authority of law itself (see page 149).

Authority is necessary in any social structure. Since all legitimate authority is from God, God's authority is present in just governments and laws. St. Paul wrote: "Let every person be subordinate to the higher authorities, for there is no authority except from God, and those that exist have been established by God. Therefore, whoever resists authority opposes what God has appointed, and those who oppose it will bring judgment upon themselves" (Rom 13:1–2). Legitimate authority in society and government denies the possibility for **anarchy**, which is always seen as an evil. Jesus himself made it clear that his disciples must respect rightful secular authorities, instructing them to "repay to Caesar what belongs to Caesar and to God what belongs to God" (Lk 20:25). Christ affirms that your first obligation is to God, but that you must also give worldly authority what it is due.

Defining Legitimate Authority

It is important to define *legitimate* authority. For example, authority is legitimate only when it "seeks the common good for the group concerned and if it employs morally licit means to attain it" (*CCC*, 1903). Thus, if an authority is unjust itself or its measures are unjust, one does not have an obligation to follow it. For example, a government that mandates the number of children families can have violates the inviolable rights of the family, and citizens do not have a moral obligation to obey its dictate. In fact, St. Thomas Aquinas would argue that a law isn't even truly a law if it goes against reason, formed by the natural law.

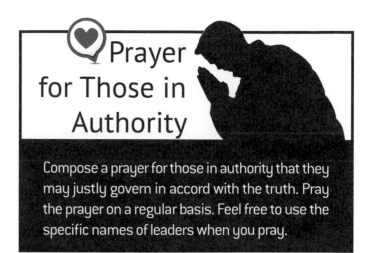

Prayer for Those in Authority

Compose a prayer for those in authority that they may justly govern in accord with the truth. Pray the prayer on a regular basis. Feel free to use the specific names of leaders when you pray.

Furthermore, the *Compendium of the Social Doctrine of the Church* (§396–398): gives guidelines on what a true authority should look like.

- *Authority must be guided by the moral law*, which is transcendent, absolute, universal, and equally binding upon all.[5] All authority must follow the divine and natural law, from which all other laws should emerge.

- *Authority must recognize, respect, and promote essential human and moral values*, "values which no individual, no majority, and no State can ever create, modify, or destroy."[6]

- *Authority must enact just laws*, that is, laws that correspond to the dignity of the human person and to what is required by reason, formed by the natural law.

Because all authority is ultimately from God, any necessary authority within human societies is subject to divine law. In other words, God's Law always trumps man-made laws. You must follow human laws only insofar as they are in accord with divine law. This is called **civil allegiance**.

---

anarchy A state of lawlessness or political disorder due to the absence of governmental authority.

civil allegiance Duty of respect and obedience owed by every person to the state of which he is a member. In the light of Christian principles, this does not mean that one must support his country in morally wrong ideologies or practices.

Your ultimate calling is to be a citizen of Heaven. When your life is pointed toward this destiny, your social interactions here on earth are informed by this reality. You must be obedient to all rightful, just authority, but this duty is only binding when the authority is legitimate and its laws are just, for those are the ones which are in accord with your final heavenly citizenship.

UNDERSTANDING the MEANING of LAW

Law is defined as reasonable regulations, issued by the proper authority, and aimed at the common good. Law is intended to promote basic human rights. Good law promotes human freedom. And, as you know, following law always brings with it corresponding responsibility on your behalf. There are several other specific definitions of law:

- Divine law (also known as Eternal Law) has its source in the Blessed Trinity. Divine law can either be natural or revealed.

- Natural law is inscribed in the human heart and known by human reason. An example is the natural knowledge that one should not take the life of another person without just cause.

- **Revealed law** is found in the ancient law (Old Testament). It is also found in the New Law (Law of the Gospel)—that is, the teaching of Christ, notably in the Sermon on the Mount. The New Law of Christ perfects the ancient law. An example of revealed law is the Beatitudes.

- Civil law is the law of the government; it should apply the natural law to the given society. An example is traffic laws that help protect innocent lives.

- Ecclesiastical law is the body of laws and regulations of the Church. It applies revealed law to the lives of Catholics. For example, in the Old Testament, God revealed that his people were to "keep holy the Sabbath." This revealed law is applied through the ecclesiastical law that mandates Catholics attend Mass on Sundays and holy days of obligation.

revealed law God's law made known in the Old Testament and the New Testament.

The Relationship between Government and the Family

In its role of protecting human rights and adhering to the principle of subsidiarity, the government will naturally interact with its citizens, both as individuals and as members of a family. The family performs functions that are valuable for the government—namely, the procreation and education of children, the passing on of culture, and the instilling of values. Hence it is accurate to say that "the family, then, does not exist for society or the State, but society and the State exist for the family."[7]

The principle of subsidiarity applies to the family, in that larger associations like the government should not interfere with functions the family can perform on its own. Also, the government must help protect the family from outside abuses.

However, family life is often at odds with society at large and, by extension, with the government. In many cases, laws are in direct opposition to the development of the family life, such as laws that promote abortion or contraception. Society and governments have a duty to honor and assist the family and to guarantee basic rights. The *Charter of the Rights of the Family* (see page 128), presented by St. John Paul II at the request of the Synod of Bishops, spelled out some of these rights. These include the right to freely choose a state of life, the right to have and educate children, the right to basic necessities like housing, and more.

As with all rights, there is a corresponding responsibility. In this case, the families have a responsibility to show society, namely the government, their great dignity and value to the world. Civilizations rise and fall based on the nature of the family, so it is a family's duty to remain thriving, so society at large may thrive.

SECTION ASSESSMENT

NOTE TAKING

Use the sentences you completed to help answer the following questions.

1. Share two responsibilities of government that help it to assure the common good for its citizens.

2. Besides parents, who are other legitimate authority figures the Fourth Commandment requires you to respect?

VOCABULARY

3. Define *anarchy*.

COMPREHENSION

4. Share an example of how divine law equates to civil law and ecclesiastical law.

5. What should be the first priority of the government?

6. Name one "right" of the family.

CRITICAL THINKING

7. Apply one of the basic rights of the family to an issue in the current news. Explain how the right addresses the issue.

Catholic Understanding of Government

MAIN IDEA

The Church does not necessarily promote a particular form of government, but acknowledges that those with democratic values are well-suited for the common good.

IN GOD WE TRUST

The Church in her nature is not a political society, nor is she bound to any government. The primary duty of the Church is the spiritual needs of her people, whereas governments exist to manage temporal affairs. Because of the necessity of religious freedom, the political society should not interfere with the Church's mission. For her part, the Church "respects the legitimate autonomy of the democratic order and is not entitled to express preferences for this or that institutional or constitutional solution,"[8] except to address religious or moral implications of their programs. Although the government and the Church are autonomous, they are not always strictly separate, in that they can cooperate to serve the needs that allow men and women to flourish.

Democratic Governments

When discussing political society, a question concerning the *best* form of government often arises. The Church does not necessarily promote a singular form of government. However, she is very clear that political communities that uphold democratic values—that is, ones that call for the involvement of citizens—are integral for upholding human rights.

Nevertheless, democratic governments are not immune to unjust policies and ideologies. That is, even a government that appears to be democratic can

NOTE TAKING

Classifying Information. Create a two-column chart like the one below. As you read the section, list both positive and negative characteristics of government.

Positive	Negative
promotes human dignity	politicians put their own needs first

The "balance of power" or "separation of powers" in government is a model that was first developed in ancient Greece. The typical balance of power, as in the United States, is among the legislative, judicial, and executive branches.

still deny the dignity of the human person and the common good. An authentic democracy does more than just involve its citizens, but it "is the fruit of a convinced acceptance of the values that inspire democratic procedures: the dignity of every human person, the respect of human rights, commitment to the common good as the purpose and guiding criterion for political life."[9]

In *Doctrinal Note on Some Questions Regarding the Participation of Catholics in Political Life* the Congregation for the Doctrine of the Faith stated: "Democracy must be based on the true and solid foundation of non-negotiable ethical principles, which are the underpinning of life in society" (§3). These principles are foundational for any society, because they concern the "integral good of the human person." Explicitly named in the document are such issues as abortion, euthanasia, protection for the rights of the human embryo, monogamous marriage between a man and a woman, protection of minors, and religious freedom.

One element of democratic governments that helps to protect human rights is its balance of power. Even in the first modern social justice encyclical, *Rerum Novarum*, written in 1891, Pope Leo XIII recognized the benefits of organizing government around the three powers of legislative, executive, and judicial branches. St. John Paul II reiterated this in *Centesimus Annus*: "It is preferable that each power be balanced by other powers and by other spheres of responsibility which keep it within proper bounds" (§44).

Within a democratic system, those in power are always held accountable to the people. This is seen in free elections of representatives and the obligation for the representatives to give account of their operations. Nonetheless, representatives are never "merely passive agents of the electors." They have freedom within their elected positions, and should always use that freedom to serve the common good.

Corruption in Political Society

Although the goal of government is to serve the common good, individual representatives of government can, at times, fall short of that ideal. Temptation to put personal gain and pursuits ahead of the welfare of the citizens can lead to corruption, with those with influence undermining rather than contributing to the common good. Responsible authority requires putting power at the true service of others by exercising such virtues as generosity, patience, moderation, and charity.

Also essential to combatting political corruption is avoiding excess bureaucratization, in which institutions become so complex and convoluted that they lose their effectiveness and their focus on the service of citizens. In other words, "the role of those working in public administration is not to be conceived as impersonal or bureaucratic, but rather as an act of generous assistance for citizens, undertaken with a spirit of service."

Totalitarianism

Directly opposed to democracies are **totalitarian** political communities (such as the former Soviet Union or Nazi Germany). When one person or group usurps power, the temptation to reject the dignity of others,

and thus the common good, is often prevalent. Totalitarianism can lead to great mistreatments of human dignity, such as genocide, and often brings abuses of the economic order, such as the rejection of private ownership of goods.

Related to totalitarianism are political communities based on religious fanaticism. Catholics believe that the truth of Christianity should permeate every aspect of society; however, the Church delineates between certain radical regimes and a Christian society. St. John Paul II also said: "Since it is not an ideology, the Christian faith does not presume to imprison changing socio-political realities in a rigid schema." And, "in constantly reaffirming the transcendent

> **totalitarian** A society in which the state exercises total control of the life and conduct of the citizens.

IMPORTANCE OF
TRUTHFULNESS

The Eighth Commandment—"You shall not bear false witness against your neighbor"—calls all people to truthfulness. Along with your individual call to truthfulness, the significance of truth within the various levels of society is also crucial. Namely, politicians (and the media) have a unique role in promoting honesty, for their words reach so many in civil society.

Truthfulness is promoted in several ways, for individuals and groups, including avoiding:

- *detraction*, which is revealing without good reason another's faults and failures;
- *perjury*, which is lying under oath;
- *calumny*, also called slander, which is telling a false story that damages another's reputation;
- *rash judgment*, in which one makes a judgment without sufficient information about another.

Also, within civil society one has an obligation to keep *professional secrets* (such as those told to a psychologist or attorney). Catholic priests must be protected by laws to maintain the sacred *seal of confession*.

ASSIGNMENT
Imagine what a society would look like if truth was not valued by institutions and individuals. Write a short fictional story that expresses what might happen.

dignity of the person, the Church's method is always that of respect for freedom."

"Dictatorship of Relativism"

Though not a political system or a form of government per se, **relativism**—which holds that there is no absolute, universal truth—is present in the political sphere whenever people claim that whatever the majority decides is what is true. In reality, truth is independent of one's opinions or emotions, even if a particular opinion is widespread. Jesus Christ, the Word of God, is the ultimate truth of God's Revelation.

St. John Paul II spoke very clearly about the need for individuals and societies to recognize objective truth and be governed by it: "It must be observed in this regard that if there is no ultimate truth to guide and direct political action, then ideas and convictions can easily be manipulated for reasons of power."[10] St. John Paul II said that such a subjective worldview as relativism can lead even democracies to a form of totalitarianism. It may at first seem that relativism is everything

but a dictatorship; however, when you allow yourself to be led by anything but the ultimate truth, that in and of itself becomes a "dictator" upon your life and freedom.

Before he was elected pope, Cardinal Joseph Ratzinger (Pope Benedict XVI) warned that a world that does not recognize objective truth is in danger of falling under a "dictatorship of relativism." He explained:

> Whereas relativism, that is, letting oneself be "tossed here and there, carried about by every wind of doctrine," seems the only attitude that can cope with modern times. We are building a dictatorship of relativism that does not recognize anything as definitive and whose ultimate goal consists solely of one's own ego and desires. (Homily of Cardinal Joseph Ratzinger, April 18, 2005)

SECTION ASSESSMENT

NOTE TAKING

Use the chart you completed to answer the following questions.

1. What are some negative and positive characteristics of government?
2. What does your list tell you about the possibility of a "perfect" government?

COMPREHENSION

3. What form of government does the Church prefer?
4. How can injustices and corruption enter into democracies?
5. What is the benefit of balance of power in government?
6. How can bureaucracy lead to corruption?

VOCABULARY

7. What are characteristics of a government that is *totalitarian*?
8. How can *relativism* be a form of totalitarianism?

SECTION 4
Politics and Conscience

MAIN IDEA
In order to support human rights and promote the common good, Catholic citizens and politicians have a responsibility to follow their informed conscience in making decisions and then acting on them.

Conscience is primarily a "judgment of reason" that allows you to determine whether certain acts are moral or immoral. Your conscience is not an entity separate from yourself that *tells* you what to do; rather, it is that part of you that *makes you aware* of what is right and wrong, attuned to the voice of God. A well-formed conscience allows you to have responsibility for your actions. If your conscience is sure about the rightness of a course of action, you must follow it in every circumstance.

However, as Blessed Cardinal John Henry Newman said, "conscience has rights, because it has duties."[11] In other words, yes, you have freedom of conscience, but you also have the duty to *correctly* form your conscience. Cardinal Newman added, "We can believe what we choose. We are answerable for what we choose to believe.[12] Here Newman doesn't defend truth-as-whatever-you-want-to-believe. Instead he states that you can choose to believe what you want, but when you choose to believe and act on something not informed by the ultimate truth of Christ, foremost expressed to you in the teaching of the Catholic Church, then you run the risk of sinful error.

NOTE TAKING

Identifying Main Ideas. As you read the section, complete an outline of the contents.

I. What Conscience Is
   A. Definition:
   B. Conscience has rights, because it has ___.
   C. With freedom of conscience is the necessity for ___ liberty.

II. What Conscience Is Not
   A. It is not merely ___ of choice.
   B. It is not ___ telling you what to do.

III. Conscientious Objection
   A. Definition:
   B. Just Resistance to Authority
      1. there is certain, grave, and prolonged violation of fundamental rights;

2.
3. such resistance will not provoke worse disorders;
4.
5. it is impossible reasonably to foresee any better solution.

IV. Participation
   A. Definition:
   B. A basic way for citizens to participate in political society is to ___.
   C. Catholic politicians must:

You are called to use your gifts of intellect and free will to pursue a *true* freedom of conscience, one that is informed by and serves the Incarnate Truth. Cardinal Raymond Burke explains:

> Sometimes the primacy of the conscience is misunderstood. If you mean that the conscience has primacy—in the sense that whatever I feel or think becomes then the right thing to do—that's false. The primacy of the conscience is related essentially to the primacy of the truth. In other words, your conscience has primacy in as much as it is conformed to the truth, and as much as it is properly informed. ("Catholic Identity," *St. Louis Review*, November 8, 2011)

Freedom of conscience is the basis of any free society, because it allows people to act out of their own volitions, not out of coercion. Because the freedom to follow one's conscience is integral to the dignity of the human person, it is essential that those who govern allow citizens to abide by their consciences, unless doing so harms another or impedes upon the consciences of others. Freedom of conscience also requires religious liberty within society. The political community must ensure everyone's right to not only worship God, but also to practice their religion in the society in which they live.

Conscientious Objection

Just as your conscience can help you choose between moral and sinful choices in your personal life, your conscience can also help you to determine the legitimacy of political authority and the morality of demands made by governments. You do not have a moral duty to follow authority that is not legitimate.

And although you have an obligation to follow just laws, the obligation does not apply to unjust ones. This refusal to follow unjust laws—called **conscientious objection**—is also a basic human right and, thus, must be respected by all in authority. Not following laws contrary to divine law is more than just a right. It is also a serious duty of conscience.

When facing situations in which just resistance to authority and unjust law is necessary, peaceful means should always be sought. Examples of peaceful protest in history include Mohandas Gandhi's movement

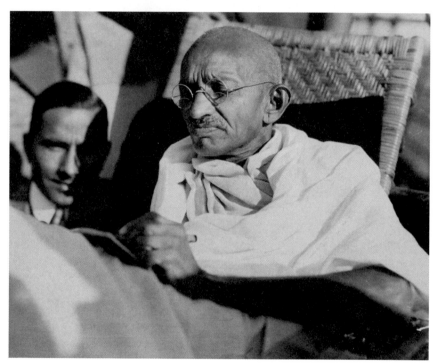

Mohandas Gandhi

for India's independence from Great Britain and the 1980s Solidarity Movement in Poland, mobilized by Lech Walesa, in which strikes, boycotts, and an underground press helped topple the communist regime in Poland. (Chapter 8 will look more in-depth at war, which is a related concept.) In other situations, armed

> **conscientious objection** The moral right to refuse to follow laws or other social constructs based on moral or religious grounds. An example is choosing not to fight in an unjust war.

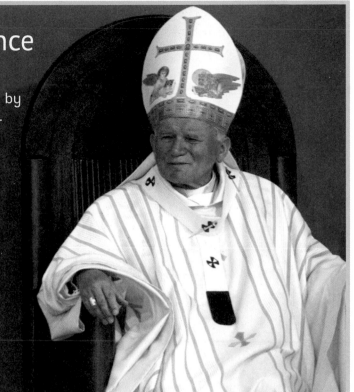

Freedom and Conscience

In *Centesimus Annus* St. John Paul II wrote:

> But freedom attains its full development only by accepting the truth. In a world without truth, freedom loses its foundation and man is exposed to the violence of passion and to manipulation, both open and hidden. The Christian upholds freedom and serves it, constantly offering to others the truth which he has known (see Jn 8:31–32). (§46)

ASSIGNMENT

- Explain the meaning of this statement in your own words.

- How does this statement relate to one's conscience in civic and political societies?

resistance to political authority can be legitimate if *all* of the following criteria, outlined in the *Catechism* (see *CCC*, 2243) are met:

1. there is certain, grave, and prolonged violation of fundamental rights;

2. all other means of redress have been exhausted;

3. such resistance will not provoke worse disorders;

4. there is well-founded hope of success; and

5. it is impossible reasonably to foresee any better solution.

Your Call to Participation

As a Catholic, you are not called to create a closed cocoon around yourself, but rather to be an active participant in your society and world in order to transform it with the presence of the Person of Christ. Your **participation** begins with your own personal responsibility, by the way you educate yourself and do your best in all of your endeavors, such as in schoolwork, in your relationships with family and friends, and in the way you care for those who need your attention. In other words, transforming society begins in your own home, school, and workplace.

On a broader plane, your role in the laity—that is, members of the Church who are not religious or priests—calls on you to participate within the various levels of society, especially the political community. One of the most fundamental ways you can participate in the political society is by encouraging and voting for political representatives who uphold and create laws that protect basic human rights. In fact, it is a moral duty to vote. The *Catechism of the Catholic Church* teaches: "submission to authority and co-responsibility for the common good make it morally obligatory to pay taxes, to exercise the right to vote, and to defend one's country" (*CCC*, 2240).

> **participation** The voluntary and generous engagement of a person in society.

That said, you are not called just to vote, but rather to vote *as a Catholic*. Indeed, your identity as a Catholic should permeate every decision of your life, especially ones of great consequence like voting. Choosing political parties and candidates takes a great amount of prayerful, thoughtful consideration. You must strive to have a conscience that is attuned to the truth of Christ and his Church so that you may vote in light of such truth.

Likewise, Catholic politicians have a special role to promote the common good and the dignity of the human person. The Church is clear that following one's Christian conscience enables politicians to have a unique perspective in secular society:

Living and acting in conformity with one's own conscience on questions of politics is not slavish acceptance of positions alien to politics or some kind of confessionalism, but rather the way in which Christians offer their concrete contribution so that, through political life, society will become more just and more consistent with the dignity of the human person. ("Doctrinal Note on Some Questions Regarding the Participation of Catholics in Political Life," Congregation for the Doctrine of the Faith)

Politicians must remember that "a well-formed Christian conscience does not permit them to vote for a political program or an individual law which contradicts the fundamental contents of faith and morals."[13]

Your call to community begins in your family, but expands to civil and political societies. Within these communities you have both rights and responsibilities. You must work to form your conscience, so that you might be more than just a passive citizen, but rather one who is active in serving the dignity of the human person and, thus, the common good.

SECTION ASSESSMENT

NOTE TAKING
Use your section outline to help you complete the following items.

1. Explain the correct notion of conscience.
2. Why is conscience more than just freedom of choice?
3. Explain the importance of participation in civil and political societies.

Section Summaries

Focus Question

What are all people's fundamental human rights, and what are the responsibilities that go with them?

Complete one of the following:

 Read and summarize paragraphs 2234–2242 of the *Catechism of the Catholic Church*.

 Research a political issue that you do not know much about. Report your findings to the class in a verbal presentation.

 Pretend you are giving a presentation to middle school students on "formation of conscience." Write ten important factors and steps to a properly formed conscience that middle school students can easily understand.

INTRODUCTION (PAGES 137–141)
Basic Human Rights

All people have dignity because they are created in the image and likeness of God, and all have rights simply by virtue of being human. The most basic of rights is the right to life. With rights come responsibilities, the foremost responsibility of which is to ensure the rights of others are upheld.

 Choose one of the rights discussed in the introduction. List three ways you can take responsibility to uphold this right.

SECTION 1 (PAGES 142–145)
Responsibilities in Civil Society

Civil society refers to most of one's interactions with communities in the world. Subsidiarity, a principle that states that the group "closest" to the person must be given primary authority and responsibility for meeting the person's needs—is integral for civil society. Also crucial for such interactions is law. Civil laws should be applications of the natural law.

 Name at least four ways you experience subsidiarity on a daily basis.

The Government and Human Rights

"Political society" or "the state" essentially refers to the government, from the most local to the most remote. The human person is the foundation of the political life. One of the crucial roles of government is to protect the dignity of the family. The importance of an authority that is just cannot be overstated. The Church is not a political community herself, although she informs the political society with her view of the human person.

 Carefully read 1 Peter 2:13–17. Explain its message about authority in your own words.

SECTION 3 (PAGES 151–154)

Catholic Understanding of Government

Governments that uphold democratic values are well suited to meet the rights of the human person. Yet even democracies can become corrupt and abuse the dignity of persons. Relativism, while not a form of government, can disrupt any government by ignoring objective truths.

 List four ways the Church and government can partner together to promote the common good and human dignity.

SECTION 4 (PAGES 155–158)

Politics and Conscience

A well-formed conscience, guided by the truth of Christ and his Church, is crucial for one's interaction with the political community. Every Catholic is called to participate in the world, especially the political community. Such participation is vital for a thriving, truth-oriented civil society.

 The *Catechism of the Catholic Church* teaches: "The education of conscience is indispensable for human beings who are subjected to negative influences and tempted by sin to prefer their own judgment and to reject authoritative teachings" (*CCC*, 1783). Explain this statement in your own words.

Chapter Assignments

Choose and complete at least one of the following three assignments to assess your understanding of the material in this chapter.

1. Church Document Summary

 Read paragraphs 152–159 in the *Compendium of the Social Doctrine of the Church*. You can access the document at www.vatican.va. For each paragraph:

- Write a two- to three-sentence summary in your own words.

- Write a question that could be used to test comprehension of the paragraph.

 Share an application idea that might help a person apply the principle in his or her own life.

2. Questions for Catholic Voters

Recent elections have raised the important issue of whether Catholics may vote for political candidates who endorse pro-abortion views. The issue is especially controversial when the candidate who is running for office identifies himself or herself as a Catholic. While the Church does not offer endorsements for candidates, she does offer "a series of questions, seeking to help lift up the moral and human dimensions of the choices facing voters and candidates."[14] Several of the questions to be asked of the candidates are listed here:

- How will the weakest in our midst—innocent unborn children—be protected?

- How will the nation resist what St. John Paul II termed a "culture of death"?

- How can you keep from turning to violence to solve some of the most difficult problems—abortion to deal with difficult pregnancies; the death penalty to combat crime; euthanasia and assisted suicide to deal with the burdens of age, illness, and disability; and war to address international disputes?

- How can society accept the reality that nearly nine million children worldwide die each year before their fifth birthday?

- How can society defend the central institution of marriage and better support families in their moral roles and responsibilities, offering them real choices and financial resources to obtain quality education and decent housing?

- How will the needs of the growing number of families and individuals without affordable and accessible health care be addressed? How can health care better protect human life and respect human dignity?

Carefully consider all of the questions, then complete the following task.

- Write a two- to three-paragraph essay explaining the common theme that connects the questions, and tell how this theme is a reflection of Catholic social teaching.

In your essay, make sure to explain why a person holding or running for political office must be accountable for his or her views on these issues, and the wider implications of his or her views. Also, make sure to include in your essay why your call to participation in society requires you to consider political leaders' views on these issues.

3. Human Rights in the News

Make a chart like the one below, listing the fundamental human rights (see pages 138–140). For each right, find a recent news story in which the right is *upheld* and another news story in which the right is *denied*. The news stories can cover events from any part of the world, and the news sources can be from the United States or international. Summarize each story in your own words. After you have completed the chart, write a short reflection on positive and negative human rights trends nationally or internationally.

Human Right	How the Right Is Upheld	How the Right Is Denied
Right to Life		
Moral and Cultural Rights		
Right to Worship God		
Right to Choose Freely One's State of Life		
Economic Rights		
Right of Meeting and Association		
Right to Emigrate and Immigrate		
Political Rights		

Faithful Disciple

Bl. Giovanni Battista Scalabrini

We are all called to uphold fundamental human rights. Some people make this call their mission. Bl. Giovanni Battista Scalabrini is one such person.

Giovanni Scalabrini was born in 1839 in Como, Italy. He was ordained a priest in 1863 and later was appointed bishop of Piacenza in 1876. As bishop, he worked tirelessly for his diocese. He visited all of the parishes, even remote ones accessible only by foot or mule. He encouraged frequent communion and Eucharistic Adoration. He worked to educate his people in the faith, with an emphasis on learning the catechism.

In Bl. Giovanni's time, Italy was experiencing a period of political tumult and widespread poverty, and often, people's basic needs were not met. To ease the suffering of his people, Bl. Giovanni undertook many works of social justice and charity. He aided the sick and visited the

Bl. Giovanni Battista Scalabrini

imprisoned. He opened an institute to help the deaf and speech-impaired and established societies to aid the women working in the rice fields of his diocese. In the great famine of 1879, he converted his own residence into a soup kitchen, selling even his own chalice and horse when the funds ran out.

Because of the hardships they faced during this time, many Italians fled the country in search of a new life in America. Between the years 1880 and 1920, some four-and-a-half million Italians emmigrated to the United States. Bl. Giovanni had a special concern for these emmigrants. He worried about their well-being in a country where they did not know the language or customs. Bl. Giovanni encouraged his pastors to dissuade their parishioners from leaving and instructed them to provide those who did leave with letters of introduction to give to the priests in the New World, so their pastoral needs would be met with more ease.

But this effort didn't seem like enough to Bl. Giovanni, so he petitioned to the pope to begin a religious community to minister to the needs of the Italian people overseas. In 1887, he founded the Congregation of the Missionaries of St. Charles Borromeo, with the mission to maintain Catholic faith and practice among Italian emigrants in the New World. The priests and religious sisters of the order worked to help keep immigrants from being exploited in their new environments. In 1901 Bl. Giovanni visited America and met with President Theodore Roosevelt to share his concerns about Italian immigrants in the United States.

Bl. Giovanni died in 1905. Today his religious order (now known as the Scalabrinians) is an international community of religious serving migrants and refugees of different cultures, religions, and ethnicities around the world. St. John Paul II beatified Giovanni Battista Scalabrini, naming him the "Father of Migrants."

 ## Reading Comprehension

1. What were some ways Bl. Giovanni met the spiritual and material needs of the persons of his diocese?

2. How did Bl. Giovanni serve Italian immigrants in the United States?

 ## Writing Task

- Imagine you are a new immigrant to America in the late 1800s. Write a first-person account of some of the challenges you might have to face. Also, what kinds of help would you need from the priests commissioned by Bl. Giovanni?

Explaining the Faith
Why does the Church talk about being involved in civil society, if there is a separation of Church and state?

Separation of Church and state does not mean separation of your faith from your life in civic society. Your beliefs should color *every* aspect of your actions. When you interact with civil society, you do not stop being Catholic. Therefore, your religion can and *should* influence your engagement in public life. God himself became incarnate *in the world*. Christ interacted with various peoples and social groups. And so, when you conform your life to his, you must follow suit and allow your faith to be manifest in every level of society. This includes civic and political societies.

 ## Further Research

- Read section 75 of the Second Vatican Council's *Gaudium et Spes*. You can access the document at www.vatican.va. Explain this quotation: "All Christians must be aware of their own specific vocation within the political community. It is for them to give an example by their sense of responsibility and their service of the common good."

Prayer
Prayer for the Protection of Religious Liberty

O God our Creator, from your provident hand we have received our right to life, liberty, and the pursuit of happiness. You have called us as your people and given us the right and the duty to worship you, the only true God, and your Son, Jesus Christ.

Through the power and working of your Holy Spirit, you call us to live out our faith in the midst of the world, bringing the light and the saving truth of the Gospel to every corner of society.

We ask you to bless us in our vigilance for the gift of religious liberty. Give us the strength of mind and heart to readily defend our freedoms when they are threatened; give us courage in making our voices heard on behalf of the rights of your Church and the freedom of conscience of all people of faith.

Grant, we pray, O heavenly Father, a clear and united voice to all your sons and daughters gathered in your Church in this decisive hour in the history of our nation, so that, with every trial withstood and every danger overcome—for the sake of our children, our grandchildren, and all who come after us—this great land will always be "one nation, under God, indivisible, with liberty and justice for all."

We ask this through Christ our Lord.

Amen.

—United States Conference of Catholic Bishops

OPTION for THE POOR AND VULNERABLE

Man Starts Over with the Help of
Catholic CHARITIES

One in every six Americans—that is, about fifty million Americans—is living in poverty. Antonio Hammond was one of them.

Hammond was homeless, staying in abandoned buildings where the rats were "fierce." Living in Baltimore at the time, he was addicted to crack cocaine and heroin. He financed his addiction by breaking into cars and by stealing copper pipes.

Eventually he ended up at a rehabilitation center that directed him to the local Catholic Charities. Hammond spent eighteen months with a Catholic Charities program called Christopher Place Employment Academy that assists recovering addicts and former prisoners. With the guidance and support he received there, Hammond was able to overcome his addiction. Now he is not only clean and sober but is also gainfully employed as a cleaner in a biotech laboratory. With the help of Catholic Charities, he has a stable place to live, a driver's license, and a car. He has even made amends with some of his estranged children.

FOCUS QUESTION

How do you SERVE CHRIST in the poor?

Chapter Overview

Introduction	An Overview of Poverty
Section 1	The Bible and Poverty
Section 2	The Scandal of World Hunger
Section 3	Working to End Poverty
Section 4	Poverty and You

INTRODUCTION
An Overview of Poverty

MAIN IDEA

The Church gives preferential treatment to the most poor and vulnerable in society. All Christians are called to the "poverty of spirit" described in the first Beatitude, with complete dependence on God for all their needs.

Do you sometimes find yourself struck by the extraordinary poverty in the world? The photo above is from Dhaka, Bangladesh. Do you hear about the problem of hunger and suddenly become grateful for your food, shelter, and clothing? Have you ever stopped to think that while you probably have everything you need to live, others living this very day on this same planet experience constant worry about the basics for survival?

The Catholic social teaching theme "option for the poor and vulnerable" is often referred to as the "**preferential option for the poor.**" This theme highlights the call to treat those who are impoverished in a special way. This preferential option is just common sense. For example, when a child is sick, or weakened and susceptible to serious health risks, the family gives the child special attention and resources until he or she becomes healthy again. Parents will make sure the child rests, eats the right foods, and visits a doctor who can prescribe the right medicines. And so it is with the poor in society. Like the sick child, they deserve particular concern because of their vulnerable position. You are called to give the poor special attention and offer the resources necessary for their human growth.

From the very example of Jesus, the Church has always had a special concern for the poor, ministering to them by providing alms, food and shelter, medical care, and education.

> **preferential option for the poor** A preferential love for the poor that allows one to give priority to the needs of the poor and to make a commitment to transform unjust social structures that are the causes of poverty.

NOTE TAKING

Concept Web. Make a concept web like the one below. In the large center circle, write a definition of poverty. In the connecting circles, write examples of material poverty and poverty of spirit.

```
( MATERIAL POVERTY ) —— ( POVERTY ) —— ( POVERTY OF SPIRIT )
```

The consistent teaching of the Church's Magisterium is that all Catholics have a responsibility to do justice by caring for the poor; that is, those who lack the necessities for a decent human life.

Forms of Poverty

The word poverty, from the Latin word *paupentas*, literally translates as pauper, or poor. Poverty is most commonly associated with the lack of means to provide for material needs or comforts, called material poverty, but other forms of poverty exist as well:

- "poverty of the soul" describes people who are hopeless about life, who may be suffering from psychological illness;

- "poverty of addiction" describes people who seek things such as possessions, prestige, beauty, and sex to fulfill a desire for lasting joy and happiness, eventually finding themselves unfulfilled; and

- "poverty of spirit" is connected with the first Beatitude and a person's dependence on God for all needs.

Further information on material poverty and the Beatitude's call to be "poor in spirit" follows.

Material Poverty

In its prime sense, material poverty is defined as "the lack of sufficient material means to meet basic human needs." This type of poverty describes a lack of the basic necessities for survival, such as nutritious food, safe drinking water, and basic health care. People in poverty may lack shelter or live in woefully inadequate, unsafe, unhealthy, and crowded conditions, often in high-crime neighborhoods.

Causes of material poverty include chronic unemployment, or jobs that do not earn workers a "living wage" that enables them to provide for their own or their families' needs. Those who are poor are typically voiceless in the political and economic sectors, where governments sometimes make decisions that perpetuate poverty and social inequality. Material poverty plagues societies around the world, from developing nations to prosperous nations such as the United States (see "Evidence of Material Poverty," pages 174–175).

Of course, material poverty looks much different in the United States than it does in, say, Somalia or Guatemala. On the whole, Americans are very rich in comparison with people in developing nations. Being blessed with wealth imposes a tremendous duty on Americans to use their wealth wisely, to avoid waste, to share their abundance with others, and to reform political, economic, and social structures that lead to, or perpetuate, economic inequality. Sadly, statistics reveal that, rather than narrowing, the gap between the rich and the poor is widening, both domestically and internationally. Rather than accepting this reality passively, seeing it as an unavoidable consequence of industrialization and modernization, you are all called to work to change it. God has blessed the earth with enough wealth and material goods to take care of the needs of all people, and you should help to ensure that all people can justly share in those blessings.

Encampments like this one in Brazil are common throughout Latin America. Many children, while returning to live with their families each night, spend the majority of their days working the streets for money and food.

Poverty of Spirit

Scripture speaks of a *positive* dimension of poverty—that is, the "poverty of spirit." In the first Beatitude, Jesus says, "Blessed are the poor in spirit, for theirs is the kingdom of heaven" (Mt 5:3).

Poverty of the spirit means depending on God for all your needs. It affirms that God alone is the sole source of all good gifts, the foremost of which are the Salvation and Redemption offered by Christ. A poverty of spirit begins with **humility**. The virtue of humility prompts people, even those who may appear materially poor, to act in gratitude for what many others take for granted. As the *Catechism* tells us, "Abandonment to the providence of the Father in heaven frees us from anxiety about tomorrow. Trust in God is a preparation for the blessedness of the poor. They shall see God" (*CCC*, 2547).

Those who are poor in spirit continually follow the example of Christ who in his Incarnation "emptied himself" (Phil 2:7) for the sake of his people: "For you know the gracious act of our Lord Jesus Christ, that for your sake he became poor although he was rich, so that by his poverty you might become rich" (2 Cor 8:9).

And so, the poor in spirit "empty themselves" by sharing their personal gifts, talents, and material blessings with others, especially those most in need. They realize that everything—food, water, air, health, family, peace, prayer, and all else—are gifts from God. Out of love, this poverty of spirit compels them to give of themselves in every aspect of their lives, so that the most defenseless and impoverished may obtain what they truly need to live in dignity as human beings and children of a loving Father.

Need for Christ

All forms of poverty are signs that the world is not perfect. This is obvious, of course, but looking a little deeper, you can see how poverty indicates the

> **humility** A virtue that avoids extreme ambition and pride and focuses rather on the acknowledgement that God is the author of all that is good.

fallenness and brokenness of the world because of Original Sin. If Adam and Eve had not sinned, humanity would not have any suffering; this includes the suffering of poverty. All suffering points to the human need for an answer; it points to *the* answer of Jesus Christ. It follows, then, that poverty ultimately shows you your need for Christ and the graces of Redemption. The Congregation for the Doctrine of the Faith reiterates this reality:

> In its various forms—material deprivation, unjust oppression, physical and psychological illness and death—*human misery* is the obvious sign of the inherited condition of frailty

Residents of the very poor indigenous village of Chuchuy, Gran Chaco, Salta, Argentina, South America

Evidence of MATERIAL POVERTY

Consider these facts and statistics about poverty worldwide:[1]

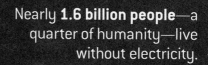

At least **80 %** of humanity lives on less than **$10 per day**.

Nearly **1.6 billion people**—a quarter of humanity—live without electricity.

About **28 %** of all children in developing countries are estimated to be underweight or stunted. The two regions that account for the bulk of the deficit are South Asia and sub-Saharan Africa.

Water problems affect **HALF** of humanity.

About 1.1 billion people in developing countries have inadequate access to water; 2.6 billion lack **BASIC SANITATION**.

Close to **HALF** of all people in developing countries suffer from a health problem caused by water and sanitation deficits.

OF THE 1.9 BILLION CHILDREN IN DEVELOPING NATIONS

 640 million (1 in 3) are without adequate shelter.

 400 million (1 in 5) have no access to safe water.

 270 million (1 in 7) have no access to health services.

 In 2003, 10.6 million died before the age of 5.

15 million are orphaned each year because their parents have died from HIV/AIDS.

174   **Foundations of Catholic Social Teaching**

In the **UNITED STATES**, the recession that began late in the first decade of the century led to some worsening statistics.[2] For example:

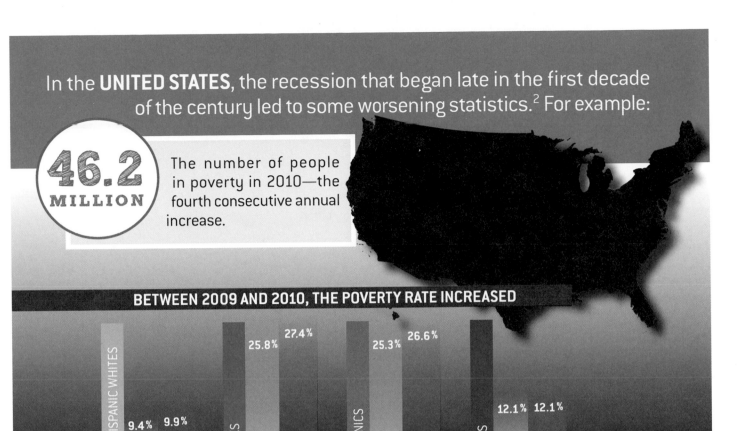

46.2 MILLION The number of people in poverty in 2010—the fourth consecutive annual increase.

BETWEEN 2009 AND 2010, THE POVERTY RATE INCREASED

NON-HISPANIC WHITES		BLACKS		HISPANICS		ASIANS	
9.4%	9.9%	25.8%	27.4%	25.3%	26.6%	12.1%	12.1%
2009	2010	2009	2010	2009	2010	2009	2010

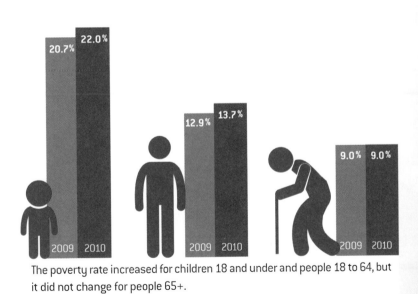

20.7%	22.0%	12.9%	13.7%	9.0%	9.0%
2009	2010	2009	2010	2009	2010

The poverty rate increased for children 18 and under and people 18 to 64, but it did not change for people 65+.

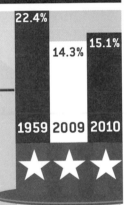

The official poverty rate in 2010 was 15.1%—up from 14.3% in 2009. The 2010 rate was 7.3% lower than the poverty rate in 1959—the first year that poverty estimates were published.

22.4%	14.3%	15.1%
1959	2009	2010

Statistics about poverty highlight the immensity of the problem and the need for a preferential option for the poor. That said, the human person must never be reduced to a number or statistic: *poverty* refers not to some anonymous group of people, but rather to millions of persons, each with great dignity and worth.

and need for salvation in which man finds himself as a consequence of original sin. This misery elicited the compassion of Christ the Savior, who willingly took it upon himself and identified himself with the least of his brethren. (*Libertatis Conscientia*, 68)

As you will see in the next sections, Christ directed his loving gaze upon the most vulnerable of society. Even more, he identified himself with the poor. And thus, you are to be inspired by his very life to treat the poor in a special way.

SECTION ASSESSMENT

NOTE TAKING

Use the concept web you created to complete the following items.

1. Define *poverty*.
2. What are some elements of material poverty? Explain and give examples.
3. How is "poverty of spirit" a positive application of poverty?

COMPREHENSION

4. What is a contemporary word to describe poverty of the soul?
5. How do the "poor in spirit" follow the example of Christ?
6. Why is material poverty scandalous?

CRITICAL THINKING

7. How does poverty show the need for Christ?

REFLECTION

8. Do you feel differently about a person suffering the "poverty of addiction" or the "poverty of the soul" than you do about someone suffering from material poverty? Explain your response.

SECTION 1
The Bible and Poverty

MAIN IDEA

The Old Testament established standards for treating the poor. Through his words and example, Christ showed great compassion for the poor and called all people to do the same.

In his encyclical marking the one-hundredth anniversary of *Rerum Novarum*, the Church's first social justice document, St. John Paul II reminded Catholics that "the Church's love for the poor . . . is part of her constant tradition."[3] Certainly, Sacred Scripture reveals God's compassion and concern for the poor. Likewise, the Church teaches of the need for a preferential option for the poor. The United States Conference of Catholic Bishops' pastoral letter *Economic Justice for All* teaches: "From the Scriptures and Church teaching, we learn that the justice of a society is tested by the treatment of the poor."[4]

Both the Old and New Testaments speak of the poor often, and describe who they are. The poor mentioned in Scripture include:

- the materially impoverished members of the lower class whom the powerful exploited;

- the afflicted and powerless;

- the hungry, the unclothed, the homeless, prisoners;

- orphans;

- lepers, whom society feared and isolated;

- sinners, such as the woman caught in adultery, who were subject to harsh penalties, even death;

NOTE TAKING

Summarizing Biblical Concepts. Create a chart like the one below. As you read the text section below, summarize what each of the following biblical concepts says about serving the poor.

Concept	What It Says about Serving the Poor
Sabbatical Year	
Jubilee Year	
Words of the Prophets	
Christ's Own Poverty	
Parable of the Good Samaritan	
Parable of the Last Judgment	
Other Parables	

WAYS TO HELP THE POOR

Choose and complete at least one of the following service projects to aid the poor or homeless in your area. Keep a written journal detailing your experience. When you have completed your effort, write a reflection discussing lessons that you learned.

- Contact Catholic Charities and learn how the organization serves the homeless in your area. Volunteer to help with one of their efforts.
- Have a fund-raising drive at your school to purchase some fast-food certificates. Donate these to a homeless shelter.
- Collect food, money, and toys to donate to a women's shelter.
- Volunteer at a soup kitchen.
- Learn about after-school programs in your area that provide tutoring for underprivileged children and volunteer as a tutor.
- Volunteer with Habitat for Humanity.

- strangers and outsiders;
- widows, who had no social status;
- tax collectors, who were shunned and no longer accepted as true sons of Abraham.

In his public ministry, Jesus, the Son of God, embraced the poor. His first public discourse announced his outreach to the neediest among them:

> The Spirit of the Lord is upon me,
> because he has anointed me
> to bring glad tidings to the poor.
> He has sent me to proclaim liberty to captives
> and recovery of sight to the blind,
> to let the oppressed go free,
> and to proclaim a year acceptable to the Lord. (Lk 4:18–19)

Jesus' prophetic voice, repeating God's love for the poor and his command for the comfortable to respond to the needy, was a message announced time and again in the New Testament.

Care for the Poor in the Old Testament

God's Chosen People, the Israelites (later called the Jews), showed their love for God by communion with, and care for, the poor in their midst. The communal nature of Israelite society included two important practices: the Sabbatical Year (the seventh year) and the Jubilee Year (every fifty years). During the Sabbatical Year, land was not to be farmed (so as not to overuse the land and render it unusable), debts from the previous six years were to be forgiven, and slaves were to be set free. Requirements of the Jubilee Year (following seven cycles of the sabbatical year) included restoring ancestral lands to families that may have lost them, and emancipating indentured servants (whose terms of servitude were unexpired). The goal of these practices was to try to maintain a balance of wealth and resources among the tribes of Israel and to raise up those held low.

Observing the Sabbatical and Jubilee years also was a practice of poverty of spirit. In fulfilling the obligations of these years, the Jewish people were reminded that they were former slaves whom a just and loving God rescued. In return, they had a duty to care for the oppressed and the poor in their midst.

Despite the ideals of the Sabbatical and Jubilee years, because the Israelites, like all people, were sinners, all too often the needs of the poor were ignored. Because of this, God sent prophets to warn the Israelites about their wickedness and to call them back to justice.

The prophet Zechariah taught the Israelites how to be just:

> Render true judgment, and show kindness and compassion toward each other. Do not oppress the widow or the orphan, the alien or the poor; do not plot evil against one another in your hearts. (Zec 7:9–10)

The prophet Amos taught that injustice would be punished:

> Hear this, you who trample upon the needy
> and destroy the poor of the land! . . .
> I will turn your feasts into mourning
> and all your songs into lamentations.
> I will cover the loins of all with sackcloth
> and make every head bald.
> I will make them mourn as for an only son,
> and bring their day to a bitter end. (Am 8:4, 10)

Time and again, the Old Testament teaches about injustice and reassures the poor that God indeed hears their cries:

> Injure not the poor because they are poor,
> nor crush the needy at the gate;
> For the LORD will defend their cause,
> and will plunder the lives of those
> who plunder them. (Prv 22:22–23)

Care for the Poor in the New Testament

The Incarnation is proof of God's love for humanity and his great love and compassion for the poor. An ancient hymn recorded in the Letter to the Philippians proclaimed that Christ Jesus,

> Who, though he was in the form of God,
> did not regard equality with God
> something to be grasped.
> Rather, he emptied himself,
> taking the form of a slave,
> coming in human likeness;
> and found in human appearance,
> he humbled himself,
> becoming obedient to death,
> even death on a cross. (Phil 2:6–8)

The Son of God became lowly and lived a life of poverty. He called no place home (cf. Mt 8:20). He relied on the generosity of others for support (cf. Lk 8:3). He died with no possessions (cf. Jn 19:23–24). Jesus freely chose this lifestyle of openness and dependence on the Father to teach about what it means to love and to sacrifice his life to gain eternal life for all humanity.

Throughout his earthly ministry, Jesus associated with the lowly and the outcast: lepers, sinners, children, tax collectors, the lame and the blind, and so on. He responded to their needs, for example, by feeding them when they came to hear his life-giving words (cf. Mk 6:30–44 and Jn 6:1–13). He healed those who were ill: people who were blind, lame, deaf, and mute—even lepers. He took pity on a widow by bringing her son back to life (cf. Lk 7:11–17).

Jesus' parables—part of his teaching that reveals the words of the Father—communicate his attitude toward the poor and lowly. For example, when asked by a rich young man to define "who is our neighbor," he told the parable of the Good Samaritan (cf. Lk

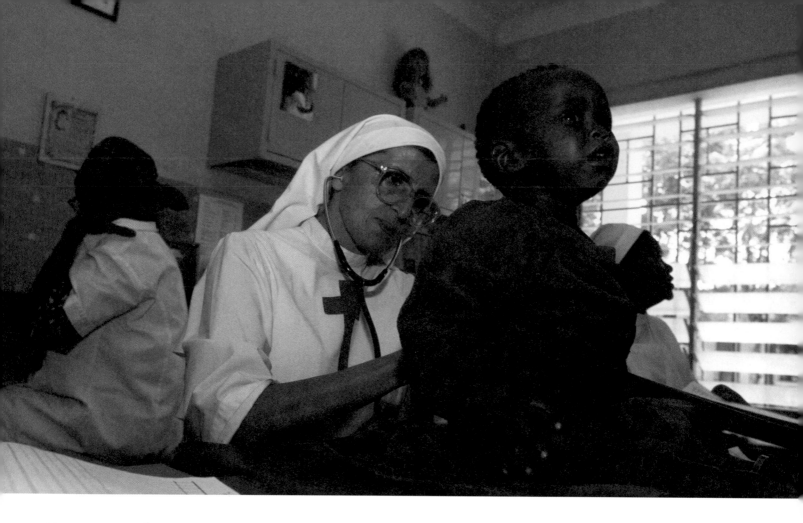

10:30–37; see photo on page 177). The hero of this parable—a Samaritan typically despised by the Jews—went out of his way to minister to the wounds of a beaten traveler. He even spent his own money to provide for his care. Through this parable, Jesus taught that you must consider everyone your neighbor, and that you are charged with helping your neighbor in need, even when doing so requires sacrifice.

Two other of Jesus' parables particularly address how a person must respond to the poor. The parable of Lazarus and the rich man (cf. Lk 16:19–31) teaches that those who ignore the needs of the poor risk eternal separation from God. The parable of the rich fool tells of keeping priorities straight: care for the poor must come before accumulation of possessions. Ultimately, a person will be judged on how he or she treats the poor. Jesus reveals this in the parable of the Last Judgment (cf. Mt 25:31–46). He said, "Amen, I say to

you, what you did not do for one of these least ones, you did not do for me" (Mt 25:45).

Jesus' standard for how to treat the poor and *all* people is both simple and compelling: "Do to others whatever you would have them do to you" (Mt 7:12). Indeed, how you treat the less fortunate (the hungry, thirsty, strangers, the ill or imprisoned) is integral to your very *salvation*. You are saved only by God's grace, but Christ was clear that you are judged on how you serve him in the least of his people. This should be a startling, life-altering reality for you. St. Rose of Lima said, "When we serve the poor and sick, we serve Jesus. We must not fail to help our neighbors, because in them we serve Jesus."[5] Bl. Mother Teresa reiterated this thought:

> Today, once more, when Jesus comes amongst his own, his own don't know him! He comes in the rotten bodies of our poor; he comes in the rich choked by their own riches. He comes in

the loneliness of their hearts, and when there is no one to love them. Jesus comes to you and me often, very, very often, we pass him by. (*Mother Teresa: An Authorized Biography*, 172)

Christians give the poor a preferential option because they love Jesus. This is the heart of the theme.

Anyone can give food to someone who is hungry, but the Christian does so because he sees Christ in that person.

SECTION ASSESSMENT

NOTE TAKING

Use the chart you created to complete the following items.

1. Explain the purposes of the Sabbatical and Jubilee Years.

2. What does the parable of the Good Samaritan tell you about how you should serve the poor?

3. How is your treatment of the poor connected with the way you will be judged by God?

COMPREHENSION

4. According the parable of the Good Samaritan, who is your "neighbor"?

5. What was Jesus' simple standard for treatment of the less fortunate?

APPLICATION

6. Look up the following Scripture verses, then explain what each tells the Israelites about who is the poor in their midst and how they are to relate to them.

    -   Deuteronomy 15:7–8

    -   Job 30:25

    -   Psalm 82:3–4

    -   Exodus 22:21

    -   Isaiah 1:17

SECTION 2
The Scandal of World Hunger

MAIN IDEA

World hunger is a result of social sin, not the world's inability to produce sufficient food supply. Catholic social teaching calls you both as an individual and as a member of society to work to eliminate the root causes of hunger.

The most basic right of each human being is the right to life. To live, people need food. Denying people the right to food is an injustice of the highest order. That is why it is essential to study in more detail the issue of world hunger in the context of a chapter on poverty.

For Christians, feeding the hungry is one of the corporal **works of mercy** (see page 315). So basic is the injunction to feed the hungry that the Second Vatican Council called attention to the saying of the Church Fathers, "Feed the man dying of hunger, because if you have not fed him, you have killed him."[6]

Worldwide, millions of people are chronically hungry and malnourished. Malnourishment is a silent killer whose effects may not be immediately obvious. A malnourished body gets enough calories to sustain life, but the subsistence level of food intake does not provide the proper amount of nutrition for a healthy life. The body turns on itself and consumes muscle, fat, and tissue for sustenance. It quickly deteriorates and becomes susceptible to disease. Brain function slows. Eventually, the chronic weight loss leads to death.

Globally, there is a clear link between hunger and poverty. Further, the chief victims of hunger and malnutrition are often the most vulnerable members of society: children, pregnant women, the sick, the elderly, refugees, and those affected by political turmoil.

> **works of mercy** Charitable actions by which we provide for the physical and spiritual needs of others.

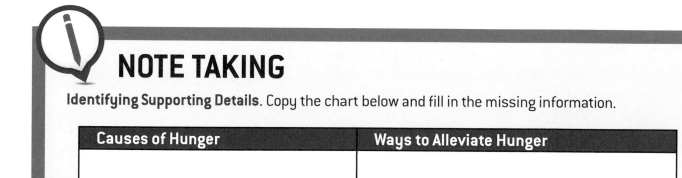

NOTE TAKING

Identifying Supporting Details. Copy the chart below and fill in the missing information.

Causes of Hunger	Ways to Alleviate Hunger

For many people in the developed world, particularly those living comfortable middle- or upper-class lives, the problem of world hunger is a formless concept, rather than a definable problem with nameable victims. Consider the following statistics about the reality of hunger:

Approximately 925 million people in the world do not have enough to eat—a greater number than the populations of the United States, Canada, and the European Union combined. In fact, 98 percent of the world's hungry live in developing countries.[7]

In 2008, nine million children died of hunger-related issues before they reached their fifth birthdays. One-third of these deaths were related directly or indirectly to malnutrition. Also, 178 million children under five were stunted or too short for their ages. Nearly 90 percent of these stunted children lived in thirty-six countries, most of them in Sub-Saharan Africa and South and Central Asia.[8]

In 2010, approximately 15 percent of US citizens lived below the poverty line. (The poverty line in 2010 for a family of four was $22,314.)

Why are so many people around the world victims of chronic malnutrition? Is it because the world is simply unable to produce enough food to feed all its people? Is the rate of population growth exceeding our farming and agriculture capacities? On the contrary, the research of many organizations, including the United Nations, shows that the world produces enough food to feed every human being. In *World Hunger—A Challenge for All: Development in Solidarity,* a pontifical council devoted to development, concludes:

> The fact that people continue to starve . . . shows that the problem is structural, and that "inequitable access is the main problem." Hunger is not a problem of availability, but of meeting demand. It is an issue of poverty. (§19)

Speaking about the injustice of world hunger to members of the United Nation's Food and Agriculture Organization, Pope Francis said, "It is a well-known fact that current levels of production are sufficient, yet millions of people are still suffering and dying of starvation. This is truly scandalous." In his encyclical, *Caritas in Veritate* ("Charity in Truth"), Pope Benedict XVI pointed to the institutional "infrastructure" needed to prevent hunger:

> Hunger is not so much dependent on lack of material things as on shortage of social resources, the most important of which are institutional. What is missing, in other words, is a network of economic institutions capable of guaranteeing regular access to sufficient food and water for nutritional needs, and also capable of addressing the primary needs and necessities ensuing from genuine food crises, whether due to natural causes or political irresponsibility, nationally and internationally. (*CV*, 27)

World Hunger—A Challenge for All addressed the root causes of hunger in considerable detail. Not surprising, the primary cause of hunger is poverty, often resulting from or perpetuated by corruption. Here are four factors that contribute to world hunger:

FACTORS CONTRIBUTING TO WORLD HUNGER

ISSUE	RELATION TO HUNGER
1. CORRUPTION	In developing nations, officials who seize power by force or attain power by privilege often do not rule with the common good in mind. Rather than developing policies that serve the public good and raise people out of poverty, they work to protect or build their own wealth. For example, rather than developing a sound economy that rewards the growing of diverse crops that could feed the entire population, they protect the raising of crops, such as sugar or coffee, that they personally profit from. Further, they may divert foreign aid intended to alleviate poverty for their personal wealth.
2. FOREIGN LOANS	Often, poor nations incur extreme debt to foreign investors. The interest on these foreign loans is usually unreasonably high, siphoning resources that could otherwise support vital development projects that serve the good of citizens. In desperate times, when money is tight or inflation is high, creditors might impose severe borrowing restrictions on the debtor nations, further plunging them into poverty and despair.
3. LAND DEGRADATION	Land degradation occurs when agricultural practices lower the capacity of the soil to support crops and, therefore, to support human life. Practices that lead to land degradation include over farming or over tilling the land, erosion because of poor drainage or poor irrigation, and lack of sustainable farming methods. Land degradation can happen in any part of the world; however, developing nations are more susceptible to the consequences and frequently lack policies or resources to remediate (or control) the problem.
4. POLITICS	Food is often used as a political or military tool. In 2011, the Somalian military withheld food from starving citizens. Thousands of people, mostly women and children, died while trying to flee to neighboring Kenya in search of food. Similarly, nations who provide foreign aid at times do so with "strings attached," requiring certain concessions ahead of providing aid.

Response to World Hunger

Catholic social teaching advocates a response to the problem of world hunger from both society and individuals. This means developing infrastructures that support education, commerce, transportation, health care, and so forth. For individuals, it means that, along with doing **works of charity**, we must also work for justice.

Changing the "Culture of Waste"

Pope Francis described the problem of world hunger as part of a "culture of waste." He said:

> This culture of waste has made us insensitive even to the waste and disposal of food, which is even more despicable when all over the world, unfortunately, many individuals and families are suffering from hunger and malnutrition. Once our grandparents were very careful not to throw away any leftover food. Consumerism has led us to become used to an excess and daily waste of food, to which, at times, we are no longer able to give a just value, which goes well beyond mere economic parameters. We should all remember, however, that throwing food away is like stealing from the tables of the poor, the hungry! I encourage everyone to reflect on the problem of thrown away and wasted food to identify ways and means that, by seriously addressing this issue, are a vehicle of solidarity and sharing with the needy. (Papal Audience, June 5, 2013)

According to a 2012 Natural Resources Defense Council report, Americans discard 40 percent of the food supply each year, and the average family throws away the equivalent of $2,275 annually. According to the report, just a 15 percent reduction in food waste would be sufficient to feed 25 million Americans annually. Everyone has a right to enough food. Depriving

> **works of charity** Actions that provide an immediate response to a person or group who is suffering or in need of the basic necessities for a dignified life.

other human beings of food is a violation of the Seventh Commandment, "You shall not steal" (Ex 20:15). This commandment "forbids unjustly taking or keeping the goods of one's neighbor and wronging him in any way with respect to his goods" (*CCC*, 2401). Eliminating the wasting of food is a critical step in addressing the problem of hunger.

Direct Aid to the Poor through the Principle of Subsidiarity

Poor people must have a say in decisions that affect them, especially regarding basic sustenance. Rich people must not exclude poor people from social and

A Sudanese mother feeds her child at a Red Cross feeding center for the malnourished.

What You Can Do for World Hunger: A Call to Self-Examination

Catholic social teaching challenges us to work to end world hunger:

> Wherever in the world God has placed them, Christians must respond to the call of those who are hungry by personally questioning their own lives. The call of the hungry urges one to question the meaning and the value of daily actions. . . . One must gauge the magnitude . . . of the consequences of all one does, even the most ordinary things, and hence appraise real responsibility. . . . [Christians must] discreetly and humbly . . . listen to and serve anyone in need. (*World Hunger—A Challenge for All: Development in Solidarity,* 66)

You can do your share in one or more of the following ways:

- Collect food for a local hunger center/food bank. Do so at a nonholiday time, remembering that people are hungry year-round, not just at Thanksgiving and Christmas.

- Volunteer your time at a local soup kitchen.

- Sponsor a food waste awareness campaign at your school.

- Assist at a local Meals on Wheels program.

- Write a letter to your congressional representative encouraging him or her to (1) support long-term solutions to the hunger problem abroad; (2) sponsor foreign-aid bills that support land reform and literacy programs; (3) inquire about our arms trading policy to poor countries so that tax dollars go for food and not guns.

- Fast from a favorite food item for a month. Donate the money you save to a hunger-fighting program.

- Examine your own eating habits. This will help you become more aware of food waste and good nutrition. It will also help you become more sensitive to hungry people in other parts of the world. You might consider replacing higher-priced processed food with less expensive, healthier options to increase your awareness of your food spending habits.

economic life. Governments must financially support international organizations that are working to solve the hunger problem. They should establish fair trade relations with poorer nations to support development. They should ensure that poor people have access to credit as a means to pull themselves out of poverty.

In addition, governments and individuals must also back emergency food aid during times of famine and other crises. St. John Paul II offered these words of instruction:

> Justice will never be fully attained unless people see in the poor person, who is asking for help in order to survive, not an annoyance or a burden, but an opportunity for showing kindness and a chance for greater enrichment. Only such an awareness can give the courage needed to face the risk and the change involved in every authentic attempt to come to the aid of another. It is not merely a matter of "giving from one's surplus," but of helping entire peoples which are presently excluded or marginalized to enter into the sphere of economic and human development. (*Rerum Novarum*, §58)

SECTION ASSESSMENT

NOTE TAKING

Use the chart you created to complete the following items.

1. List four causes of hunger.
2. Discuss two moral responses to the hunger problem.

COMPREHENSION

3. What are some effects of malnourishment?
4. Who are the chief victims of hunger and malnourishment?
5. How did Pope Francis describe the problem of world hunger?

RESEARCH

6. Check with agencies that provide up-to-date statistics on world hunger (e.g., Bread for the World, United Nations' World Food Program). Report on two new facts you discovered about world hunger.

SECTION 3
Working to End Poverty

MAIN IDEA
A plan to eradicate poverty centers on the corporal and spiritual works of mercy and includes bringing Christ to the world through the actions of almsgiving, sharing fairly the world's resources, and evangelization.

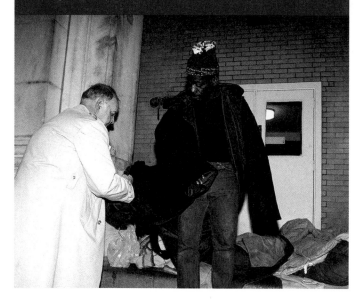

Recall that poverty is an aspect of human suffering that is a result of the Fall of humankind. Jesus said, "You will always have the poor with you, but you will not always have me" (Mt 26:11). This verse does not mean one should not work to alleviate poverty, but rather it is a call to Christian realism.

Jesus himself chose not to eliminate the poverty of his time. Neither did he spend a lot of time explaining the causes of poverty. Instead, Jesus showed compassion for the poor, and went about caring for the immediate needs: hunger, thirst, and several kinds of illness. He also addressed spiritual poverty by calling followers to leave their old lives behind to follow him (see page 193 for more information on spiritual poverty).

Poverty is a by-product of Christ's enemy, Satan. Though efforts to defeat poverty are laudable, it will never be possible to totally eliminate all poverty. This will only happen with the Second Coming, when Christ will be with his people forever.

Nevertheless, it remains a requirement of the Christian life to do what Jesus did, work to end the immediate and far-reaching effects of poverty. The United States Conference of Catholic Bishops named as a high social priority increasing active participation in economic life by those who are presently excluded or vulnerable. "The human dignity of all is realized when people gain the power to work together to improve their lives, strengthen their families, and contribute to society" (*Economic Justice for All,* §91).

NOTE TAKING

Summarizing and Giving Examples. Copy the table below. Write a definition for each term or concept in your own words. In the third column, share an example of how each principle can be practiced in today's world.

Principle	Definition	Example
Works of Mercy		
Universal Destination of Goods		
Almsgiving		
Evangelization		

Cardinal Timothy M. Dolan's recent "Letter to Bishops on Economic Situation" (which can be found under the "Unemployment and Poverty" link on the USCCB website) suggests many pastoral responses to poverty. His first recommendation is this: "The best way out of poverty is a living wage."

Corporal and Spiritual Works of Mercy

A good summary of how individuals, and even groups, can serve all the needs of the poor are the corporal and spiritual works of mercy, which are listed in the column to the right.

The corporal works of mercy provide help for the needs of the body (see photo on page 188). Addressing physical necessities should be more than just well-wishing that these needs will be someday met; instead, it includes active involvement in providing for them. "If a brother or sister has nothing to wear and has no food for the day, and one of you says to them, 'Go in peace, keep warm, and eat well,' but you do not give them the necessities of the body, what good is it?" (Jas 2:15–16). If you care for others only in word and not in deed, then you are not truly carrying out the corporal works for mercy. You must put your words into action. You must practice what you preach.

Nevertheless, providing for the physical needs of the poor does not excuse one from addressing their spiritual needs. A person may seemingly be materially satisfied, and yet may be enduring a certain poverty of the spirit, such as great loneliness, ignorance, or distance from God. You are called to reach out to all of these types of poverty as well. And sometimes this may prove to be more difficult than addressing material poverty. Admonishing sinners or forgiving hurts done unto you can often take more human effort working with God's grace than donating food to the hungry. In examining the works of mercy, you must be careful

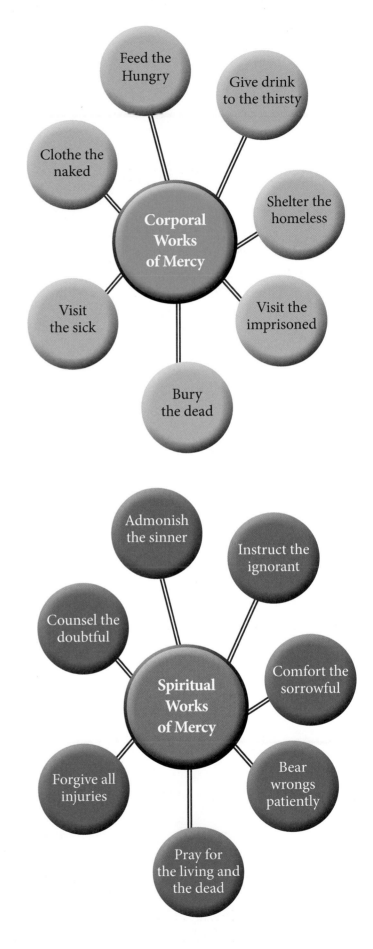

not to strictly delineate the poor into categories, such as "well, this person has physical needs, but this other person has spiritual needs." Instead, many times someone has needs in both "categories," so to speak. And in reality, *everyone* has spiritual hardships.

Justice and Almsgiving

A second principle for ending poverty is **almsgiving**. "Giving alms to the poor is one of the chief witnesses to fraternal charity: it is also a work of justice pleasing to God" (*CCC*, 2447). Almsgiving traditionally refers to giving to the poor, be it buying a meal for a homeless person or supporting organizations that give aid to areas affected by natural disasters. But one can also look at almsgiving in a broad sense, which involves addressing the social and political dimensions that cause the poverty. In this case, almsgiving would take on a dimension of justice.

In justice, each person is compelled to ask these questions: "Why are the people I am giving alms to poor?" and "How can I help to change what caused this poverty?" Part of this interplay between charity

> **almsgiving** Freely giving money or goods to the poor as an act of penance or fraternal charity. Almsgiving, together with prayer and fasting, are traditionally recommended to foster the state of interior penance.

and justice is aiding the materially poor with the skills and structures that they need in order to help themselves rise out of this impoverished state. St. John Paul II wrote:

> It is a strict duty of justice and truth not to allow fundamental human needs to remain unsatisfied, and not allow those burdened by such needs to perish. It is also necessary to help these needy people to acquire expertise, to enter the circle of exchange, and to develop their skills in order to make the best use of their capacities and resources. (*Centesimus Annus*, 34)

The corporal and spiritual works of mercy are usually categorized as works of *charity*, which are indispensable. That said, you cannot forget about the call to *justice*. In justice, no one can overlook the plights

Workers sort clothing at a sorting facility at Goodwill Industries in Astoria, New York.

of those in need, especially if one is able to address those plights.

Universal Destination of Goods

Another principle meant to alleviate property is defined as the "universal destination of goods." This principle teaches that the goods of the earth should be divided to ensure freedom and dignity of the human person, so that all might meet basic human needs. "Goods" means more than just food or other natural resources. Although these types of property will always be of value, especially in the modern world, the idea of "property" takes on a new dimension and includes "knowledge, technology, and know-how."[9] And so, when the Church speaks about the universal destination of *goods*, it includes more than just physical resources.

The universal destination of goods has its basis in Scripture. God gave humans dominion over the earth and the command to "fill the earth and subdue it" (Gn 1:28). Ultimately, the earth and all it contains belongs to God. However, he has allowed his people to participate in his dominion by allowing them to be stewards of his creation. "God gave the earth to the whole human race for the sustenance of all its members, without excluding or favoring anyone."[10]

Human beings cannot exist, let alone flourish, without material goods; they are "absolutely indispensable if he is to feed himself, grow, communicate, associate with others, and attain the highest purposes to which he is called."[11] And thus, based on the principle of the common good, all human beings must have

access to created goods. Pope Leo XIII wrote in *Rerum Novarum*:

> Whoever has received from the divine bounty a large share of temporal blessings, whether they be external and material, or gifts of the mind, has received them for the purpose of using them for the perfecting of his own nature, and, at the same time, that he may employ them, as the steward of God's providence, for the benefit of others. (*RN*, 22)

You should see your goods as not merely your own, but "common" to others, in that others can benefit from your property. Practicing this principle includes

using your own possessions moderately, so that you can share with guests, the sick, and the poor.

For example, part of any money you earn should be earmarked for the needs of the poor. Also, a portion of the hours in your week should be dedicated to direct service of those in need. In this case, "those in need" may be people in your community you don't know personally or family members or friends who need you to assist them in either in their material or spiritual poverty. Your service of, and sharing with, the poor is not to come merely out of your excess, but rather it emerges from the rights of others to these goods and to your time. St. Gregory the Great said, "When we attend to the needs of those in want, we give them what is theirs, not ours. More than performing works of mercy, we are paying a debt of justice."[12] The Second Vatican Council document *Gaudium et Spes* explains further:

> On the other hand, the right of having a share of earthly goods sufficient for oneself and one's family belongs to everyone. The Fathers and Doctors of the Church held this opinion, teaching that men are obliged to come to the relief of the poor and to do so not merely out of their superfluous goods. (*GS*, 69)

Right to Private Property

It is important to be extremely clear that the universal destination of goods is *not* an encouragement of socialism (a system in which the government controls all goods and means of production; socialism will be addressed more closely in Chapter 7). You have the right to own things, but as with all rights, private ownership comes with responsibility. In this case, the responsibility is to share with others, especially the less fortunate. The origin of this responsibility is the reality that everything you have—even nonmaterial goods like ideas and talents—are ultimately from God.

In other words, just because your friend owns a nice car and you do not, you have no right to your friend's car. Instead, this principle calls you again and again to the *just use* of your own goods, not the unjust seizing of others' things.

This is a tricky balance to maintain in your life: you have the right to own things, but you also have a duty to share with others. To understand such a seeming contradiction, you need to return to the virtue of charity. Out of *love*, you are impelled to *freely* share even that which is "rightly" yours with those who lack resources.

St. Thomas Aquinas further explained that, "it is lawful for a man to hold private property; and it is also necessary for the carrying on of human existence."[13] Acquired in a just manner, private ownership is necessary in keeping with the common good. Private property is an extension of human freedom; it can help you to assure your individual and family autonomy. That said, you need to use your resources in a way that is not simply for your own private gain, but also for the common good. Property is a *means* to one's human fulfillment and serving of the common good, not an end in itself. St. Thomas Aquinas added, "Man should not consider his material possessions as his own, but as common to all, so as to share them without hesitation when others are in need."[14]

Evangelization

In discussing solutions for poverty, it is important not to forget to pay special attention to poverty of heart, or spiritual poverty. Bl. Mother Teresa pointed out that spiritual poverty can be even *worse* than material poverty, in that it creates an intense suffering:

> But in the West you have another kind of poverty, spiritual poverty. This is far worse. People do not believe in God, do not pray. People do not care for each other. You have the poverty of people who are dissatisfied with what they have, who do not know how to suffer, who give in to despair. This poverty of heart is often more difficult to relieve and to defeat. In the West you have many more broken homes, neglected children, and divorce on a huge scale.

One solution to alleviate spiritual poverty is **evangelization**, a "most profound duty of the Church."[15] As you learned previously, poverty chiefly is a sign of one's need for Christ and his truth. Thus, you cannot serve your neighbors without bringing Christ and his Gospel to them. Even an atheist can perform outward acts of service to the poor; however, it is not *charity* in the truest sense, in that it is not compelled by a love that ultimately comes from God, who *is* love (1 Jn 4:8). Without the love of Christ driving you, your actions are empty and do not hold the profound meaning of those compelled by charity.

Pope Benedict XVI made it clear that when you evangelize *and* serve the material needs of the less fortunate, you are following Christ's own example:

> Proclaiming the Gospel, [the Church] takes seriously human life in the full sense. . . . To be indifferent to the temporal problems of humanity would mean "to forget the lesson which comes to us from the Gospel concerning love of our neighbor who is suffering and

> **evangelization** The proclamation of Christ and his Gospel (Greek: *evangelion*) by word and the testimony of life in fulfillment of Christ's command.

in need (*Evangelii Nuntiandi*, 31); it would not be attuned to Jesus' conduct, who "went about all the cities and villages, teaching in their synagogues and preaching the Gospel of the Kingdom, and healing every disease and every infirmity" (Mt 9:35). (Message for World Mission Sunday, 2011)

Evangelization and addressing other forms of poverty are not mutually exclusive. Again, like so many other realities within Catholic social teaching, it is a "both/and" duty, not an "either/or" task.

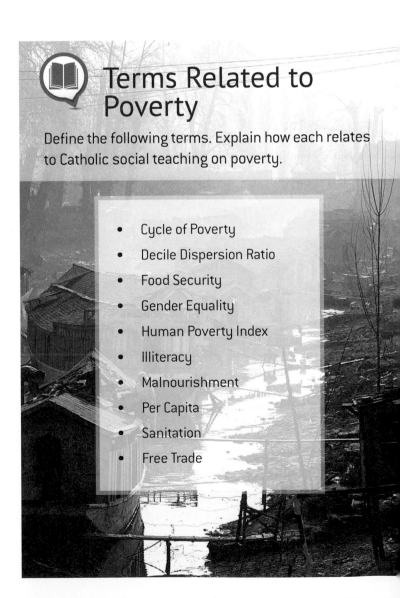

Terms Related to Poverty

Define the following terms. Explain how each relates to Catholic social teaching on poverty.

- Cycle of Poverty
- Decile Dispersion Ratio
- Food Security
- Gender Equality
- Human Poverty Index
- Illiteracy
- Malnourishment
- Per Capita
- Sanitation
- Free Trade

This section offered four principles as solutions to end poverty. To review:

1. Practice the corporal and spiritual works of mercy.

2. Give alms both out of charity (love) and justice.

3. Be a steward of God's gifts to you; share the blessings you have received from God with others.

4. Share the Good News of Jesus Christ with others, especially those with spiritual need.

SECTION ASSESSMENT

NOTE TAKING

Use the chart you created to help you complete the following items.

1. What are the two types of works of mercy?

2. How is the principle of the "universal destination of goods" applied in today's society?

3. What is an example of almsgiving?

COMPREHENSION

4. What did Cardinal Dolan suggest was the best way out of poverty?

5. What is the most profound duty of the Church?

6. How can almsgiving take on the dimension of justice?

7. What does it mean to be a steward of the goods of the earth?

8. How is evangelization a deterrent against spiritual poverty?

FILL IN THE BLANK

9. Providing for the material needs of the poor does not excuse one from addressing a person's _____ needs.

10. Private property is an extension of human _____.

CRITICAL THINKING

11. "An atheist's act of service to the poor is not charity in the truest sense." Explain the meaning of this sentence.

APPLICATION

12. Explain the balance between the universal destination of goods and the right to own private property.

SECTION 4
Poverty and You

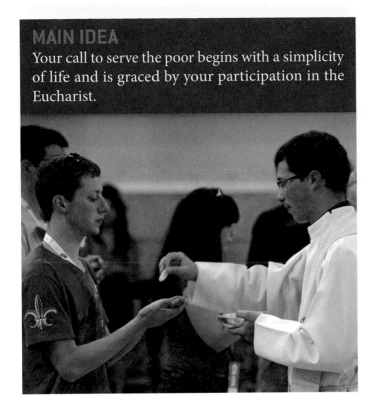

MAIN IDEA
Your call to serve the poor begins with a simplicity of life and is graced by your participation in the Eucharist.

Church history is dotted with a long list of saints who have taken up the call to serve the world's poorest and most vulnerable people. But you can't say "the Church practices a preferential option for the poor" without making this option a priority in your own life. Honestly, for you to serve the poor, it means more than reading statistics about poverty and *feeling* a sense of remote compassion. Although compassion is certainly a start, you are called to serve Christ in the poor *right before you every day*.

In Fyodor Dostoevsky's classic novel *The Brothers Karamazov*, a wise monk said, "The more I detest men individually the more ardent becomes my love for humanity." What this means is that sometimes it is easy to "love humanity," but it is extremely difficult to love individual persons put before you in your daily lives. Don't forget Jesus' words: "Whatever you did for one of these least brothers of mine, you did for me" (Mt 25:40). It is absolutely crucial to become involved in community and global efforts to end material poverty, but you cannot forget that the task begins in the way you treat the poor in your own life.

Simplicity of Life

A significant part of learning to live a life in service to the poor is with your own simplicity of life and moderation of goods. It is not wrong to have material possessions and wealth; however, it is wrong to allow owning things and "getting ahead" to take priority over serving

NOTE TAKING

Finishing the Sentence. Label a section in your notebook as "Section 4 Summary." Copy each sentence listed below in your notebook. As you read the section, complete the sentence with the word(s) that make it complete.

- Practicing the preferential option for the poor begins with _____.
- A significant part of learning to live a life in service to the poor is with your own simplicity of _____ and _____ of goods.
- The Church reminds her people that they are merely _____, not ultimate owners of their goods.
- When you are dismissed to "go forth" from the Mass, you must bring _____ to others.
- Living in a self-centered way is one of the effects of _____ _____.

A Poor Church for the POOR

On March 13, 2013, Cardinal Jorge Mario Bergoglio, S.J., was seated in the Sistine Chapel next to Cardinal Claudio Hummes, Archbishop Emeritus of Sao Paolo, Brazil, when "things were looking dangerous." The two cardinals were attending the papal conclave, and Cardinal Bergoglio realized he was about to be elected pope.

When the votes were officially counted and Cardinal Bergoglio had received the necessary two-thirds majority, Archbishop Hummes stood and hugged the new pope. He also whispered, "Don't forget the poor."

It was then that Jorge Mario Bergoglio knew that he would choose the name Francis:

> And those words came to me: the poor, the poor. Then, right away, thinking of the poor, I thought of Francis of Assisi. Francis is also the man of peace. Francis gives us this spirit of peace, the poor man who wanted a poor Church. How I would love a Church that is poor and for the poor. (Audience to Representatives of the Communications Media, March 16, 2013)

JOURNAL ASSIGNMENT

- What do you think Pope Francis means when he says that he "would love a Church that is poor and for the poor"?

- In your own words, write a prayer for the "Church that is poor and for the poor."

---

the dignity of the human person. Catholics must be a witness of treasure beyond these earthly ones. The *Catechism of the Catholic Church* is clear that loving the poor is "incompatible" with selfish use of goods (*CCC*, 2445).

Again and again the Church reminds her people that they are merely *stewards*, not ultimate owners of their goods. St. John Chrysostom once exhorted, "Not to enable the poor to share in our goods is to steal from them and deprive them of life. The goods we possess are not ours, but theirs."[16] Even if one does not have

much, it is blessed to give even a little. This is witnessed in the example Jesus recounted of the poor widow who donated pittance in comparison to rich people who put large sums of money into the Temple treasury:

> Calling his disciples to himself, he said to them, "Amen, I say to you, this poor widow put in more than all the other contributors to the treasury. For they have all contributed from their surplus wealth, but she, from her poverty, has contributed all she had, her whole livelihood." (Mk 12:41–44)

The Eucharist and the Commitment to the Poor

The liturgical life of the Church is not separate from her life of charity and justice. The *Catechism of the Catholic Church* is clear that reception of the Eucharist *commits* the Church to the poor. It quotes St. John Chrysostom:

> You have tasted the Blood of the Lord, yet you do not recognize your brother. . . . You dishonor this table when you do not judge worthy of sharing your food someone judged worthy to take part in this meal. . . . God freed you from all your sins and invited you here, but you have not become more merciful. (*CCC*, 1397)

Because you have this great privilege of receiving the very Body of Christ, you must be compelled to serve him in the least of his people. Jesus *is* the satisfaction for all of the world's hungers: "I am the bread of life; whoever comes to me will never hunger, and whoever believes in me will never thirst" (Jn 6:35).

The Eucharist is not meant to be an isolated affair among Catholics who simply enjoy one another's and the Lord's company. Rather, the Eucharist is meant to help the Church become Christ's Body so he may continue his work of feeding people to satisfy not just their spiritual hungers, but also their physical hungers.

Translated to action, this means that at Eucharist (including during the Prayers of the Faithful), you are to pray for the needs of the world. But when you are dismissed to "go forth" from the Mass, you must bring Christ to others. Minimally, this means you must respond to those in your local community, nation, and world who are crying out for help. Their cries must not go unanswered. You must become Christ's hands and his feet to feed the hungry—and to clothe the naked, give drink to the thirsty, and so forth. Not to do so is to receive the Eucharist unworthily.

All of this demands a conversion of heart from selfishness. Living in a self-centered way is one of the effects of Original Sin. On the other hand, selflessness, the opposite of selfishness, is a characteristic of a disciple of Jesus Christ. Justice can sometimes require the giving up of some of one's own privileges and goods so others can have at least the chance to live and to participate in the community. This can be tough to do in a consumer society that measures people by what they have, not who they are.

Remember, before God *everyone* is poor. God is the only source of goodness. People who lack the basics are often more aware not only of this, but also that their God-given human dignity can never be taken from them.

The *Catechism of the Catholic Church* teaches, "Our Lord warns us that we shall be separated from him if we fail to meet the serious needs of the poor and the little ones who are his brethren" (*CCC*, 1033). In the face of the tragedy of poverty in all of its forms, you are called to commit to your own simplicity of life, so that you may have the freedom and resources to give of yourself to the poor. Ultimately, however, you should not be motivated by mere "duty" or "obligation." Rather, "the love of Christ impels us" (2 Cor 5:14).

SECTION ASSESSMENT

NOTE TAKING

Each of the following statements is false. Use the finished sentences you completed as part of the Note Taking to help you rewrite each statement to make it true.

1. Practicing the preferential option for the poor begins with the saints.
2. You are called to give up ownership of all your possessions in order to be a Christian disciple.
3. Pope Benedict XVI said that goods people possess truly belong to the poor.

COMPREHENSION

4. What is loving the poor incompatible with?
5. How does reception of the Eucharist commit one to the poor?
6. How is serving the poor rooted in selflessness?

REFLECTION

7. Reread the Scripture quotation about the poor widow (Mk 12:41–44) on page 196. What is the greatest gift of yourself that you can offer to the Lord?

Section Summaries

Focus Question

How do you serve Christ in the poor?

Complete one of the following:

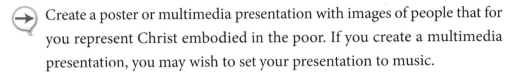 Create a poster or multimedia presentation with images of people that for you represent Christ embodied in the poor. If you create a multimedia presentation, you may wish to set your presentation to music.

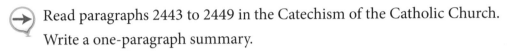 Read paragraphs 2443 to 2449 in the Catechism of the Catholic Church. Write a one-paragraph summary.

 Read the following Scripture passages and respond to the questions.

MARK 10:17–31: THE RICH YOUNG MAN

Why was it difficult for the rich young man to give up his possessions?

How can a rich person get to Heaven? Explain.

LUKE 12:13–21: SAYING AGAINST GREED AND THE PARABLE OF THE RICH FOOL

What is the meaning of this parable?

Rewrite this parable in a modern context.

ACTS 2:44–47; 4:32–35: LIFE IN THE CHRISTIAN COMMUNITY

How did the early Christians deal with poverty?

MARK 12:38–44: DENUNCIATION OF THE SCRIBES

What message might Jesus' words have for individuals? For greater society?

INTRODUCTION (PAGES 171–176)

An Overview of Poverty

Poverty is most often associated with an absence of material possessions. This includes a lack of basic necessities, including nutritious food, safe drinking water, health care, and shelter. Catholics are required by a mandate of Christ to work to end poverty. The Catholic social teaching theme "option for the poor and vulnerable" highlights the call to treat those who are impoverished in a special way. Poverty is also associated with psychological issues such as loneliness and addiction. "Poverty of spirit" is a positive dimension of poverty that flows from the first Beatitude and encourages an acceptance of Divine Providence.

 Keeping in mind the call to be poor in spirit, list some of the things in your life for which you are grateful to God.

SECTION 1 (PAGES 177–181)

The Bible and Poverty

Throughout Salvation History, God has called his people to provide for the needs of the poor. This call is embodied in Christ: he lived a life of poverty, and attended to the needs of the most vulnerable of his time. Christ makes it very clear that this type of self-gift is crucial to discipleship.

 Carefully and prayerfully read Christ's teaching on the Last Judgment in Matthew 25:31–46. Write down the verses that impact you the most and why.

SECTION 2 (PAGES 182–187)

The Scandal of World Hunger

Linked to material poverty is the pressing issue of hunger. Hunger and malnutrition are two of the worst effects of poverty. World hunger is a result of social sin. Catholic social teaching calls us as individuals and as a society to work to eliminate the root causes of hunger.

 With the permission of your parents, fast for a day. Eat only three small meals with no snacks. When you experience hunger pains, pray for those who endure hunger every single day. Journal about your experiences.

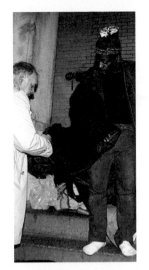

SECTION 3 (PAGES 188–194)

Working to End Poverty

The traditional corporal and spiritual works of mercy are a good summary of the Christian response to both material poverty and poverty of the soul. Within the service of the poor, there is a duty to evangelize. One concept that is important to keep in mind while looking to end poverty is the universal destination of goods, which upholds the right to private property, but calls each person to give of his or her goods to those less fortunate.

 Choose one corporal or one spiritual work of mercy. Prayerfully perform it somehow in your life. Write a paragraph about your experiences.

SECTION 4 (PAGES 195–198)

Poverty and You

Ending poverty begins with *you*. Foremost, it starts with living a life of simplicity, so you are more free to see the needs of others. Serving Christ in the poor is rooted in receiving him in the Eucharist.

 Compose a prayer of thanksgiving for the material and spiritual blessings you have been given. Share your prayer with Christ before the Blessed Sacrament. Ask him for the wisdom and courage to see him in the least of his people.

Chapter Assignments

1. Assessing the Cost of Healthy Eating

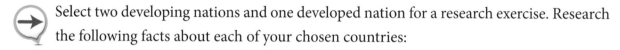

Locate a copy of the United States Department of Agriculture's plan for healthy eating that indicates the proper proportion of daily helpings of fruit, vegetables, grains, protein, and dairy products. Using the plan as a guide, construct a five-day menu of meals for a family of four. Include some variety in meal and food options. Record your menu in a chart listing breakfast, lunch, and dinner for each day. Next, take your menu to a grocery store. Bring a calculator with you. Assess the five-day cost of eating the meals on your menu. Where there are item choices to be made—for example, three ounces of expensive steak, or a less-expensive chicken breast to fulfill the protein requirement—select the less expensive option. Record your findings. Display them on a chart or in a multimedia presentation. Share the menu and costs with the class. Include a summary of what you have learned about the cost of healthy eating.

2. Researching Worldwide Poverty

Select two developing nations and one developed nation for a research exercise. Research the following facts about each of your chosen countries:

- What is the country's population?
- What is the country's population density?
- What percent of the population is hungry?
- What is the fertility rate?
- What is the infant mortality rate?
- What is the life expectancy at birth?
- What is the GNP (Gross National Product) per capita?

Find one other interesting fact about each country, such as when the country was founded or, if applicable, its history of colonialism. Then report your findings to the class.

Finally, write a one-page report addressing what you learned about poverty and about the following: connections between poverty and life expectancy, connections between poverty and infant mortality. Then share your ideas for how rich nations can help poor nations overcome poverty, and how individuals can contribute to helping solve the problem through works of charity or works of justice, or both. Your report should reflect the theme of Catholic social teaching, "option for the poor and vulnerable." You are encouraged to incorporate references to Scripture and other Church documents.

3. Researching and Promoting Catholic Charitable Organizations

 Research three Catholic organizations that serve the poor, such as:

- Pontifical Council *Cor Unum* for the Human and Christian Development
- Catholic Relief Services
- Catholic Charities USA
- Catholics Confront Global Poverty
- Catholic Campaign for Human Development

Create a bulletin board display (or, alternatively, a poster board display) that promotes the work of the three organizations. Include photos and printed information describing each organization. Also, advertise ways teenagers can participate in the the work of these groups.

Faithful Disciple

St. Gemma Galgani

St. Gemma Galgani is a saint most widely known for her extraordinary mystical experiences. And yet, much of her heroic abandonment as a disciple of Jesus Christ is witnessed in her example of accepting poverty with great humility.

St. Gemma Galgani was born in 1878 in a small Italian town. Her mother Aurelia died of tuberculosis when Gemma was only eight. Her awareness of poverty was present from an early age:

St. Gemma Galgani

> Whenever I went out, I asked Papa to give me some money, and if, as sometimes was the case, he refused, I had at least bread and clothes to give away. It was God's will I should meet these poor people, and every time I went out I encountered some three or four of them. To those who called at the house I gave clothing or whatever I could lay my hands on. . . .

In St. Gemma's young life, she knew relative economic prosperity. Her father, Enrico, was a successful pharmacist. He had always been a generous man; he gave of his resources to the less fortunate. Sadly, however, people did not make good on the loans he gave them. This, coupled with the medical bills from his wife's illness, led the Galgani family into destitution. All of his property was seized; the creditors even searched Gemma's own pockets and purse and took the few coins she had.

Very soon after this turn of events, Enrico was diagnosed with cancer. Gemma took care of him and comforted him throughout his illness. He died when Gemma was only nineteen. Gemma and her brothers and sisters were left as orphans in abject poverty. She became like a mother to her siblings. They stayed with an aunt for a while, but she, too, was very poor. The Galganis had to rely completely on the generosity of others, even for a few scraps of bread.

This situation might lead many people to despair, but Gemma's reaction was the opposite. She saw everything—even her poverty and sorrows—as gifts from God. She allowed her suffering to bring her closer to Christ. She always put her family before herself, even with the little food they received. A relative testified about Gemma, "No matter how small it was, Gemma always reserved the smallest portion for herself."

Gemma later had extraordinary mystical experiences. She is even reported to have received the stigmata—that is, the visible wounds of Christ, on her hands. She greatly wished to become a nun, but her poor health prevented this. She spent her final years in deep prayer and union with Christ on the Cross. In 1903 she contracted tuberculosis and died quietly in the company of her parish priest at the young age of twenty-five.

St. Gemma Galgani was beatified in 1933 and canonized in 1940, only thirty-seven years after her death. Because of her own difficult experiences, many people who are poor or unemployed ask for the intercession of St. Gemma Galgani.

Reading Comprehension

1. What were the events that changed the course of life for the Galganis?

2. How did St. Gemma view the poverty her family experienced?

3. Why couldn't St. Gemma become a nun?

Writing Task

- Answer the following questions: How can suffering bring one closer to Christ? In what ways can you offer up the small or more significant sufferings of your life to deepen your relationship with God?

Explaining the Faith

Why shouldn't we look out for ourselves first? Why do we have to serve the poor?

God looks out for every human being. He brings you into being, guides you in this life, and draws you to want communion with him forever. Evidence of his concern can be found in the way your family, friends, Church, and community support you and others with the necessities of life—physical and spiritual.

Living in a self-centered way is one of the effects of Original Sin. God created you to live and act in a way that is centered on him and others, not merely yourself. Selflessness, rather than selfishness, is the characteristic of a disciple of Jesus Christ, who is the living embodiment of what it means to live in a self-giving manner.

Further Research

- Read paragraph 1931 from the *Catechism of the Catholic Church*. What does it mean to look upon your neighbor as "another self"?

Prayer
Prayer for Generosity

Lord Jesus, teach me to be generous.

    Teach me to serve you as you deserve,

To give and not count the cost,

To fight and not to heed the wounds,

To toil and not to seek for rest,

To labor and not to seek reward,

Except that of knowing that I do your will,

Amen.

                —St. Ignatius of Loyola

THE DIGNITY OF WORK AND THE RIGHTS OF WORKERS

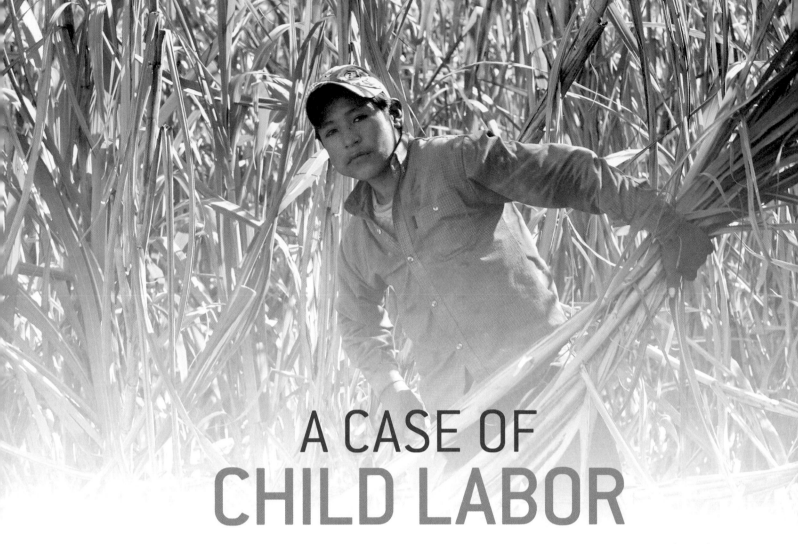

A CASE OF
CHILD LABOR

The United States has strict laws regarding child labor. Still, sometimes, abuses occur and workers are subject to conditions and requirements that stretch or break the law; for example, laws having to do with the age of the worker and the hours and tasks a younger person is asked to do.

A teen from North Carolina identified as Marcos S. reflected on the work he did cutting Christmas trees full time. He began working when he was twelve years old. In this case, not only did he regularly use a chainsaw without training, he was also in the fields when the trees were being sprayed with insecticides. Marcos recalled:

> You're right there. . . . There are people with big tanks on their back and they go around. They did it when I was working. It smelled so bad. The guys that spray—they don't even wear masks.

For the most part, Marcos said that he worked on different crops throughout the year on weekends and school vacations, but it was during the Christmas tree harvest that he was asked to miss school to work. "But in school there's a limited number of times you can be absent. Then I have homework to catch up on. I go to work, I come home. I stay up late to get it done." To date, nobody in Marcos's family has made it past tenth grade, but he has plans to go further.[1]

FOCUS QUESTION

How are the **DIGNITY of WORK** and the **RIGHTS OF WORKERS** related to your own **DIGNITY** as a person?

INTRODUCTION
The Nature of Work

What are your views about work? Do you see work as a great duty, a higher calling? Or do you see work as just a day-to-day drudgery? Do you ever think about the rights and duties of employers and employees? Have you ever considered the fact that Jesus Christ himself worked?

These questions fit well with the theme of Catholic social teaching, "the dignity of work and the rights of workers." Work is a participation in God's creative action. Work strikes at the very core of one's humanity, in that it can become an expression of one's talents and capacities; it is a "fundamental dimension of human existence on earth."[2] That said, work can also become subject to great abuses, especially when it loses sight of the rights and dignity of the worker.

Issues involving the meaning of work and the rights and importance of workers are the subject of this chapter. The chapter also examines the strengths and weaknesses of the world's major economic systems and rules for operating the economy. Section 1 explores the origins, purposes, and benefits of work.

Dimensions of Work

Work, or labor, is a sustained effort with the intent to produce or accomplish something. Work can involve jobs that require physical labor, such as plumbing or construction; or, work may not involve much physical

NOTE TAKING

Summarizing the Section. Take notes as you read the section. Create an outline as in the pattern below.

I. Dimensions of Work
  A. Objective
    1.
    2.
  B. Subjective
    1.
    2.
II. Origins of Work
  A. Present from Creation
    1.
    2.

  B. Not a Punishment
    1. Without the Fall, work would not be accompanied by suffering
III. Duties and Benefits of Work
  A. Duties
    1.
    2.
  B. Benefits
    1.
    2.
    3.

labor, but can still be mentally laborious, as with accounting or writing. Not all work is compensated for in the same way, if at all. For example, a stay-at-home mother does not receive compensation. And, as you know, neither does a student. All types of work involve two dimensions, objective and subjective.

The **objective dimension of work** refers to the product or outcome of work, the *object*. This includes the means used to accomplish a task. Thus, tools, technology, machinery—as well as the products of research, farming, industry, and the many service-oriented activities—are part of the objective aspect of work.

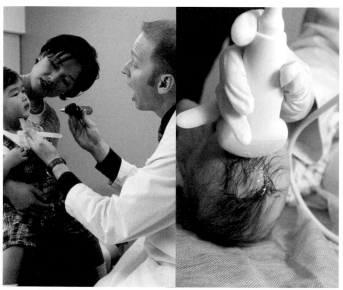

Both of these objective aspects of a pediatrician's work can enhance his dignity as a person.

The **subjective dimension of work** refers to the *subject*, the human person, and his or her involvement in the work. The value of human work, and the basis of its dignity, rests in the person, not in the work being done (the objective aspect). Consider these examples that differentiate between the two dimensions of work:

- Think of the work done by an executive secretary. The secretary organizes meetings, types up reports, and screens phone calls, to mention a few tasks. This is the objective part of work. The person doing the work—in this case, the secretary, is the subject of the work. The true value of this work is how it helps the secretary to grow and to develop as a

person and how the work done by the secretary benefits others in the organization.

- Take another example: a pediatrician. The pediatrician's care of children is the objective aspect of the work. The pediatrician is the subject doing the work. The value of the work is tied into whether it enhances or detracts from the doctor's dignity as a person and how it enhances or detracts from the dignity of the patients, those the doctor serves. That is, does the work help the person develop as a human being? Does the person participate in God's creative activity, bringing benefit to humanity and order to creation?

The bottom line is this: work exists for human beings; human beings do not exist for work. The purpose of work is to help individuals reach their own potential and to support of the human dignity of those their work serves. Because the person is the central focus of work, the human laborer has priority over **capital**.

Any political or economic system that makes the objective element of work its god violates the human person. For example, unbridled capitalism is immoral and contrary to God's plan because it makes profit its god, and it treats workers as mere instruments of production and not as persons with human dignity. Similarly, economic systems like socialism or communism that subordinate individual workers and their rights (the subjective dimension) to the work being done (the objective dimension) are likewise immoral. Section 2 of this chapter looks more closely at economic systems.

> **objective dimension of work** The product or outcome of work.
>
> **subjective dimension of work** The human person and his or her involvement in work.
>
> **capital** The natural resources God has given people to use as well as to all the means of producing and developing them.

Origins of Work

Work was present as a part of humans' lives even before the Fall; God's first instructions were for Adam and Eve to "subdue the earth" (Gn 1:28) and "cultivate and care for" God's creation (Gn 2:15). St. John Paul II explained that in "carrying out this mandate, every human being reflects the very action of the Creator of the universe."[3]

Thus, work itself is not a punishment from the Fall, but instead, humans now *toil and suffer* in work because they live their lives in a fallen world. Only by the sweat of the brow (Gn 3:19) can you reap the rewards of labor. If Adam and Eve had not sinned, you would still work, but your work would not be marked by arduousness. This "suffering" refers not only to the personal effort required of work, but also the tensions, conflicts, and injustices that can arise within working environments.

Duties and Benefits of Work

You have a duty to work. There are also great benefits that come from work. Because you live in a human community and are called to communion with others, you are not exempt from contributing your due in order to live at the expense of others. St. Paul exhorts you to work, so as to "not depend on anyone" (1 Thes 4:12). He also wrote that "if anyone was unwilling to work, neither should that one eat" (2 Thes 3:10). There will be times in your life in which dependency upon another is necessary, but you should always put forth your best effort, so that you do not abuse the charity of others.

Likewise, within this responsibility, you are called to share the fruits of your work. The poor, by virtue of their poverty, have a right to accept such charity. This does not excuse the poor from doing everything possible to find gainful employment. The *Catechism of the Catholic Church* states that "everyone should be able to draw from work the means of providing for his life and that of his family, and of serving the human community" (*CCC*, 2428).

Work is not only for others; it is for the good of the worker too. St. John Chrysostom wrote that "idleness is harmful to man's being, whereas activity is good for his body and soul."[4]

In *Economic Justice for All*, the United States Conference of Catholic Bishops stressed the threefold moral and positive benefits of work:

1. *Work benefits you as a human person.* Work is a fundamental means for you to express and to develop yourself as a human being, a unique creature of God.

2. *Work benefits you as a provider.* Work is the ordinary way for you to provide for your material needs. This is especially true for heads of families who must feed, clothe, shelter, and educate their children.

3. *Work benefits you as a member of society.* "Finally, work enables people to contribute to the well-being of the larger community. Work is not only for one's self. It is for one's family, for the nation, and indeed for the benefit of the entire human family" (§97). St. John Paul II put it this way: "Work serves to add to the heritage of the whole human family, of all the people living in the world."[5]

In brief, work enables all people to fulfill their human destiny, to provide for themselves and their families, and to help the rest of society by sharing their gifts.

JESUS: A Man of Work

Jesus' life on earth was filled with words and deeds that affirmed the value of work. In fact, he devoted most of his life to manual labor in the carpenter's shop of his foster father, St. Joseph (cf. Mt 13:55).

Jesus chose workers to travel alongside him, notably fishermen and even a tax collector. In his parables on the Kingdom of God, Jesus often referred to a variety of human workers including shepherds, farmers, doctors, sowers, householders, servants, stewards, fishermen, merchants, laborers, scholars, and investors. In one of the parables, the parable of the talents (see Matthew 25:14–30), Jesus condemned the useless servant who buried his talents in the ground and praised those servants who are found hard at work and using their gifts to the fullest.

Jesus also described his own mission as work. After being persecuted for healing a man on the Sabbath, Jesus responded, "My Father is at work until now, so I am at work" (Jn 5:17). Truly, in performing this deed on the Sabbath, Jesus reinvigorated its meaning as a day that should be used by all to dedicate themselves to God and to others. He explained: "The sabbath was made for man, not man for the sabbath. That is why the Son of Man is lord even of the sabbath" (Mk 2:27–28).

Jesus taught that a person should not be enslaved by work. Like everything else in life, work should find its proper place and perspective. Work only has meaning if it is oriented to the Kingdom of God. Consider what Jesus said to Martha when she was upset for being left to do all the household work while her sister Mary sat at the foot of Jesus listening to him speak: "Martha, Martha, you are anxious and worried about many things. There is need of only one thing. Mary has chosen the better part and it will not be taken from her" (Lk 10:41–42).

Christ's greatest work was his work of Redemption, his once-and-for-all Sacrifice on the Cross that remains ever present for your life today. Christ's Sacrifice is an unmerited gift. Uniting your own work to Christ is a way you can participate in the grace of his gift.

Work as a Share in the Cross of Christ

In your life as a student, you have discovered that work, be it manual or intellectual, can be hard. Most jobs involve some suffering. This could be evidenced in things like long hours, an unpleasant supervisor, physical labor, time away from family or from other pursuits, and so on. The toil connected with work is part of a person's journey here in this life. In its own way, the pain and sufferings of earthly work prepare you for the final trials you will face approaching death.

Also, work is a way to unite your suffering and sacrifice to the Cross of Christ Jesus. Through work, you can share in God's saving plan for the world. Your earthly work can help you participate in the work of your own Redemption. Working is a way to strengthen your relationship with Jesus and join him in his threefold mission of prophet, priest, and king:

This work of salvation came about through suffering and death on a cross. By enduring the toil of work in union with Christ crucified for us, man in a way collaborates with the Son of God for the redemption of humanity. He shows himself a true disciple of Christ by carrying the cross in his turn every day in the activity that he is called to perform. (*Laborem Exercens*, §27)

You carry only a small part of Christ's Cross when you offer up the toil that is associated with work. However, because of the Resurrection of Christ, through your work, you can find a glimmer of the new life that God has prepared for you. "Work can be a means of sanctification and a way of animating earthly realities with the Spirit of Christ" (*CCC*, 2427).

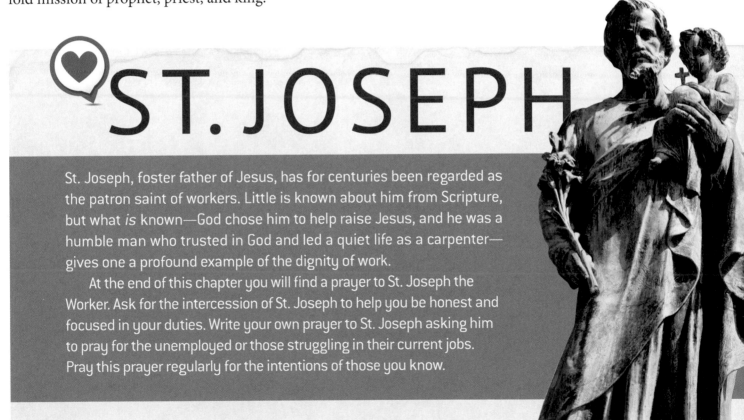

ST. JOSEPH

St. Joseph, foster father of Jesus, has for centuries been regarded as the patron saint of workers. Little is known about him from Scripture, but what *is* known—God chose him to help raise Jesus, and he was a humble man who trusted in God and led a quiet life as a carpenter—gives one a profound example of the dignity of work.

At the end of this chapter you will find a prayer to St. Joseph the Worker. Ask for the intercession of St. Joseph to help you be honest and focused in your duties. Write your own prayer to St. Joseph asking him to pray for the unemployed or those struggling in their current jobs. Pray this prayer regularly for the intentions of those you know.

SECTION ASSESSMENT

NOTE TAKING

Use the notes for this section to complete the following items.

1. Define *work*.

2. What is the purpose of work?

3. What are three benefits of work?

COMPREHENSION

4. Cite evidence from Scripture to show that Adam and Eve worked before the Fall.

5. Cite two examples from the letters of St. Paul that explain the necessity of work.

REFLECTION

6. How can suffering bring you closer to God?

7. What is your favorite lesson about work from the words and teachings of Jesus? Tell why.

APPLICATION

8. Share your own example to explain the objective and subjective dimensions of work.

SECTION 1
Rights and Abuses Associated with Work

As noted in the previous section, everyone has the duty to work. The corresponding right to this duty is the right of

> suitable employment for all who are capable of it. The opposite of a just and right situation in this field is unemployment, that is to say, the lack of work for those who are capable of it. (*Laborem Exercens*, §18)

A job is critically important for two reasons. First, a job helps a person earn a living. This is especially important for parents who are obliged "to provide as far as possible for the physical . . . needs of their children" (*CCC*, 2252). Second, work helps a person achieve human fulfillment. This is why people often experience a great loss of personal dignity when they cannot find jobs:

> Unemployment almost always wounds its victim's dignity and threatens the equilibrium of his life. Besides the harm done to him personally, it entails many risks for his family. (*CCC*, 2436)

Every economic system that desires justice and the common good must aim for full employment for its

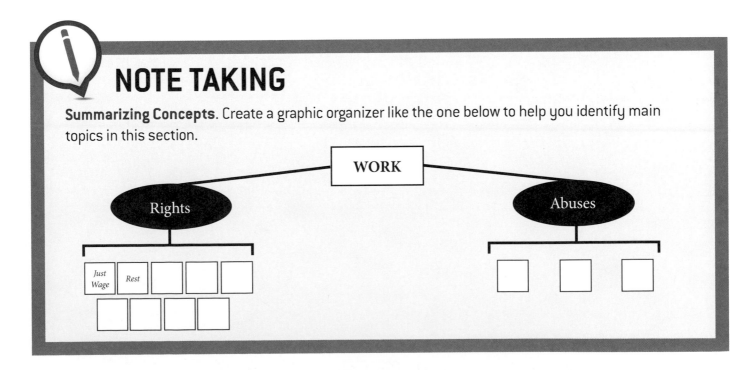

NOTE TAKING

Summarizing Concepts. Create a graphic organizer like the one below to help you identify main topics in this section.

citizens. In the words of the United States Conference of Catholic Bishops:

> Full employment is the foundation of a just economy. The most urgent priority for domestic economic policy is the creation of new jobs with adequate pay and decent working conditions. We must make it possible as a nation for everyone who is seeking a job to find employment within a reasonable amount of time. Our emphasis on this goal is based on the conviction that human work has a special dignity and is a key to achieving justice in society. (*Economic Justice for All*, §136)

However, most societies fail in such a goal of employment for all those who want, or need, to work. As of early 2014, the unemployment rate in the United States was at about 6.6 percent.[6] This number did not reflect those persons who are "underemployed," that is, those who are working but not being compensated in accord with their education and experience. The Church sees lack of employment as a "huge obstacle on the road to human and professional fulfillment."[7] Those who are unemployed or underemployed run the risk of "being marginalized within society, of becoming victims of social exclusion."[8]

The Church emphasizes the need for specialized, ongoing education and training throughout one's life as means for protecting workers from unemployment. She also challenges the government to create conditions and policies that encourage employment opportunities. The government's duty is not necessarily to guarantee employment for everyone, but rather to encourage individual initiative and business opportunities by "creating conditions which will ensure job opportunities, by stimulating those activities where they are lacking or by supporting them in moments of crisis."[9]

Business owners and employers are an essential part of the employment equation. For their part, business owners or employers have the right to make a profit for the risks they take in investing their money. These profits guarantee the future of the business, which, in turn, creates employment opportunities and provides wages for workers. However, profits are not supreme. The right to make profits is tempered by the obligation to do so responsibly. For example, in running their enterprises, employers must "consider the good of persons and not only the increase of profits" (*CCC*, 2432). In addition, businesses must consider that they are "responsible to society for the economic and ecological effects of their operations" (*CCC*, 2432).

UNEMPLOYMENT STUDY

Check the current national unemployment rate and the unemployment rate for your state through the US Department of Labor's Bureau of Labor Statistics. Then interview an unemployed person you know. Report on the ups and downs of his or her experience of trying to find employment. Combine both parts of your research into an oral or written presentation.

SPECIAL CONCERNS IN THE WORKPLACE

THE CHURCH ADDRESSES SPECIFIC CONCERNS WITH REGARD TO THE NEEDS OF FAMILIES, WOMEN, AND IMMIGRANTS IN THE WORKPLACE.

WORK IS INTEGRAL FOR THE DEVELOPMENT OF *FAMILIES*, WHICH ARE THE FOUNDATIONAL COMMUNITY OF ALL SOCIETY.

Work provides the sustenance needed to raise children and provide for their human development. Therefore, it is necessary for business owners, labor organizations, and the government to promote family life and avoid hardships that require people to work multiple jobs, endure difficult hours, and travel great distances away from their family.

THE CHURCH SEES *WOMEN* AS HAVING A "FEMININE GENIUS"—THAT IS, SPECIAL QUALITIES THAT ONLY THEY POSSESS.

The Church is adamant that this femininity is needed in every sector of society, which includes the workplace. Thus, women must have access to advancement and professional formation.

IMMIGRANTS CAN OFTEN FILL A LABOR NEED THAT THOSE CURRENTLY IN THE COUNTRY CANNOT MEET.

The Church strictly condemns exploiting such workers, because they deserve the same labor rights as natives. Furthermore, they are to be helped in becoming integrated in society, which often includes efforts to reunite families. More information on immigration will be presented in Chapter 8.

Any of these groups, and all workers in general, are guaranteed certain rights in the workplace. Correspondingly, employers must avoid abuses that violate workers' rights and dignity. These topics are discussed in the next section.

Basic Rights of Workers

Based on the dignity of the human person, the Church clarifies certain rights of workers that employers must honor. The *Compendium of the Social Doctrine of the Church* lists nine basic rights:[10]

1. The Right to a Just Wage

It is important to note that a **just wage** is *not* merely what the worker will agree to, because often, in desperation, people may assent to wages that are well below what is fair for their work. Rather, wages should:

> guarantee man the opportunity to provide a dignified livelihood for himself and his family on the material, social, cultural and spiritual level, taking into account the role and the productivity of each, the state of the business, and the common good. (*Gaudium et Spes*, §67)

Today, at a minimum, this should include a wage high enough to meet food, clothing, and shelter needs, and to provide for transportation, education, and some form of recreation. St. John Paul II suggested a "family wage"—that is, "a single salary given to the head of the family for his work, sufficient for the needs of the family without the other spouse having to take up gainful employment outside the home."[11]

2. The Right to Rest

The first creation story in the Book of Genesis reveals that God rested after the work of creation was complete, sanctifying the seventh day of the week as a holy day (cf. Gn 2:2–3). This divinely appointed "Sabbath rest" underscores the right of workers to proper rest. Rest should also include a holiday or vacation taken once a year or possibly several other shorter breaks throughout the year.

Rest from work can, and should, elevate the human spirit by giving people the time on the Lord's Day to worship a loving God in humility and thanksgiving for all the gifts bestowed during the previous week. Catholics have the obligation to do so by participating in Mass on Sunday. Resting from the toil of a job is also a great opportunity to strengthen family life, to spend time with friends, and to cultivate the mind.

3. The Right to a Safe Workplace

Companies must make efforts to keep their employees safe, even in professions that are intrinsically hazardous. Keeping in mind the principle of subsidiarity, the government should have safeguards and penalties in

place to prevent and punish violations against one's health and safety.

4. The Right That One's Personality Should Be Safeguarded

No one should be forced to perform any task on the job that violates one's conscience.

5. The Right to Appropriate Subsidies to Aid Unemployed Workers

Aid should be provided to those who are unwillingly unemployed and their families.

6. The Right to a Pension and to Insurance

Employers have the obligation to help provide insurance for the medical care of employees, whether from illness or work-related injuries. Catholic social teaching holds that health care is a basic human right because it flows from the sanctity of human life and is essential to human dignity.

The issue of accessible and moral health care for all remains one of the most important of the day. Despite the basic right of all people to health care, rising medical costs have nearly made offering health care insurance prohibitive for many employers. Many reforms are still needed to cost structures for treatments and medicine; to tort law, to limit frivolous lawsuits that lead to rising costs; and to insurance costs so that coverage can truly be universal.

7. The Right to Social Security Connected with Maternity

Recalling the comments about women in the workplace in the previous section, the Church is clear that, in the workplace, the role of mother should never be hindered. This includes adequate compensation and job security after giving birth.

8. The Right to Assemble and to Form Associations

Associations of workers are often known as "unions." The Church upholds that unions are not always necessary, but when they are the best way to uphold the dignity of workers, people have the right to form them. Unions exist to help workers defend and secure other rights due them—like fair wages, decent working conditions, adequate rest, and so forth.

Unions must always serve the dignity of the human person; their struggles must always aim at the common good: "this struggle should be seen as a normal endeavor 'for' the just good . . . not a struggle 'against' others."[12] The Church also emphasizes that those in a union should not be politically coerced because of this particular association.[13]

9. The Right to Strike

By definition, a strike is a temporary work stoppage by employees to secure higher pay or better working conditions from employers. Given the "proper conditions and within just limits," strikes can be morally

While the number of coal miners in the United States has dwindled in recent years, the United Mine Workers union (above) continues to petition for safety for its members as well as pension and health care rights for both current and retired miners.

PLANNING a BUDGET

BASIC MONTHLY EXPENSES	AMOUNT
Rent/Mortgage	
Utilities (electric, gas, water, trash)	
Phone/Internet/Television	
Food	
Clothing	
Transportation	
Child Care	
Entertainment	
Insurance (property, life, health)	
Taxes (federal, FICA, state, local)	
MONTHLY TOTAL	
YEARLY TOTAL (MONTHLY TOTAL × 12)	

Using the information provided in the section on just wages, work on a budget for a family of four living in your area of the country. Assume the family has two children, three years old and seven years old. What are the family's monthly expenses? How much money would this family need to live on per year with a decent standard of living? What would be a just wage?

Additional Information and Questions

- Assume a work year of 2,000 hours (50 weeks × 40 hours per week). What should be the minimum hourly wage for the head of the household for the family to meet its basic needs?

- What is the actual minimum wage mandated by law for this year?

- Is it possible for one wage earner to support this family on the minimum wage?

- Is it possible for an individual to live on the minimum wage?

- If the answer to either of the preceding two questions is no, what are some possible remedies for this situation?

Check your figures against the Catholic Campaign for Human Development's Poverty USA link on the United States Conference of Catholic Bishops website: http://www.usccb.org/about/catholic-campaign-for-human-development/. Click on the Poverty USA link.

acceptable. However, there are occasions when a strike may be abused for illegitimate reasons, including political purposes. An example of an abusive strike would be to shut down the essential services of a community (e.g., hospitals), thereby gravely endangering the human welfare. The *Catechism of the Catholic Church* explains:

> Recourse to a *strike* is morally legitimate when it cannot be avoided, or at least when it is necessary to obtain a proportionate benefit. It becomes morally unacceptable when accompanied by violence, or when objectives are included that are not directly linked to working conditions or are contrary to the common good. (*CCC*, 2435)

Remember, all the rights associated with work are accompanied by responsibilities for the three major parties involved in the employment process: employers, employees, and the government (primarily through regulations). When all three work together there is an opportunity to promote human dignity of individuals within families, local communities, and nations.

Abuses against the Dignity of Work

Although work has the potential to be a positive expression of a person's gifts and talents, it also presents possibilities for the abuse of workers and their rights. Millions of workers in the United States and around the world experience workplace abuses every day, including being forced to work long hours, in unsafe conditions, and for extremely low wages. In the following subsections we'll take a look at workplace abuses with regard to children and to adults.

Child Labor

Child labor, defined as very young children being forced to work in conditions detrimental to their mental and physical development, is denounced by the Church as a form of violence, even slavery.[14] In *Rerum Novarum*, the first social encyclical, Pope Leo XIII explicitly condemned child labor:

> And, in regard to children, great care should be taken not to place them in workshops and factories until their bodies and minds are sufficiently developed. For, just as very rough weather destroys the buds of spring, so does too early an experience of life's hard toil blight the young promise of a child's faculties, and render any true education impossible. (§42)

Unfortunately, the social ill Pope Leo XIII decried in 1891 is not a relic of the nineteenth century. The International Labor Organization estimates that 215 million children currently work full-time in developing countries—one out of every six children in the world. Recent decades have seen a decrease in child labor for children ages five to fourteen in the Asian-Pacific region, Latin America, and the Caribbean. Tragically, however, the trend is reversed in Sub-Saharan Africa, where the number of young children working is increasing, so that among those ages four to seventeen, one in four works.

Instead of learning and growing, these children are working long hours, often in dangerous conditions. The International Labor Organization has identified the worst forms of child labor as enslavement, selling or trafficking children, bondage because of family debt, forced labor, recruitment of children for use in armed conflict, the use of children for prostitution or the making of pornography, using children to produce and sell drugs, and any work that is likely to harm the health, safety, or morals of children.[15]

Besides the story of Marcos S. that began this chapter, consider also the story of teenage boy Gurmeet Kumar of India, who works ten to fifteen hours at a time stitching soccer balls at five cents per hour. Gurmeet was sold into "debt bondage" after his mother incurred a $100 debt, trying to buy medicine for Gurmeet's younger brother, who later died. The interest

Since the beginning of the Afghanistan war in the early part of the century, upwards of 40,000 children in the Afghan capital of Kabul have been forced to miss school and work in the streets. "I would love to go to school, but I can't. There is no one else in my family to work except me," said Zabi, a ten-year-old boy selling shopping bags in a crowded market, to an international reporter.

charged and incurred on this small loan is so high that the loan doubles every few months. Gurmeet may even pass the debt on to his own kids. Debt bondage is really a form of slavery.[16]

Abuses in Adult Labor

Adults also suffer from labor exploitation. For example, in factories in El Salvador (see photo above), workers earn an average of only eight cents for every twenty-five dollar athletic shirt they produce for sale in the United States. The workers frequently work in unsafe and oppressive conditions, and experience harassment and intimidation. Workers who speak out against unjust conditions or express concern are often fired.

Workplace abuses happen in the United States, too. For example, the US meat industry has been criticized by a human rights agency for permitting hazardous working conditions at meat plants and using illegal tactics to suppress employee efforts to report abuses and injuries. A detailed 175-page report claimed that meat packers, who hold what is often cited as one of the most dangerous factory jobs in America, face a real danger of losing a limb or their lives because of unsafe work conditions. The report also documented

that companies often deny workers' compensation to injured employees, and "intimidate and fire workers who try to organize, and exploit workers' immigrant status in order to keep them quiet about abuses."[17]

Fraud and Other Offenses

Other forms of abuse against the nature of work occur when employees are unjust to the employer or the company itself has fraudulent practices. A modern example of the latter is business fraud, sometimes known as "white collar crimes." This includes moral and ethical violations such as misleading advertising, tax evasion, excess and irresponsible spending, and other wasteful practices.

Individual workers can also abuse their labor opportunities by not putting forth their best effort or by using, or taking, company property for themselves without permission. Both of these practices are a form of stealing, in that an employee is taking what rightfully belongs to the employer, or not working to meet the expectations on which his or her pay is based.

For teens, unethical work practices—and forms of stealing—might include actions such as texting or talking on the phone rather than attending to the work they were hired to do (for example, babysitting a young child). Or perhaps while working at a restaurant, a young person may give free food and drinks to his or her friends without permission. Just as in the preceding examples, such behavior is a form of stealing, and is unjust and immoral.

SECTION ASSESSMENT

NOTE TAKING

Use the graphic organizer you completed to answer the following questions.

1. If you were to prioritize the rights of workers, which would you rank first? Explain.

2. What is the purpose of the "right to rest"?

COMPREHENSION

3. Name a statistic associated with child labor that you find most shocking. Explain your response.

4. Name two reasons employment is a necessity.

5. What constitutes a just wage?

6. What are some health care reforms needed in the United States?

7. Why does the Church support the right of workers to form unions?

8. Why is work integral for the development of families?

9. What is a "family wage"?

10. What are some examples of "white collar crime"?

ANALYSIS

11. What can the government do to decrease unemployment? How can business owners and employers offer lasting solutions?

APPLICATION

12. Share an example of a job for the head of the household that would not inflict hardship on a family with a father, mother, and three children.

SECTION 2
Justice and Economic Society

Related to the issue of work is the overall economy of a society. Chapter 5 spoke at length about civil society and political society (government); both of these interact greatly with economic society. The world of economics is vast and multifaceted.

The Church does not necessarily endorse a certain economic system over another, but she does critique or laud certain aspects of economic life. Namely, she upholds the right of everyone to economic initiative. The *Catechism of the Catholic Church* teaches that "everyone should make legitimate use of his talents to contribute to the abundance that will benefit all and to harvest the just fruits of his labor" (*CCC*, 2429). The Church exalts individual freedom and private property, while still seeing the necessity for public services. The Church is also clear that justice—in all its forms (commutative, distributive, legal)—must be applied to the economic sphere.

Your faith should be a part of every aspect of your life, and this includes your interaction with the economy. Pope Benedict XVI said, "Every economic decision has a moral consequence."[18]

Two Economic Systems

The economic system you are probably most familiar with is capitalism, in which means of production are controlled by private individuals and companies. Although the Church supports individual initiative and ownership of private property, in *Rerum Novarum*, Pope Leo XIII condemned capitalism that has absolutely no regulations and restrictions. St. John Paul II said that such "unbridled capitalism" leads to "instances of contracts between employers and

NOTE TAKING

Synthesizing Main Ideas. Write the following words in your notebook. As you read this section, write a definition or example that explains the word in the context of the reading.

   capitalism
   socialism
   regulation
   consumerism

employees which lack reference to the most elementary justice regarding the employment of children or women, working hours, the hygienic condition of the workplace and fair pay."[19]

In other words, if business practices are unregulated, there is a potential for workers to be exploited and their rights denied. Although assisted by government, private individuals and associations like labor unions have the responsibility to protect the dignity and rights of workers to participate in honest and efficient work.

In *Rerum Novarum*, Pope Leo XIII also spoke out against socialism, a system of economics in which all means of production are controlled by the government. When a government tries to control everything, including the economy, abuses against the human person often occur. Pope Benedict XVI elucidated that "we do not need a state which regulates and controls everything, but a state which, in accordance with the principle of subsidiarity, generously acknowledges and supports initiatives arising from the different social forces and combines spontaneity with closeness to those in need."[20]

Human Person: Not Just a Money-Maker

The purpose of any economy is to serve the person, not the converse, "for man is the source, the center, and the purpose of all economic and social life."[21] St. John Paul II emphasized that, although humans do indeed produce and consume goods, they should not be reduced to the roles of producers and consumers:

> Economic freedom is only one element of human freedom. . . . when man is seen more as a producer or consumer of goods than as a subject who produces and consumes in order to live, then economic freedom loses its necessary relationship to the human person and

ends up by alienating and oppressing him. (*Centesimus Annus*, 39)

Each person has to constantly guard against the dangers of **greed**. You are exhorted by the Tenth Commandment not to covet your neighbor's goods. It is important to delineate between owning material possessions and being controlled by them.

Have you ever heard someone say, "Money is the root of all evil"? In fact, that is a misquotation of Scripture. In truth, Scripture says: "the *love* of money is the root of all evils" (1 Tm 6:10). The inclusion of the word "love" is important: it shows that money is not inherently bad and that it is instead one's inordinate attachment to money—and the material goods of this earth—that becomes evil and sinful. St. Paul warns against such greediness:

> Tell the rich in the present age not to be proud and not to rely on so uncertain a thing as wealth but rather on God, who richly provides us with all things for our enjoyment. Tell them to do good, to be rich in good works, to be generous, ready to share, thus accumulating as treasure a good foundation for the future, so as to win the life that is true life. (1 Tm 6:17–19)

St. John Paul II also spoke out about **consumerism**, which is marked by an excessive accessibility of material goods (see photo on page 226), which can be easily acquired and then easily discarded without concern, because there are always more "things" to be had. Consumerism leads to what Pope Francis has called a "culture of waste." St. John Paul II explained

---

greed Also known as avarice; the desire for earthly goods beyond what we need. Greed is a sin against the Tenth Commandment.

consumerism A social and economic order that encourages the purchase of goods in ever greater amounts.

10 PRINCIPLES OF ECONOMIC LIFE

The following ten principles, drawn from documents of the United States Conference of Catholic Bishops (e.g., *A Place at the Table: A Catholic Recommitment to Overcome Poverty and to Respect the Dignity of All God's Children* and *Economic Justice for All*), papal encyclicals, and the *Catechism of the Catholic Church* (2458–2462), help to create a framework of Catholic economic life. Study and take notes on the list. You may want to rewrite a principle in your own words or cite an example that helps you remember and understand it. Finally, complete the exercise that follows.

1. The economy exists for the person, not the person for the economy.

2. Moral principles should shape economic life. Choices and institutions should be judged by how they protect or undermine human life, and the dignity of the human person, and whether they serve the family and the common good.

3. A basic way of measuring the morality of any economy is how the poor and vulnerable are faring.

4. Each person has a right to life and the basic necessities of life (e.g., food, shelter, education, health care, safe environment, economic security).

5. All people have the right to economic initiative, to productive work, to just wages and benefits, to decent working conditions. They also have the right to join unions or other associations.

6. To the extent that they can, all people have a corresponding duty to work, a responsibility to provide for their families' needs, and the obligation to contribute to the broader society.

7. In economic life, free markets have both clear advantages and limits and governments have essential responsibilities and limits. Voluntary groups have irreplaceable roles, but they cannot substitute for the proper working of the market and the just policies of the state.

8. Society has a moral obligation, including conforming government actions to the principle of subsidiarity when necessary, to assure opportunity, meet basic human needs, and pursue justice in economic life.

9. Workers, owners, managers, stockholders, and consumers are moral agents in economic life. By personal choices, initiative, creativity, and investment, individuals enhance or diminish economic opportunity, community life, and social justice.

10. The global economy has moral dimensions and human consequences. Decisions on investment, trade, aid, and development should protect human life and promote human rights, especially for those most in need wherever they might live on this globe.

EXERCISE

Consider the following scenarios. For each, list the most important principle, criterion, or direction from the preceding list that you think must absolutely be considered in deciding in favor of, or against, the proposed action. Provide reasons for your choices.

- Congress is proposing an income tax cut.
- An auto company is proposing to move its factory to Mexico.
- A soft-drink company is considering a vigorous ad campaign in an underdeveloped country.
- You are considering investing a $500 gift from your grandparents in a company that has sweatshops in a developing country.
- To ensure the viability of the Social Security system for future generations, political leaders are considering cutting benefits to current recipients by 20 percent.

consumerism this way: "An object already owned but now superseded by something better is discarded, with no thought of its possible lasting value in itself, nor of some other human being who is poorer."[22] A consumerist mindset is prevalent in today's society. However, the relentless pursuit of material possessions often leads to the realization that the things of this earth can never bring full satisfaction. Your true fulfillment is in union with God.

SECTION ASSESSMENT

NOTE TAKING

Use your completed Note Taking assignment to write sentences in your own words to explain the following concepts:

1. *socialism*
2. *consumerism*

COMPREHENSION

3. How should moral principles shape economic life?

CRITICAL THINKING

4. Based on the feature "Ten Principles of Economic Life," write a personal statement of belief on what you consider to be the ideal economic system for a Catholic.

ANALYSIS

5. Of consumerism, St. John Paul II wrote: "The more one possesses the more one wants, while deeper aspirations remain unsatisfied and perhaps even stifled."[23] Answer the following:

   • What do you think St. John Paul II meant by this statement?

   • In what ways do you fall prey to the mentality he describes?

   • What are some concrete steps you can take today to be less materialistic and more focused on "deeper aspirations"?

SECTION 3
Work and You

Catholic social teaching tells us that, along with its importance as a way to make a living, work is a form of continuing participation in God's creation. Thus, the goal of work is not simply to "earn a paycheck"; rather, work can help in your personal development. And yet, many people let themselves be enslaved by their work. If through work you are serving anything other than God, then work can become an idol; that is, something that takes the place of God as the ultimate purpose of your life. Work as an idol can complicate your life in many ways, such as neglecting family or faith in pursuit of a career. Or it often manifests itself in focusing on only the material wealth associated with work. The *Compendium of the Social Doctrine of the Church* says,

> One must not succumb to the temptation of making an idol of work, for the ultimate and definitive meaning of life is not to be found in work. Work is essential, but it is God—and not work—who is the origin of life and the final goal of man. (§266)

Work is an integral part of life, but it is not the purpose of life. Union with God is the purpose of life. Jesus expressed this many times in his ministry. You are to be concerned chiefly with your Salvation and the Kingdom of Heaven. Once this is your priority, everything else falls into place.

NOTE TAKING

Identifying Details. Make a table like the one below to keep track of important details about the main concepts covered in this section: Keeping the Lord's Day, Careers and Vocations, and Choosing a Career. One item in each column has been done for you.

Keeping the Lord's Day	Careers and Vocations	Choosing a Career
• God rested to give his people an example to do the same. • • •	• Careers are not the same as vocations, but they interact. • • •	• Pray • • •

Keeping the Lord's Day

It can be difficult to put work in its proper place within your life. To help keep work in its proper perspective, God gave his people the gift of the Sabbath. God himself rested on the seventh day. He did not need to rest, but in doing so, he showed that the Sabbath is different from other days, and that on that day, attention should be focused on matters of the spirit, rather than on labor. The Lord's Day, as it is called in the New Covenant, is a time to truly live in the reality of Christ's Resurrection by resting from unnecessary work, ultimately by engaging in worship and prayer, and by spending time with family and friends.

To keep this day unique, you are to refrain from participation in "work or activities that hinder the worship owed to God, the joy proper to the Lord's Day, the performance of the works of mercy, and the appropriate relaxation of mind and body" (*CCC*, 2185). Family and social needs can legitimately excuse one from Sunday obligations, but legitimate excuses should not become habits.

Rest from work can, and should, elevate the human spirit by giving people the time on Sunday to worship a loving God in humility and thanksgiving for all the gifts bestowed during the previous week. Catholics have the obligation to worship God by participating in Mass on Sunday. Resting from the toil of a job is also a great opportunity to strengthen family life, to spend time with friends, and to cultivate the mind.

St. John Paul II warned that today's society has become one that exalts "the weekend," in place of the Lord's Day, in that people view the week as revolving around the relaxation of the weekend instead of the sacred rest of Sunday. You can probably relate to this. When Friday afternoon comes along, chances are your focus is on "the weekend," instead of on the holiness of Sunday.

Of course, there is nothing wrong with looking forward to the weekend. St. John Paul II was clear that the weekend is a good reality, because people need the rest from work it offers. However, he warned that Christians are called to *more*—to be people of the Lord's Day, not merely of "the weekend." The focus of

your week should always be directed toward Sunday, because it is the *Lord's Day*. This is similar to how your earthly lives should always be pointed to the definitive rest of Heaven. And so, ultimately, the Lord's Day should be a day that is a witness of, and points to, the never-ending Sabbath of Heaven.

Careers and Vocations

There are many other positive aspects of work to consider. Work provides a chance for you to develop your personality and to grow as a human person. It also helps you contribute to the common good; that is, to make society a better place for everyone. Through your work, you can share in God's creative activity and help to develop this beautiful world he gave for the benefit of all.

Currently, your best preparation for the world of work is to study hard during your high school years. This is the time in your life to learn and to practice the fundamental skills that you will need to survive and thrive in an increasingly complex society. These are also the years to learn what you are good at and what interests you so you can begin to explore possible careers and professions.

Ideally, your work will not be mere toil or simply a job. Hopefully you will choose a career or profession that matches your interests and abilities. Also, it's important to consider how a job or career may interact with your life's **vocation**. Your primary Christian vocation is to love and serve God by loving and serving other people. Further, there are some more specific ways Christians accomplish this vocation.

- The *laity* seeks God's Kingdom by engaging in daily, worldly tasks and directing these to God's will. For example, a husband would want a job that provided well for his family, but also gave him enough time to spend with them.

- There are *priestly and religious vocations* dedicated to the service of the Church.

> **vocation:** The call to holiness emanating from Baptism to live out your Christian destiny in this world and the next. Vocation also refers to a special call to share in the mission of the Church, especially as a priest or consecrated religious.

- Related to career, a woman may be called to be a *religious sister*, but she may also have talents in the field of education; therefore, she discerns that a religious community that has the apostolate of teaching would be the best for her.

Unfortunately, contemporary society sometimes ignores the important vocation of parenthood, especially the role of mothers who have the awesome responsibility of bringing forth new life. Full-time mothers are sometimes made to feel that they are less valuable as persons, because they are not in the workforce. However, the Catholic tradition greatly values the role of mothers and teaches that society needs to respect their irreplaceable contribution. St. John Paul II addressed the role of motherhood under the topic of work while also advocating for the possibilities for mothers to remain at home to care for their children:

> Experience confirms that there must be a social re-evaluation of the mother's role, of the toil connected with it, and of the need that children

Many times a career and vocation go hand in hand.

have for care, love and affection in order that they may develop into responsible, morally and religiously mature and psychologically stable persons. It will redound to the credit of society to make it possible for a mother—without inhibiting her freedom, without psychological or practical discrimination, and without penalizing her as compared with other women—to devote herself to taking care of her children and educating them in accordance with their needs, which vary with age. Having to abandon these tasks in order to take up paid work outside the home is wrong from the point of view of the good of society and of the family when it contradicts or hinders these primary goals of the mission of a mother. (*Laborem Exercens*, §19)

Choosing a Career

Since you were a child, people have probably asked you, "What do you want to be when you grow up?" At this stage in your life, that question becomes more pressing.

This chapter has focused on the Church's teaching on work and the rights of workers. Have you been thinking about your own future and how you might best use your talents to make a living? What kind of work would you like to do?

Here is something else to consider: Have you ever thought about how the career you choose will help promote justice? If so, how would you practically implement your plan? How do you begin the process of career selection?

These are all good questions. It is never too early to begin looking into your future. Some ideas to get you started follow:

PRAY

As God has a plan for you, you need to stay in touch with him throughout your life.

Ask for the guidance of the Holy Spirit to help you know how you are supposed to use your gifts for other people.

DETERMINE
YOUR INTERESTS AND ABILITIES

List what you do well; for example: math, mechanics, writing, sports, art, music, listening, and helping others.

List also what kinds of activities you are interested in; for example: being outdoors, reading, working with your hands, growing things, tinkering with cars, cooking, socializing with others, and teaching others.

RESEARCH
THE TYPES OF JOBS THAT MATCH YOUR SKILLS AND INTERESTS

Consult the Internet, libraries, career and guidance counselors; and family friends, relatives, and neighbors who work in your fields of interest.

GAIN EXPERIENCE

Do volunteer work and learn from professionals in the field.

Search for summer or after-school jobs in your area of interest.

WORK ON A
LONG-RANGE CAREER GOAL

Find an occupation that matches your skills and interests and determine the educational requirements necessary to enter this career. Research some schools or programs that can get you the education you need to enter your chosen career and map out some strategies for achieving your goal.

As you begin to discern your vocation and choose your job or career, remain committed to hope and prayer that all people who are facing hard times will be able to find work. Keep these words of Pope Benedict XVI in mind for your journey:

On this earth there is room for everyone: here the entire human family must find the resources to live with dignity, through the help of nature itself—God's gift to his children—and through hard work and creativity. (*Caritas in Veritate*, §50)

Investigating a Service Profession

Select a service profession (e.g., health care, teaching, social advocacy, police) and arrange to shadow a worker through the course of a workday. Make note of the ways this profession helps to meet the needs of others, especially those who are disadvantaged. Write a report detailing your experience. Alternatively, if you are not able to shadow a worker, interview a person in this profession outside of his or her regular working hours. Write a report that details how service of others occurs on the job.

SECTION ASSESSMENT

NOTE TAKING

Use the notes from each column of the table you created to help you answer the following questions.

1. What is the Sabbath known for in the New Covenant?

2. What is your best preparation for your future career at present?

3. Name two important steps in deciding your career.

COMPREHENSION

4. Describe ways you can keep the Lord's Day. Include activities you should participate in and those you should refrain from.

5. What is the difference between a career and a vocation?

6. What are the Church's views on the vocation of parenthood?

CRITICAL THINKING

7. Explain what St. John Paul II meant when he said that Christians are to be people of the Lord's Day, not merely people of "the weekend."

REFLECTION

8. After consideration of your personal interests and skills, describe a career path that you might choose. What are some steps you could take now, and in the future, to reach this career goal?

Section Summaries

Focus Question

How are the dignity of work and the rights of workers related to your own dignity as a person?

Complete one of the following:

 Read paragraphs 2427 to 2436 in the *Catechism of the Catholic Church*. Summarize them in a good paragraph.

 Choose three of the "Ten Principles of Economic Life" and create a poster that illustrates how they contribute to dignity in a person.

 Read the following Scripture passages and respond to the questions:

PROVERBS 6:6–11

1. Whom should you imitate when you work?

2. What will happen to you if you are too lazy?

MATTHEW 24:45–51

3. What is the payoff for a vigilant worker?

2 THESSALONIANS 3:10–12

4. What is the problem in the community that Paul addresses?

5. What instruction does he give?

JOHN 6:28–29

6. What is the work of Jesus' followers?

INTRODUCTION (PAGES 211–216)

The Nature of Work

Work has immense dignity; for through work we can be developed as human persons. It has both an objective dimension (the work being completed) and a subjective dimension (the worker himself). Work can benefit the human person and society and be a share in the Cross of Christ.

 List five things you do for work (at school, in a part-time job, or at home) that are difficult and that you do not like to do. Create a schedule for getting them done in the coming week. Offer them up in prayer as a contribution to the Cross of Christ.

SECTION 1 (PAGES 217–225)
Rights and Abuses Associated with Work

One has a duty to work, but also a *right* to work. Work should not interfere with the development of the family and individual rights. Catholic social teaching addresses many rights of workers—such as the right to a just wage, the right to a safe work environment, and the right to strike—and workplace abuses, such as child labor. Catholic social teaching also recognizes the responsibilities of workers, such as the duty to give honest work for their pay.

 Choose three rights of workers covered in this section. For each, provide an example of how the right can be upheld in the modern workplace.

SECTION 2 (PAGES 226–229)
Justice and Economic Society

Although the Church does not endorse one particular economic system, she does make it clear that systems that deny or abuse the basic rights of human persons, such as the right to private property, are immoral. Even within just economic systems, such as capitalism, abuses can occur. The Church reminds her people that the economy exists for the person and that the person should not be reduced to merely a moneymaker.

 Explain the difference between the following statements: "Money is the root of all evil" and "The *love* of money is the root of all evils." Describe what the distinction means in your own life.

SECTION 3 (PAGES 230–234)
Work and You

God has given his people the Sabbath, or Lord's Day, to worship him and rest from their usual work. Keeping the Lord's Day helps us keep from making work an idol. Your career interacts with your vocation. In order to decide your own job, you need to pray first; next, research the particular career; and then gain experience in your chosen field.

 Make a list of four careers you could realistically see yourself doing someday. Pick one of them to research further.

Chapter Assignments

1. Summarizing *Laborem Exercens* ("On Human Work")

St. John Paul II's 1981 encyclical *Laborem Exercens* was issued on the ninetieth anniversary of *Rerum Novarum*. In this encyclical, St. John Paul II focused on work as the way for people to earn their daily bread. He taught that work is one of the characteristics that distinguish humans from other creatures. Locate this document at www.vatican.va. Write a one-sentence summary for each of the main subsections (numbers 16–23) of Part IV, Rights of Workers.

IV. RIGHTS OF WORKERS

16. Within the Broad Context of Human Rights

17. Direct and Indirect Employer

18. The Employment Issue

19. Wages and Other Social Benefits

20. Importance of Unions

21. Dignity of Agricultural Work

22. The Disabled Person and Work

23. Work and the Emigration Question

2. Imagining the Objective and Subjective Dimensions of Work

Review the two dimensions of work: objective and subjective (see pages 211–212). Then create a multimedia presentation or a mural that highlights images from both dimensions. For example, images associated with the objective dimension of work might include tools, technology, and machinery. Images for the subjective dimension of work would focus on the human worker, especially focusing on his or her dignity. If you create a multimedia presentation, you may wish to provide music as well as narration or captions that explain the two dimensions of work and highlight the "bottom-line" meaning of work: work exists for human beings; human beings do not exist for work.

3. Media Evaluation

Choose an episode from a television program or a movie that depicts a place of employment (such as an office, a restaurant, or a police station). The workplace can be the focus of the whole show or just a segment of it. Evaluate whether the work and workers depicted correspond to the Catholic view of the dignity of work. Present your findings to the class in an oral presentation. You may want to include clips from the episode or movie to illustrate your points.

Some questions to consider:

- Do the workers seem fulfilled by their work? Why or why not?

- Are the relationships between the coworkers affirming of the dignity of the human person?

- Does the work performed by the characters affect society as a whole? How so?

As you consider the episode and the preceding questions, consider the following:

- the nature of work described in the Introduction of this chapter

- the rights and abuses of work described in Section 1 of this chapter; this includes the struggle of consumerism

Faithful Disciple

St. Giuseppe Moscati

St. Giuseppe Moscati

For the person called to live "in the world"—that is, those members of the laity of the Church—his or her employment should not be separate from his relationship with Christ and pursuit of Heaven. Instead, the job should be in accord with the path to sainthood. Such was the case with St. Giuseppe Moscati, a devoted doctor.

Known as the "Holy Physician of Naples," Giuseppe Moscati was born in 1880 to an aristocratic family. When Giuseppe was thirteen, his older brother, a lieutenant in the army, sustained severe head trauma when he fell from a horse, resulting in recurring epilepsy. Giuseppe helped care for his brother at home, an experience that led to his interest in medicine. It also helped him realize the limits of human powers and the need for God.

Giuseppe began his medical studies in 1897. Following his graduation, he practiced medicine at a hospital in Naples while teaching university courses too. He had incredible skill in treating and curing patients, and was able to combine both traditional medicine and some of the new findings in the world of biochemistry.

Even more remarkable than his great proficiency with medicine was the love and compassion with which he treated his patients. He truly saw each person as having great worth and dignity. St. Giuseppe saw his job as an apostolate, which means "work done for the Lord." Before treating each patient, he would pray and place himself in God's presence. He would also encourage his patients to receive the sacraments. He said, "One must attend first to the Salvation of the soul and only then to that of the body." Giuseppe once wrote to a young doctor:

> Remember that you must treat not only bodies, but also souls, with counsel that appeals to
> their minds and hearts rather than with cold prescriptions to be sent in to the pharmacist.

St. Giuseppe Moscati would often treat poor and homeless patients free of charge. Sometimes he would even secretly leave some of his own money under their pillows. Regarding these acts of charity, he said, "What have we that has not been given us by our Lord? Woe to us if we do not make good use of God's gifts!"

When Mount Vesuvius erupted in 1906, St. Giuseppe personally helped carry some frail, elderly persons from a hospital before it collapsed under the weight of the volcanic ash. He was also known to have helped saved many cholera patients during the 1911 epidemic.

St. Giuseppe Moscati had a deep prayer life. He attended daily Mass and also had a great devotion to the Blessed Mother. His faith informed all that he did. He once wrote to a medical colleague:

> Only one science is unshakeable and unshaken, the one revealed by God, the science of the hereafter! In all your works, look to Heaven, to the eternity of life and of the soul, and orient yourself then much differently from the way that merely human considerations might suggest, and your activity will be inspired for the good.

St. Giuseppe Moscati died peacefully in 1927 at the age of forty-six. Many medical miracles have been attributed to his intercession. One such miracle was the healing of a young ironworker who was dying of leukemia. Not long after the victim's mother encountered St. Guiseppe Moscati in a dream, her son went into remission.

St. Guiseppe is a witness that a person's work is not separate from his or her calling to sainthood; indeed, work can even be a vehicle through which to serve Christ by serving his people.

Reading Comprehension

1. How did St. Giuseppe Moscati's career and his Catholic faith work together?

2. How did St. Giuseppe show compassion in his work as a physician?

Writing Task

- At the canonization of St. Giuseppe Moscati, St. John Paul II described his work as a physician in this way: "In addition to the resources of his acclaimed skill, in caring for the sick he used the warmth of his humanity and the witness of his faith." Imagine a profession you would like to have some day. How could you use the "warmth of your humanity" and "witness of your faith" in this job?

Explaining the Faith

Isn't the degree of a person's success and achievement really measured in terms of financial security and wealth?

While many people build their lives on such an approach, Jesus Christ teaches you that the greatest achievement in life is growth in holiness and virtue and becoming more like him. Real happiness is found in fulfilling God's plan for you; true and lasting fulfillment is never found in money or material possessions. People who find the fulfillment in life that leads to inner peace and joy are those mature enough to understand that what really matters is God's infinite love for you and what he has taught you about himself and the meaning of life.

 ## Further Research

- Read paragraphs 2535 and 2536 of the *Catechism of the Catholic Church*. Explain the difference between rightly desiring things and when that desire "exceeds the limits of reason."

Prayer

Prayer to St. Joseph the Worker

Glorious St. Joseph, model of all who are devoted to labor, obtain for me the grace to work in the spirit of penance in expiation of my many sins; to work conscientiously by placing love of duty above my inclinations; to gratefully and joyously deem it an honor to employ and to develop by labor the gifts I have received from God, to work methodically, peacefully, and in moderation and patience, without ever shrinking from it through weariness or difficulty to work; above all, with purity of intention and unselfishness, having unceasingly before my eyes death and the account I have to render of time lost, talents unused, good not done, and vain complacency in success, so baneful to the work of God. All for Jesus, all for Mary, all to imitate thee, O patriarch St. Joseph! This shall be my motto for life and eternity.

—St. Pius X

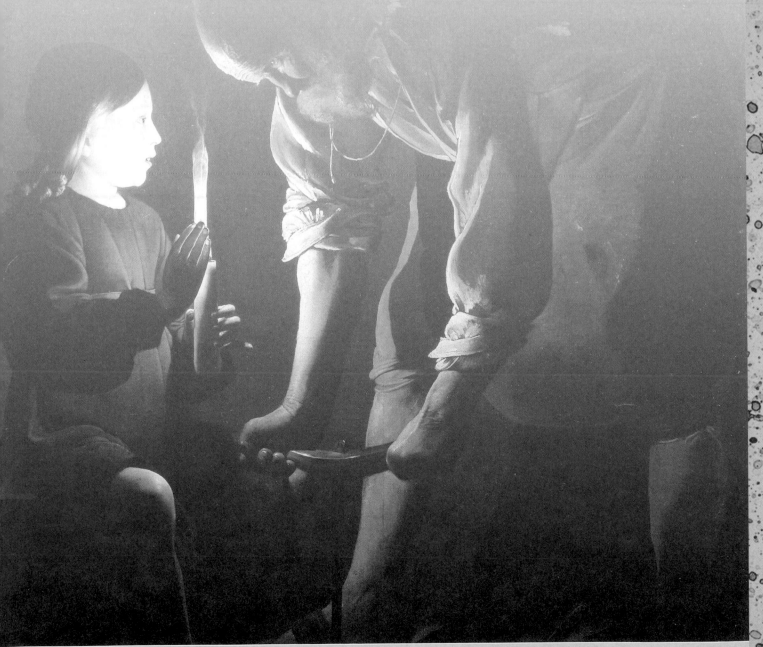

SOLIDARITY

Man Takes Off Shoes in SOLIDARITY

Six years ago Roberto Santiago took off his shoes. And he has not put them on again since.

It is not that he cannot afford shoes; instead, he does not wear them to unite himself with the poor around the world. Santiago, a Catholic and resident of Portland, Oregon, sees his act as a personal reminder to be grateful. And he hopes that his witness helps bring awareness to those suffering from severe poverty, especially in developing countries.

He told Catholic News Service, "It's just a very small act of solidarity. It gives me a little bit of a way to stay connected and be appreciative for what I have."

When Santiago steps on something sharp, it is a reminder for him to pray for people who are suffering. When he is asked to leave establishments that require footwear, he remembers to pray for the homeless or other marginalized people.

He has also found it to be a conversation starter about poverty with both adults and children. One time a child who asked Santiago about his bare feet even took off his own shoes and offered them to Santiago.

Roberto's wife, Anne, supports his decision. "It's an interesting thing he does to keep himself humble and a reminder of where his place is in the world," she said. "In the United States, we are so focused on our perspective that we don't realize how 75 percent of the world lives. It's very different from the comforts that we have."[1]

FOCUS QUESTION

How is your life INTERWOVEN with the lives of others?

INTRODUCTION
What Is Solidarity?

MAIN IDEA
Solidarity is the realization that all people are interconnected as part of one human family. It is a mark of catholicity and a moral virtue.

Solidarity is a theme of Catholic social teaching that highlights each individual's need to work for the common good. All humans are interconnected, because they are made in God's image. Solidarity is the reason you have compassion for those you have never met. It is the reason you give special attention to the poor. Solidarity involves people coming together in a more committed unity. It is a bond of interdependence between individuals and groups that transcends race, religion, or any other dividing factor, including language, as in the case of the missionary priest in the photo at left, who works with the deaf in Cambodia.

The United States Conference of Catholic Bishops point out that, "We are one human family, whatever our national, racial, ethnic, economic, and ideological differences. We are our brothers' and sisters' keepers, wherever they may be."[2] St. John Paul II linked the notion of solidarity with Pope Leo XIII's call to *friendship*, Pope Pius XI's term *social charity*, and Pope Paul VI's encouraging of a *civilization of love*.[3] In other words, loving one's neighbor has universal implications.

The *Compendium of the Social Doctrine of the Church* insists that solidarity is linked to the self-giving of charity; it "translates into the willingness to give oneself for the good of one's neighbor, beyond any individual or particular interest" (§194). St. Paul also wrote of solidarity, exhorting Christians to live out their profound connection with others:

> If there is any encouragement in Christ, any solace in love, any participation in the Spirit, any compassion and mercy, complete my joy by being of the same mind, with the same love, united in heart, thinking one thing. Do nothing out of selfishness or out of vainglory; rather, humbly regard others as more important than yourselves, each looking out not for

NOTE TAKING

Making Connections. Create a model like, or similar to, the one below. In each section, tell how solidarity is linked to each of the other elements.

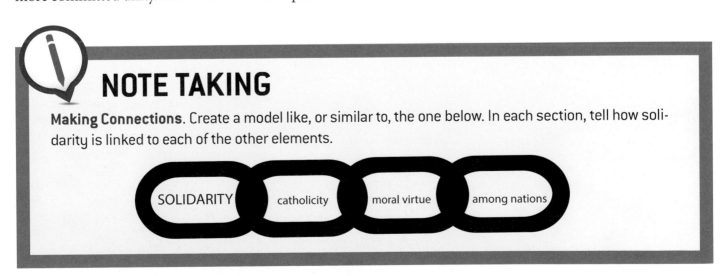

SOLIDARITY — catholicity — moral virtue — among nations

his own interests, but [also] everyone for those of others. (Phil 2:1–4)

In his analogy of the Body of Christ, St. Paul emphasized that everyone is united,

so that there may be no division in the body, but that the parts may have the same concern for one another. If [one] part suffers, all the parts suffer with it; if one part is honored, all the parts share its joy. (1 Cor 12:25–26)

Solidarity requires a commitment to the common good of *all* people. This effort is not only a personal one. In solidarity, the world's richer nations must make a conscientious effort to promote development of the poorer ones. This effort "involves sacrificing the positions of income and of power enjoyed by the more developed economies" so there will be "an overall human enrichment to the family of nations."[4]

Solidarity and Catholicity

Solidarity can rightfully be connected with a mark of the Church: catholicity. Recall that the word *catholic* means "universal." The Church is universal in two ways. First, she is universal because Christ is present in her and will always remain so. Second, the Church is catholic, or universal, "because she has been sent out by Christ on a mission to the whole of the human race" (*CCC*, 831).

Pope Francis connected this common mission of catholicity and solidarity—specifically solidarity with the poor—to the gift of Christ Catholics receive in the Eucharist: "Jesus speaks in silence in the mystery of the Eucharist and each time reminds us that following him means to come out of ourselves and not make our life our possession, but a gift to him and to others."[5]

DR. MARTIN LUTHER KING JR. ON SOLIDARITY

On Christmas Day, 1967, Dr. Martin Luther King Jr. gave a moving sermon on peace in the last of a series of speeches produced for, and aired on, CBS radio. Note the connections between peace and solidarity in this portion of the speech:

> It really boils down to this: that all life is interrelated. We are all caught in an inescapable network of mutuality, tied into a single garment of destiny. Whatever affects one directly, affects all indirectly. We are made to live together because of the interrelated structure of reality. Did you ever stop to think that you can't leave for your job in the morning without being dependent on most of the world? You get up in the morning and go to the bathroom and reach over for the sponge, and that's handed to you by a Pacific Islander. You reach for a bar of soap, that's given to you at the hands of a Frenchman. And then you go into the kitchen to drink your coffee for the morning, and that's poured into your cup by a South American. And maybe you want tea: that's poured into your cup by someone Chinese. Or maybe you're desirous of having cocoa for your breakfast, and that's poured into your cup by a West African. And then you reach over for your toast, and that's given to you at the hands of an English-speaking farmer, not to mention the baker. And before you finish eating your breakfast in the morning, you've depended on more than half the world. This is the way our universe is structured; this is its interrelated quality. We aren't going to have peace on earth until we recognize this basic fact of the interrelated structure of all reality.[10]

ASSIGNMENT

After reading the passage from Dr. King's speech, complete the following two-part assignment:

1. Select three types of food that you regularly eat for breakfast or lunch. Trace each back to its origins, and note how many people from different places were involved in producing it. Create a flowchart showing how the production moved from its origins to your table. (Remember, for example, that before a cow became a hamburger, someone provided the cow its feed and land to graze.)

2. Rewrite Dr. King's statement with food items and examples from your own experience.

Lately, the Catholic truths of solidarity have been viewed through new lenses like the globalization of economic markets and the explosion in communication networks. These modern phenomena help everyone to see that all people are members of one human family who depend on each other. Catholics must increasingly become aware that catholicity means universality in all of these contemporary areas.

Solidarity as a Moral Virtue

St. John Paul II emphasized that solidarity is much more than a "feeling of vague compassion or shallow distress at the misfortunes of so many people, both near and far."[6] It is more than just a mere sentiment of feeling sorry for the poor people or thinking it is sad that people in developing countries don't have adequate health care.

Instead, solidarity is a moral virtue of *true, resolute compassion* that leads you to action; "it is a firm and persevering determination to commit oneself to the common good; that is to say to the good of all and of each individual, because we are all really responsible for all."[7] In other words, solidarity is more than just a feeling; it is a resoluteness that becomes manifest in action. Solidarity guides the ordering of laws, market regulations, and judicial systems.

When you develop this virtue of solidarity in your life, you are able to transform the societies in which you live and to overcome any negative attitudes or structures of sin that have become rooted in these societies. These attitudes, St. Paul John II pointed out, are only conquered when you "lose yourself" for the other person.

As with all virtues, the perfect embodiment of solidarity is found in the person of Jesus Christ. He is the perfect model of virtue because he is the perfect man. He is humanity at its best. He is so one with humanity, that he emptied himself to the point of death on a Cross (Phil 2:8). He is truly Emmanuel, "God is with us," in that he took upon himself all of humanity, even its suffering. In the Incarnation, the Second Divine Person of the Trinity entered into solidarity with every human being.

And thus, it is only through Jesus that all social challenges can find meaning; indeed, through his grace, society "can be rediscovered as a place of life and hope, in that it is a sign of grace that is continuously offered to all and because it is an invitation to ever higher and more involved forms of sharing."[8] And this reality gives you a deeper perspective of your neighbor and the nature of true solidarity; you must love everyone with the love of Christ.

The Challenge of Solidarity in the Modern World

Even in the modern world, with its rapid ability to communicate instantly, there exist stark inequalities between developing and first-world countries. The *Catechism of the Catholic Church* suggests some of the causes of this divide are "abusive if not usurious financial systems, iniquitous commercial relations among nations, and the arms race" (*CCC*, 2438).

Rich nations have a moral responsibility toward those that are less fortunate, especially countries suffering because of historical and societal circumstances beyond their control (such as ravages of war or famine). In this, solidarity becomes an act of *both* charity and justice.[9] Help can come in the form of direct aid (donations of food, clothing, shelter, medical aid), especially after catastrophes, such as a natural disaster. In addition, help should move beyond immediate aid, and into reforming international economic institutions and relationships to determine and rectify the *causes* of the poverty and other social ills.

Also, nations, like individuals, need to do more than merely provide material help; instead, they must work to satisfy the need for God, which is "fundamental to any full development of human society" (*CCC*, 2441). This does *not* mean people have to convert in order to receive aid; in fact, freedom of conscience is essential to Catholic social teaching. Instead, bringing Christ and his truth to other nations begins with one's own example. When you are serving others out of genuine charity, and your actions and words reflect this, then this evangelization will occur naturally.

SECTION ASSESSMENT

NOTE TAKING

Refer to the sentences you completed as part of your notes for this section to answer the following questions.

1. How is solidarity linked with catholicity?
2. What does it mean to say that solidarity is more than just a feeling?
3. What does global solidarity mean for rich nations?

COMPREHENSION

4. What image did St. Paul use to show that people everywhere are united?
5. What did St. John Paul II say was the only way to overcome negative attitudes or structures of sin that are rooted in society?
6. In what ways do some countries need more than merely immediate material assistance?

APPLICATION

7. What are some challenges to solidarity in the modern world?
8. Share at least three ways the challenges you named can be overcome.

SECTION 1
Solidarity and Immigration

MAIN IDEA

A person has a right to emigrate to another country, especially if his or her rights are not being upheld. Society at large, on the other hand, has the right to regulate and enact laws regarding immigration.

Solidarity and the immigration issue are naturally linked. Because everyone is guaranteed basic rights (e.g., the right to food, water, shelter, jobs, religious freedom etc.), sometimes it is necessary for individuals, and especially families, to migrate to other nations to assure these rights are upheld.

In order to understand the details around the immigration issue, it is first essential to clarify terminology. *Emigration* is migration from the perspective of leaving one's country. One emigrates *to* somewhere else. On the other hand, *immigration* is migration from the perspective of the country receiving those who are moving. For example, if someone migrated from England to the United States, those in England would see him as an *emigrant,* while those in the United States would see him as an *immigrant.*

A Catholic Perspective on Immigration

Catholic tradition has long upheld the scriptural call to "welcome the stranger" (see Matthew 25:35) and "the foreigner" (see Exodus 22). The *Catechism of the Catholic Church* explains:

> The more prosperous nations are obliged, to the extent they are able, to welcome the foreigner in search of the security and the means of livelihood which he cannot find in his country of origin. Public authorities should see to it that the natural right is respected that places

NOTE TAKING

Summarizing Cited Works. Create a chart like the one below. As you read this section, summarize what each of the following cited works says about immigration.

Citation	What Passage Says about Immigration
CCC, 2241 (part one)	
CCC, 2241 (part two)	
John Paul II, Message for World Migration Day	

a guest under the protection of those who receive him. (*CCC*, 2241)

Often, people emigrating from developing countries are perceived by those in the more developed countries to which they immigrate as "a threat to the high levels of well-being achieved thanks to decades of economic growth."[11] However, immigrants often support the economies of the countries to which they migrate, such as by filling a labor need. In other words, it is possible for them to *help*—not always hinder—the countries where they settle. That said, immigrants should never be exploited and should be given the same rights as other workers.

Even though persons have a right to migrate, countries also have a right to regulate such immigration. Authorities must keep in mind the common good for those whom they govern, and must be prudential in developing laws regarding immigration. Furthermore, immigrants must adhere to such regulations and other laws of the country to which they are migrating. The *Catechism of the Catholic Church* explains:

Political authorities, for the sake of the common good for which they are responsible, may make the exercise of the right to immigrate subject to various juridical conditions, especially with regard to the immigrants' duties toward their country of adoption. Immigrants are obliged to respect with gratitude the material and spiritual heritage of the country that receives them, to obey its laws and to assist in carrying civic burdens. (*CCC*, 2241)

Remember that everyone has a duty to follow just laws, which include just immigration laws. For this reason, the Church condemns illegal immigration.

St. John Paul II poignantly connected immigration to the importance of solidarity. He challenges you to work for the spiritual and physical needs of every human person, based on everyone's dignity as made in God's image and likeness:

In the Church no one is a stranger, and the Church is not foreign to anyone, anywhere. . . . Solidarity means taking responsibility for those in trouble. For Christians, the migrant is not merely an individual to be respected in accordance with the norms established by law, but a person whose presence challenges them and

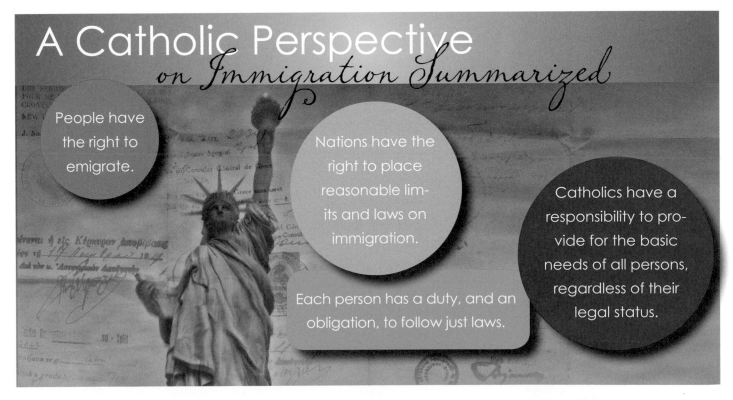

A Catholic Perspective on Immigration Summarized

People have the right to emigrate.

Nations have the right to place reasonable limits and laws on immigration.

Each person has a duty, and an obligation, to follow just laws.

Catholics have a responsibility to provide for the basic needs of all persons, regardless of their legal status.

whose needs become an obligation for their responsibility. 'What have you done to your brother?' (See Genesis 4:9). The answer should not be limited to what is imposed by law, but should be made in the manner of solidarity.[12]

CASE STUDY: Immigration

A much-debated social justice issue concerns who should be permitted to cross the borders of the United States. Should this "nation of immigrants" be generous in accepting new citizens? Whom should the government accept? What should the limits be on immigration?

A parallel issue involves what to do with immigrants who have already entered the United States illegally or without the proper documentation.

From a Catholic perspective, there is room for debate. The Church understands both sides of this tension: people have the right to emigrate, *and* a country has a right to impose laws and limitations on immigration. Therefore, it takes prudential deliberation to determine the just or unjust nature of immigration laws.

In April 2010, Arizona Governor Jan Brewer introduced one of the toughest laws against illegal immigration in the history of the United States. One of the most controversial parts of the law was that authorities could request immigration papers from anyone they stopped as a suspect for breaking another law. Many Arizonians expressed concern that the law could lead to racial profiling, with US citizens being asked to provide documentation based on their appearance.

Jan Brewer, governor of Arizona

Proponents of the law explained that the state of Arizona was spending upwards of three billion dollars annually to provide education, health benefits, and incarceration for immigrants without receiving any tax dollars back from the same group. At the time, Arizona was home to nearly a half million illegal immigrants. It has more illegal border crossings than any other state.

A district judge struck down part of the law before it went into effect: police would not be required to determine the immigration status of anyone they stop or arrest; it would not be a crime to be without one's immigration papers; it would not be a crime for illegal immigrants to seek work. The Supreme Court upheld this in 2012.

The border between the United States and Mexico stretches for almost 2,000 miles.

BASIC QUESTIONS FOR DEBATE

- Should a prosperous nation like the United States welcome those seeking religious or political asylum or people wanting better economic opportunities to provide for their families? Or is it not practical for the United States to take in more citizens?

- Do you think of your country as a lifeboat that will capsize if you allow others to scramble aboard? Or do you see it as one that has been blessed with so much wealth and resources as to be able to help feed the hungry and give opportunity to the many?

- How do you feel about some of the arguments people often give for supporting tough anti-immigration legislation? (For example: Illegal immigrants cost money because they use services such as health care and education, and take jobs from US citizens.)

PROPOSED SOLUTIONS

The United States Conference of Catholic Bishops laid out a vision for a just immigration policy in their 2003 document, *Strangers No Longer: Together on the Journey of Hope.* On July 14, 2010, Bishop Gerald Kicanas of Tucson, Arizona, went before the United States Congress House Subcommittee on Immigration, Citizenship, Refugees, Border Security, and International Law, and used talking points from that document to explain how imperative it is to reform the immigration system. He proposed the following solutions to the committee to take back to the full body of Congress:

Bishop Gerald Kicanas, Archdiocese of Tucson

- Work together on a comprehensive package that would legalize undocumented migrants and their families in the United States;

- Provide legal means for migrants to enter the United States to work and support their families;

- Reform the system whereby immigrants come to the United States to be reunited with close family members;

- Restore due process protections to immigrants that were taken away under the *Illegal Immigration Reform and Immigrant Responsibility Act* of 1996;

- Perhaps most importantly, the United States must work with Mexico and other nations to address the root causes of migration, so that migrants and their families may remain in their homelands and live in dignity.[13]

RESEARCH

Choose and complete one assignment from Group A and one assignment from Group B.

GROUP A

- What do you know about the home countries of your parents or their ancestors? Where did they come from? Why did they leave their homeland? When did they immigrate to the United States? Research these questions by speaking with older family members. Also, check a history book to discover the attitudes of Americans toward immigrants at the time your ancestors arrived.

- The Pew Hispanic Center estimates that, as of March 2011, there were 11.1 million illegal or unauthorized immigrants in the United States, down from a peak of 12 million in 2007. About 58 percent of unauthorized immigrants are from Mexico.[14] Research and report on current government plans to extend citizenship to undocumented immigrants. What approaches are more consistent with the virtue of solidarity proposed by the United States Conference of Catholic Bishops?

GROUP B

- Share your opinion on the following statement: "It is un-Christian to close our borders."

- What types of basic human services should the government allow for immigrants already in the country illegally?

SECTION ASSESSMENT

NOTE TAKING

Use the summaries you created for the major citations from this section to answer the following questions.

1. What are the moral obligations of prosperous countries in regard to immigration?
2. What are the obligations of immigrants in their new country?
3. What did St. John Paul II say in regard to the treatment of all immigrants?

COMPREHENSION

4. Explain the difference between emigration and immigration.
5. What are some ways in which immigrants can help the countries where they settle?
6. What are some responsibilities of authorities who regulate immigration?

CRITICAL THINKING

7. Imagine you are the pastor of a Catholic parish. A man shows up at the parish office door and explains that he is an immigrant who just arrived from Mexico. His wife and two children are standing near the curb. What steps would you take in response to the man and his situation?

SECTION 2
Solidarity and Peace

The virtue of solidarity and peace—one of the fruits of the Holy Spirit (cf. Gal 5:22–23) are related. Working for peace and being a peacemaker is a goal of Christian living. In the Beatitudes, Jesus preached, "Blessed are the peacemakers, for they will be called children of God" (Mt 5:9).

In his encyclical *Caritas in Veritate*, Pope Benedict XVI wrote: "Love—*caritas*—is an extraordinary force which leads people to opt for courageous and generous engagement in the field of justice and peace" (§15). These words echoed the famous statement of Bl. Pope Paul VI at the 1972 World Peace Day: "If you want peace, work for justice."

Any discussion of peace in this world must include clarification about what is morally permissible for war. Nevertheless, peace is more than the absence of war. Peace is truly the work of justice and is achieved through acts of love or charity on behalf of all people, especially the poor.

The *Compendium of the Social Doctrine of the Church* reiterates that, as with all social justice, the pursuit of peace is rooted in the dignity of the human person:

> Peace is threatened when man is not given all that is due him as a human person, when his dignity is not respected and when civil life is not directed to the common good. The defense and promotion of human rights is essential for the building up of a peaceful society and the integral development of individuals, peoples and nations. (§494)

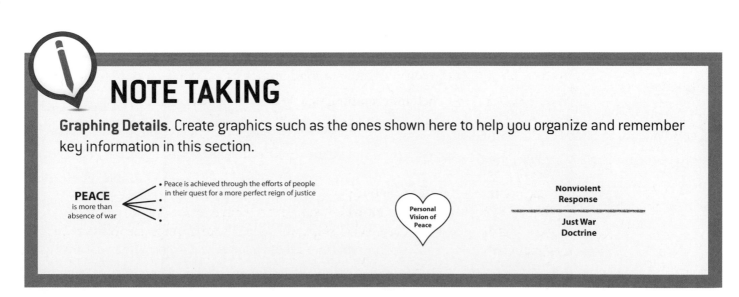

NOTE TAKING

Graphing Details. Create graphics such as the ones shown here to help you organize and remember key information in this section.

PEACE is more than absence of war
- Peace is achieved through the efforts of people in their quest for a more perfect reign of justice
- .
- .
- .

Personal Vision of Peace

Nonviolent Response

Just War Doctrine

Defining Peace

Peace is, ultimately, a blessing of Jesus Christ, a fruit of the Holy Spirit. It is "the tranquility of order" (*CCC*, 2304). Peace results from both justice *and* love. Peace exists when people are treated with dignity, are allowed to communicate freely, and relate to each other lovingly as brothers and sisters.

Peace for the earth is the image and fruit of the peace of Christ that was won for you when he sacrificed his life on the Cross. The gift of his Life, Death, and Resurrection reconciled you to God and one another. The fruit of reconciliation is the peace of Christ (cf. *CCC*, 2305).

Several teachings on peace can be drawn from the Second Vatican Council document *Gaudium et Spes*. The document makes the following points on human efforts to define and achieve peace, besides the aforementioned "peace is more than the absence of war":

- Peace is achieved through the efforts of people in their quest for a more perfect reign of justice.

- Peace must be built up continually.

- Because of sin, achieving peace requires a constant effort.

- Peace is a fruit of love that even goes beyond what justice can provide.

In other words, by being more than the absence of war or trouble, peace means helping others enjoy all the good life has to offer. For the individual, this translates to peacemaking as an active, not passive, lifestyle. A peacemaker has to look for a variety of ways to make the local and larger community a better place to live.

Peace in Your Life

To be a peacemaker, peace must begin in your heart. Peace starts with you, then it can spread to families, and then other associations within society, until the whole world has been transformed.[15]

St. John Paul II said, "To pray for peace is to open the human heart to the inroads of God's power to renew all things."

However, because all people are prone to sin, peace is difficult to attain. It requires conversion of mind and heart that leads to openness to God's healing grace working within you. St. Paul wrote in the Letter to the Romans:

> Do not conform yourself to this age but be transformed by the renewal of your mind, that you may discern what is the will of God, what is good and pleasing and perfect. (Rom 12:2)

In *The Harvest of Justice Is Sown in Peace*, the United States Conference of Catholic Bishops noted two sets of virtues to help people be more peaceful. On the one hand, you must—like Jesus—be humble, gentle, and patient with people. On the other hand, you must be strong, active and bold in spreading the Gospel of peace. This Gospel of peace is best exemplified when you forgive and love your enemies and, in a spirit of generosity, perform good deeds for them. Jesus commands, "But rather love your enemies and do good to them. . . . Be merciful, just as [also] your Father is merciful" (Lk 6:35–36).

Peacemaking is enhanced further by practice of the virtues, habits that empower you to be good. Think about how the virtues can help you to be more of a peacemaker. For example,

- *Faith* and *hope* enable you to put your trust in God, not yourself.

- *Courage* and *compassion* move you to action.

- *Humility* and *kindness* empower you to put others' needs first.

- *Patience* and *perseverance* help you stay the course as we fight for justice.

- *Civility* and *charity* enable you to treat others with respect and love.

Finally, prayer is essential for developing a spirituality of peacemaking (as in the gathering for peace shown in the photo on page 255). In prayer, God can calm your anxieties, challenge you to greater compassion and love for others, and energize you to keep working for peace despite frustration, setbacks, and defeats. Prayer teaches many important lessons:

> Prayer for peace is not an afterthought to the work of peace. It is of the very essence of building the peace of order, justice, and freedom. To pray for peace is to open the human heart to the inroads of God's power to renew all things. With the life-giving force of his grace, God can create openings for peace where only obstacles and closures are apparent; he can strengthen and enlarge the solidarity of the human family in spite of our endless history of division and conflict. To pray for peace is to pray for justice, for a right-ordering of relations within, and among, nations and peoples. It is to pray for freedom, especially for the religious freedom that is a basic human and civil right of every individual. To pray for peace is to seek God's forgiveness, and to implore the courage to forgive those who have trespassed against us. (St. John Paul II, World Day of Peace Message, 2002)

Legitimate Circumstances for War

Of course, any discussion about peace must also address war. In every era of history, including today, Christians have lived in a sinful world that is, at times, a violent world. Violence is one response to conflict; its antidote is peace. Jesus' command to be peacemakers applies to all today.

War is never the preference. Consider these pleas from recent popes:

NOTHING IS LOST BY PEACE; EVERYTHING MAY BE LOST BY WAR.

—POPE PIUS XII

IT IS HARDLY POSSIBLE TO IMAGINE THAT IN AN ATOMIC ERA, WAR COULD BE USED AS AN INSTRUMENT OF JUSTICE.

—ST. JOHN XXIII

NEVER AGAIN SOME PEOPLES AGAINST OTHERS, NEVER AGAIN! . . . NO MORE WAR; NO MORE WAR!

—BL. POPE PAUL VI

WAR IS NOT ALWAYS INEVITABLE. IT IS ALWAYS A DEFEAT FOR HUMANITY.

—ST. JOHN PAUL II

WAR BRINGS ON WAR! VIOLENCE BRINGS ON VIOLENCE.

—POPE FRANCIS

Just War Doctrine

If you recall from Chapter 3, self-defense is not only an option, but it is a grave duty for one who is responsible for the lives of others (cf. *CCC*, 2265). Just as a husband has a right and a duty to protect himself and his family from a violent intruder, so too do those who have legitimate authority have a duty to protect the citizens they govern, and sometimes that protection requires military action. However, such action must be justifiable—that is, it must meet the conditions of a just war.

The Church has developed criteria to help determine when war is justified and morally permissible. The Church's just war doctrine addresses the following:

1. the conditions under which armed force might be used in conflict;
2. the limits that should constrain resort to force;
3. ethical norms to restrain damage caused by military forces in a war.

As is true of all Church efforts at peacemaking, just war assessments always begin with a strong presumption against the use of force. However, the doctrine sets out those conditions that enable properly constituted governments to use force when the common good demands it to protect human dignity and human rights. As you will see, the circumstances in which a war would be truly just are rare and difficult to meet.

CRITERIA OF A JUST WAR

The Church holds that all of the following criteria must be met before a government can legitimately declare war and subsequently use lethal force:

JUST CAUSE

The damage inflicted by the aggressor on a nation or a community of nations must be lasting, grave, and certain. If a situation threatens the lives of innocent people, if basic human rights are violated, or if there is an imminent need for self-defense, then there would be just cause.

Adolf Hitler was leader of the Nazi Party during World War II.

LEGITIMATE AUTHORITY

Those declaring a war of defense have the legitimate responsibility to represent the people and are entrusted with the common good.

The President of the United States, as Commander in Chief of the nation's armed forces, can order troops to battle. However, the president must have the approval or consensus to declare war.

RIGHT INTENTION

War is waged for the best of reasons and with a commitment to postwar reconciliation with the enemy. Needless destruction, cruelty to prisoners, and other harsh measures are not tolerated.

During the Civil War, Abraham Lincoln and the Union Army fought to abolish slavery.

PROBABILITY OF SUCCESS

The odds of success should be weighed against the human cost of the war. The purpose of this criterion is to prevent irrational use of force or hopeless resistance when either will prove futile anyway.

United States troops organized in battle during the Korean conflict.

PROPORTIONALITY

The damage to be inflicted and the costs to be incurred by the war must be proportionate to the good expected. Armed conflict must not produce evils and disorders graver than the evil to be eliminated. For example, if a large number of people would be killed over a dispute that only slightly affects the combatant nations, the decision to go to war would violate proportionality.

The graves of soldiers at a French battlefield after World War I are reminders of the ultimate sacrifice of war.

LAST RESORT

War must be a last resort, justifiable only if all peaceful efforts have been tried and exhausted and there are no alternatives.

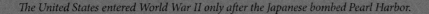

The United States entered World War II only after the Japanese bombed Pearl Harbor.

STANDARD OF RESTRAINT IN A JUST WAR

The Church's just war doctrine also imposes a moral standard of restraint once there is armed conflict. Just because the declaration of the war is just does not mean that all warfare within the said war is just. This standard during war includes:

IMMUNITY OF NONCOMBATANTS

Civilians may not be the object of direct attack. Military strategies must avoid and minimize any indirect harm inflicted on noncombatants.

Civilians, facing regular bombing runs by the Nazis, evacuated their homes in North London during World War II.

PROPORTIONALITY

The military should use the minimum force necessary to obtain military objectives so as to avoid undue "collateral" damage to civilians and property.

The Soviet freighter Anosov, rear, being escorted by a US Navy plane and the destroyer USS Barry, while it leaves Cuba during the Cuban missile crisis of 1962.

RIGHT INTENTION

Political and military leaders must always see that peace with justice is the only reason for the use of arms. Vengeful acts and indiscriminate killing—committed by individuals, military forces, or governments—are forbidden and immoral. Therefore, mass extermination of a people, nation, or ethnic minority is morally reprehensible and gravely sinful. Furthermore, blind obedience to unjust orders, such as participation in genocide, cannot excuse one's responsibility for participating in heinous crimes.

Clothes from the 1994 genocide are on display at a memorial in Rwanda.

Applying the principles of a just war requires the virtue of **prudence**. It also requires resisting the various political forces that can affect the accuracy of the information that is needed for a nation or an individual to make a decision about the morality of a particular war. For example, military strategies that involve air strikes that target civilian infrastructures or the use of overwhelming force usually contradict the **principle of proportionality** and the necessity of sparing noncombatants from violence.

Although, in a violent society that fosters a culture of death, it can become more difficult to apply these principles in an honest and a restrained way, there are some acts that may never be permitted in a war:

- Any act of war aimed indiscriminately at entire cities or extensive areas and their populations.

- Any act that has great potential for widespread and indiscriminate destruction.

prudence The moral virtue by which a person is inclined toward choosing to do good and avoiding evil.

principle of proportionality The rule that requires the damage inflicted and the costs incurred in a war (or a particular action in war) to be commensurate with the good expected.

conscientious objectors People who refuse to join the military or participate in a war based on moral or religious grounds. Conscientious objectors must be open to other forms of service.

conscientious objection The moral right to refuse to follow laws or other social constructs based on moral or religious grounds. An example is choosing not to fight in an unjust war.

A Preference for Nonviolence

Nonviolence is always preferable to war. However, nonviolence should not be confused with passivity; that is, it does not mean a "sit-back-and-do-nothing" approach to confronting evil. Nonviolence requires courage, patience, action, creativity, and a passionate commitment to seeking justice and truth no matter what the price. Nonviolence combats injustice and resists evil by using peaceful means like dialogue, negotiations, protests, boycotts, civil disobedience, strikes, citizen resistance, and the like. The *Catechism of the Catholic Church* (2306) explains the unique mission of the practice of nonviolence.

In the past, nonviolence was often seen as simply an individual option to resist war and other violent actions. For example, **conscientious objectors** (COs) are people who refuse to engage in armed conflict. Historically, one type of CO opposes all war on principle. A second type refuses to participate in wars considered to be unjust. Members of the Society of Friends (Quakers) and the Mennonite religion usually are COs of the first type. Many young American men who protested the Vietnam War in the 1960s and 1970s were COs of the second type because of their belief in the injustice of that particular war. Conscientious objectors choose alternative forms of service in lieu of refusing to participate in armed conflict. The Catholic tradition supports **conscientious objection** to unjust wars. In fact, all Catholics must object to unjust wars.

Conscientious objectors serve their country in other ways; in this case as a road crew.

These acts include decisions about the use of nuclear weapons. The United States Conference of Catholic Bishops' document, *The Challenge of Peace*, points out that there are major problems in trying to apply just war doctrine to any kind of nuclear war. For example, it is difficult to imagine any situation in which the first strike using nuclear weapons could be justified. The US Catholic Bishops further question whether there can be such a thing as a "limited nuclear war." They argue that one criterion of just war teaching is that there must be reasonable hope of success in bringing about peace and justice, and question whether this reasonable hope can exist once nuclear weapons have been used. In such cases, the good ends (defending one's country, protecting freedom) cannot justify immoral means (the use of weapons that kill indiscriminately and threaten whole societies).

Further, the *Catechism of the Catholic Church* (2314–2317) warns that the arms race does not ensure peace. Rather, it aggravates the causes of war; namely, it contributes to injustice, excessive economic and social inequalities, envy, distrust, and pride. The accumulation, production, and sale of arms endangers international peace and imposes a grave injustice for the poor and needy. Further, over-armament intensifies the threat of conflict and squanders money that should be spent on the care of citizens, especially the poor.

Today, nations are beginning to realize that nonviolent actions have the power to bring about change, even under repressive dictatorial regimes. Successful examples of nonviolent action in the middle to latter half of the twentieth century included:

- Mohandas Gandhi's (1869–1948) nonviolent protests (what he termed "truth and firmness") helped lead to India's independence from British colonial rule in 1947.

- The Solidarity Movement in Poland in the 1980s, mobilized by Lech Walesa, used strikes, labor meltdowns, prison hunger strikes, boycotts, marches, and the power of an underground press to topple a communist regime.

- In 1986 the People Power Movement in the Philippines led a four-day nonviolent protest that brought down the Marcos dictatorship in the Philippines. As part of the protest, Filipino citizens, armed with rosaries, knelt in front of armored tanks sent to intimidate them.

- In 1989–1992, massive nonviolent resistance to a coup attempt against Mikhail Gorbachev as well as other nonviolent actions helped bring freedom to states forced by communist regimes to be part of the former Soviet Union.

- In 2000, hundreds of thousands of Serbian protestors nonviolently seized hold of the parliament building, ending dictatorship in their nation. This was a culmination of two years of nonviolent struggle led by a youth movement. Free elections followed this changeover.

- In 2003, Liberian women united across tribe, religion, social class, and ethnicity to end the civil war in their country that had killed more than 200,000 people. They dialogued with warlords, shut down the capital, and held weekly prayer services. They eventually persuaded the president to attend peace talks, which eventually led to an agreement. The president was later indicted for war crimes. The women stayed organized and helped elect the country's first female president.

These nonviolent revolutions prove the power of systematic, organized, nonviolent activity. The American bishops support the belief in solving problems and conflicts with nonviolent means. They also call for the promotion of education, research, and training in nonviolent ways to combat evil.[16]

♥ Nonviolence in Action

Here are some suggestions for promoting peace through nonviolent actions:

1. Pray for peace daily. Use the Prayer for Peace of St. Francis of Assisi:

> Lord, make me an instrument of your peace.
> Where there is hatred, let me sow love;
>   where there is injury, pardon;
>   where there is doubt, faith;
>   where there is despair, hope;
>   where there is darkness, light;
>   where there is sadness, joy.
> O Divine Master, grant that I may not seek
>   so much to be consoled as to console;
>   to be understood, as to understand,
>   to be loved, as to love.
> For it is in giving that we receive,
>   it is in pardoning that we are pardoned,
>   and it is in dying that we are born to
>   eternal life.

2. Become an "instrument of peace" by learning about the causes of conflict, war, and the like. Amass some data about the economic and political factors that cause nations to fight. Keep informed about some of the hot spots of conflict in the world by setting online alerts. Keep a log of short-term and long-term solutions being undertaken to curb the violence in these areas.

3. Learn the positions of your representatives in the House of Representatives and the Senate on weapons spending versus foreign aid for development. Write to encourage them to work against the arms race and other policies that cause international conflict. Post letters or comments in online news sources that promote peaceful solutions.

4. "Sow love" by being gentle in how you treat others: your family members, fellow classmates, students from other schools, your coworkers, and others you meet each day.

5. Where there is personal injury to you, learn to pardon the offender. Celebrate the Sacrament of Penance regularly.

6. Engage in the corporal works of mercy. For example, support an organization like Catholic Relief Services that works to alleviate some of the suffering of people at home and abroad.

7. Shed light by dispelling ignorance. Learn about people who are different from you. For example, read a book that reveals the current social situation in another country. Correspond with a student in another part of the world. Attend an ethnic festival in your area to learn about the customs of a nationality with which you are unfamiliar.

8. Console and understand others when conflict arises by trying to resolve tension nonviolently. Don't use inflammatory words or gestures. If your efforts meet with little success, ask for someone to act as a mediator.

9. Love by befriending a lonely person at school, by verbally defending a member of a minority who is being badmouthed, by volunteering at a meal distribution center, by organizing a fund-raising project for a peace-and-justice group, etc.

Just War Doctrine and the War on Terrorism

The day-to-day calm of citizens of the United States and many other countries changed on September 11, 2001, when Islamic extremists hijacked jets and used them as weapons of destruction in New York City, Pennsylvania, and Washington, DC. On that day, Americans came face to face with a new kind of threat with which the international community has had difficulty dealing; namely, terrorist organizations that are not themselves organized states. The international legal system has established norms to discipline sovereign states that violate human rights. But how should countries respond to terrorist organizations and atrocities like those committed on 9/11/01?

St. John Paul II defined **terrorism** as "the intention to kill people and destroy property indiscriminately, and to create a climate of terror and insecurity, often including the taking of hostages."[17] Terrorist actions or threats to commit violence against innocent people are used to sow fear or to further the ideological purposes of the terrorist group. These tactics include kidnapping and hostage-taking. In his World Day of Peace Message in 2002, St. John Paul II said,

> Terrorism is built on contempt for human life. For this reason, not only does it commit intolerable crimes, but because it resorts to terror as a political and military means it is itself a true crime against humanity.

terrorism A systematic use of subversive strategies aimed at the destruction of material goods or the killing of people in order to coerce certain actions or decisions.

Terrorist actions are objectively a grave evil that can *never* be justified. Governments have the right of self-defense against terrorists. But, on the other hand, repressive and punitive operations are not the final solution. The fight against terrorism must also include political, economic, and educational solutions that change the social conditions from which many terrorists come. Individual nations and the international community must find ways to prevent, monitor, and suppress attacks on civilian populations. Furthermore, governments must adhere to international laws about human rights and ban attempts to undermine these rights. Recall that a good end, or purpose, for doing something can never justify evil means to attain it. This is why, for example, the torture of suspected terrorists can never be permitted.

The most effective remedy for the scourge of terrorism is to remove its causes, which are complex. These causes include poverty, powerlessness, oppression, and the abuse of basic human rights. These dire situations can make people more receptive to terrorism as a solution for problems. Responding to terrorism with revengeful acts will only breed more hatred and violence rather than get at the root of the problem. Nations must band together to promote the common good. They must respect international law and cooperate with organizations like the United Nations because laws, treaties, and the participation of the UN are widely respected means of achieving peace among nations.

For all people of good will, forgiveness is needed for solving the problems of individuals and peoples. There is no peace without forgiveness.

SECTION ASSESSMENT

NOTE TAKING

Use the graphic reminders you created to help you complete the following items.

1. "Peace is more than the absence of war." Name two points that support this statement.

2. Explain what it means to say that peace originates in one's own heart.

VOCABULARY

3. Define *principle of proportionality*.

4. How is prudence essential to putting just war principles into practice?

5. What are some objectives of terrorism?

COMPREHENSION

6. Name three solutions that must accompany the military response to terrorism.

CRITICAL THINKING

7. How is the Church's teaching on war related to her teaching on self-defense?

8. List and describe the six criteria of a just war in your own words. Choose one criterion and name an example from a recent conflict in the news.

SECTION 3
Discrimination: An Offense against Solidarity

MAIN IDEA
Discrimination that denies the basic dignity of the human person is an offense against the virtue of solidarity. Discrimination can be manifest in attitudes of prejudice and the actions of racism.

Because all human beings are created in God's image and likeness, all share equal dignity. Discrimination involves harmful actions against the targeted groups or individuals, and denies their fundamental human rights. Discrimination is an offense against human solidarity.

This means that any form of discrimination, be it regarding sex, race, color, social conditions (like poverty and social class), age, language, handicap, or religion, is to be strongly condemned. Someone else's condition, albeit different from your life situation, cannot be the basis for treating someone with any less human worth. Such a command extends to those in authority; civil laws must treat everyone as equal in dignity.

Prejudice

The attitude that leads to discrimination is often called **prejudice**. One can be prejudiced against another person based on many factors, but usually at the root of prejudices is a lack of knowledge about the person or

> **prejudice** A preconceived opinion formulated without consideration of known factors and usually based on erroneous knowledge.

NOTE TAKING

Concept Web. As you read this section, make a concept web like the one below. Define the terms related to discrimination.

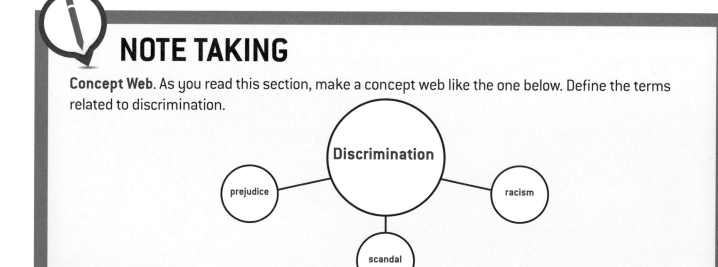

A LESSON IN LOVE

An old Rabbi once asked his pupils how they could tell when the night had ended and the day begun.

"Could it be," asked one of the students, "when you can see an animal in the distance and tell whether it's a sheep or dog?"

"No," answered the Rabbi.

Another asked, "Is it when you can look at a tree in the distance and tell whether it's a fig tree or a peach tree?"

"No," answered the Rabbi.

"Then, when is it?" the pupils demanded.

"It is when you can look on the face of any man or woman and see that it is your sister or brother. Because if you cannot see this, it is still night."

his or her situation. Prejudice is the false attitude; discrimination is the action that flows from it.

Racism

One of the most evident forms of prejudice is **racism**, which is a false, discriminatory attitude toward another because of his culture or race. The sinful reality of racism leads to the mistreatment of people based on their race, color, national origin, religion, place of birth, or ancestry. This mistreatment can obviously take place on a person-to-person basis whenever one person misjudges and discriminates against another. You may be aware of incidents around your school or on a team where someone was targeted with harsh words or behavior based on his or her race.

Racism can also be institutional, that is, legalized or tolerated in the very structures of society, favoring the majority and hindering the success of the minority. In the United States, slavery of African Americans was the most notorious example of institutional racism.

Since then, America has fought a Civil War, passed an amendment that guarantees the basic human rights of all people regardless of race, handed down Supreme Court decisions banning segregated schools and approving some forms of **affirmative action**, and passed Civil Rights legislation. Although the United States has made much progress in its efforts to eradicate racism, its institutions are still not entirely free of its insidious effects.

> **racism** A belief that race determines human traits and abilities and that a particular race is inherently superior or inferior to another; and the discrimination that stems from those beliefs.
>
> **affirmative action** Policies and programs established to correct past discrimination in educational and employment opportunities directed against women, African Americans, and members of other minorities.

Racism—whether individual or institutional—has many negative effects. The United States Conference of Catholic Bishops pointed out that racism is a sin that

- divides the human family,
- blots out the image of God among specific members of that family,
- violates the fundamental human dignity of those called to be children of the same Father (*Brothers and Sisters to Us*, §9).

Racism mocks the words of Jesus, who said to treat others as you would like them to treat you. Ultimately, racism denies the truth of the dignity of each human being revealed by the mystery of the Incarnation.

Scandal

Scandal has been used previously to describe the outrageousness of injustices like hunger, poverty, and abortion. Scandal is another example of discrimination.

Scandal is a grave offense when someone leads another to do evil. For example, think about the man who insists his girlfriend have an abortion. Or, consider the scandal of a drug dealer pushing illegal and addictive drugs on a younger child.

Though more subtle than other offenses, scandal is still an attack on the dignity of the human person. Christ warns, "Whoever causes one of these little ones who believe in me to sin, it would be better for him to have a great millstone hung around his neck and to be drowned in the depths of the sea" (Mt 18:6).

> **scandal** An attitude or behavior that leads another person to sin.

SECTION ASSESSMENT

NOTE TAKING

Use the concept web you created for this section to complete the following items.

1. Why is discrimination an offense against solidarity?
2. Share examples of each of the following: prejudice, racism, and scandal.

COMPREHENSION

3. What is usually the root of prejudice?
4. Describe individual racism and institutional racism.
5. Explain how someone engaging in discrimination can also be guilty of the sin of scandal.

APPLICATION

6. Read Matthew 5:43–48. Then answer the following questions: What is the meaning of this passage? How could the application of this passage reduce racial tensions?

Section Summaries

Focus Question

How is your life interwoven with the lives of others?

Complete one of the following:

 Check with your diocesan missionary office for the names of priests, sisters, brothers, or laypeople who are serving in the foreign missions. Write to one of them and ask for ideas on how you can help them in their work.

 Create a connection web (like a family tree) that shows how you have relationships through first-, second-, and third-degree connections with a number of different people worldwide.

 Read paragraphs 1939 to 1942 from the *Catechism of the Catholic Church*. Explain the section in a one-paragraph summary.

INTRODUCTION (PAGES 245–249)

What Is Solidarity?

Solidarity is a realization of one's unity with all of humanity put into practice. It is a reminder that everyone, regardless of physical location, is one's "neighbor." It is a moral virtue and an attribute of catholicity.

 Make a list of some people you don't think of as your neighbors. How might recognizing these people as neighbors make a difference in your treatment of all people?

SECTION 1 (PAGES 250–254)

Solidarity and Immigration

The Church recognized the right of people to emigrate, as well as the rights of nations to regulate such immigration.

 Read and summarize paragraph 2433 of the *Catechism of the Catholic Church* in your own words.

Solidarity and Peace

Peace should always be the aim of every society. There are certain circumstances in which a country has a duty to protect its own people. The Church's just war doctrine describes the criteria for a war to be justified and not intrinsically evil.

 List four ways you can foster peace in the societies in your life (such as family, school, neighborhood, city).

Discrimination: An Offense against Solidarity

Discrimination based on factors such as race or culture is morally impermissible. Every human being is made in God's image and likeness and has intrinsic dignity. Racism is an especially insidious form of prejudice. Racism and discrimination can be a form of scandal.

 Write a prayer that asks God for true charity and generosity, especially toward those who are different from yourself.

Chapter Assignments

1. Catholic Relief Services and the Fair Trade Program

 Catholic Relief Services (CRS) was founded at the end of World War II by the United States Conference of Catholic Bishops to serve survivors of the war in Europe. The agency's mission today remains to bring relief and aid to the impoverished and disadvantaged living in many places throughout the world.

Research Catholic Relief Services. Pay special attention to the CRS Fair Trade Program. In contrast to the usual trading system, which looks to the bottom line and often exploits low-income workers in other nations, Fair Trade puts into practice the virtue of solidarity by respecting human dignity and promoting global economic justice. The goal of Fair Trade is to connect Americans to the persons in other nations who actually make products used in the United States. Using products sold by the CRS Fair Trade program is an opportunity to provide more direct support to merchants in impoverished nations. Note this strategy for providing help through CRS:

1. Write a two- to three-page report with an overview on Catholic Relief Services' Fair Trade program.

2. Find out where the persons responsible for buying coffee for your school or parish currently purchase it. Tell them about Fair Trade coffee and request that they give serious consideration to buying coffee from a Fair Trader. (CRS lists many of them on their website.) You may offer a copy of your research to assist the person or persons in their decision making.

3. Share the results of your efforts to implement Fair Trade coffee at your school.

2. How Interdependent Are We?

 Dr. Martin Luther King Jr. wrote, "It really boils down to this: that all life is interrelated. We are all caught in an inescapable network of mutuality, tied into a single garment of destiny. Whatever affects one directly, affects all indirectly." Find a story from literature, film, history, or the contemporary news that supports or challenges these words. Intersperse examples from your own experience or the experience of someone you know to answer the question, "How interdependent are we?"

- Write a one-page essay that answers the question while summarizing the story you have chosen. Your essay should explicitly address the virtue of solidarity.

3. Deliberate Acts of Kindness

 Respect, solidarity, caring for the poor, and harmonious family life all thrive when kindness is present. Kindness is much more than just "niceness." Synonyms for the word *kindness* include: good will, tenderness, compassion, humanity, gentleness, goodness, generosity, and favor.

A popular concept in modern society is "random acts of kindness." Although doing random acts of kindness is a great start, Christian acts of kindness are *more* than just random. Instead, they are deliberate and purposeful, because your acts are to be impelled by the love of Christ.

- Devise a plan for "*deliberate* acts of kindness." Your active goodness for others will help build the virtue of solidarity.

- Create an art project (e.g., poster, photo display, painting) that depicts the far-reaching ripples of your acts of kindness on the world around you.

Faithful Disciple

Bl. Franz Jägerstätter

Bl. Franz Jägerstätter

"Actions speak louder than words." An enduring example of this time-tested principle was an Austrian farmer, Bl. Franz Jägerstätter, who, at the age of thirty-seven, was executed for refusing to enter Hitler's army. By refusing to succumb to social pressure, Franz did what he thought was right in the face of evil. He followed his conscience, saying he would rather die following the Lord's teaching than live and betray what he knew was the right thing to do.

Bl. Franz Jägerstätter was born out of wedlock on May 20, 1907. His father was killed in World War I. Franz's birthplace was the small Catholic village of St. Radegund on the border of Austria and Germany. He took the Jägerstätter name from a farmer who eventually married his mother and adopted him. Franz grew up on a farm, and like most of his peers, left school at the age of fourteen.

As a young man, Franz had a wild side. Franz enjoyed fighting, bowling, playing cards, dancing, and women. At the age of twenty-seven, he fathered a child out of wedlock, as had his own father. The birth of this child, however, converted Franz from his immoral living and set him on a transformative spiritual journey.

Franz made a pilgrimage to a local shrine and even considered entering a religious order. However, he returned to the farm and married a loving wife with a similar religious outlook. Franz became active in his local church and worked there in maintenance. He would often be heard singing religious songs or reciting the Rosary as he worked in the fields or walked to the church. He went to daily Mass and often fasted until noon out of deep respect for the Blessed Sacrament. At a sacrifice to his own family, he shared food with the poor living in his area.

When Hitler marched into Austria, Franz Jägerstätter was the only one in his community who voted against the *Anschluss* (the annexation of Austria by Germany in March 1938). He saw Hitler as an evil man who wanted allegiance to him to replace allegiance to Christ Jesus. When his contemporaries, even leading Catholics, would salute "Heil Hitler!" rather than "Jesus is Lord!" Jägerstätter would often reply, "*Gruess Gott!*" which means "God's greetings!"

In February 1943, Franz received a draft notice. By then he had three young daughters, the oldest of whom was only six. Franz refused to serve in the army of the Third Reich. His neighbors thought him a fanatic. Even his pastor, a good priest who also opposed Nazism, urged him to serve for the sake of his family. The local bishop joined in, arguing that Franz was not knowledgeable enough to oppose the government's position. Franz continued to refuse to submit himself to what he considered an evil regime. He was eventually imprisoned for his convictions.

During Franz's imprisonment, his wife encouraged him to change his mind, as did the prison chaplain. After six months in prison, Franz Jägerstätter still would not relent. He underwent a military trial in Berlin. He was sentenced to death by decapitation.

Franz left behind only thirty-three pages of collected writings. In one letter he composed from prison, he wrote:

> Today one can hear it said repeatedly that there is nothing any more an individual can do. If someone were to speak out, it would only mean imprisonment and death. True, there is not much that can be done anymore to influence the whole course of world events. . . . But as long as we live in this world, I believe it is never too late to save ourselves and perhaps some other soul for Christ. . . . Do we no longer want to see Christians who are able to take a stand in the darkness around us in deliberate clarity, calmness, and confidence—who, in the midst of tension, gloom, selfishness, and hate, stand fast in perfect peace and cheerfulness—who are not like the floating reed which is driven here and there by every breeze—who do not merely watch to see what their friends will do but, instead, ask themselves, "What does our faith teach us about all this," or "Can my conscience bear this so easily that I will never have to repent?"[18]

On August 8, 1943, Bl. Franz Jägerstätter was given one last chance to sign a paper left by prison authorities that would have spared his life. He refused and told the chaplain, "I am completely bound in inner union with the Lord." Bl. Franz remained calm while taken to the scaffold for the execution.

Franz's body was cremated at the prison in Berlin. Three years later the ashes were taken to St. Radegund Church in his home village where they were buried in a war memorial inscribed with his name and the names of sixty other local citizens who died in World War II.

In 2007, Pope Benedict XVI issued an apostolic statement declaring Franz Jägerstätter a martyr. He was beatified later in the same year.

Reading Comprehension

1. Explain Franz Jägerstätter's conversion back to God.

2. How did Bl. Franz follow his conscience?

3. What argument did the bishop give that Bl. Franz should rethink his position?

Writing Task

- In a letter from prison, Franz Jägerstätter wrote: "The true Christian is to be recognized more in his works and deeds than in his speech. The surest mark of all is found in deeds." Describe the deeds of someone you know that mark that person as a Christian.

Explaining the Faith

Isn't not fighting back or getting even with someone who hurts or offends you a sign of weakness?

Choosing not to fight back or "get even" with someone who hurts you is not necessarily a sign of weakness, in that it often takes more courage and strength to "turn the other cheek" (Mt 5:39) through forgiveness. Being a person of the Beatitudes requires the strength of God's grace. So to be a peacemaker, you need God's help. Jesus Christ, in his life and his teaching, challenges you to see the truth that strength is to be measured in terms of virtue, not worldly power. He himself did not fight back and he forgave his executioners; this showed true strength. Many Christian martyrs courageously took on the example of Christ, and show us the strength and power that only faith and God's grace can give.

 ## Further Research

- Read paragraphs 2259 to 2262 of the *Catechism of the Catholic Church*. Answer: How has the prohibition of violence been understood throughout Salvation History?

Prayer
Prayer for Peace

Let us, then, pray with all fervor for this peace which our divine Redeemer came to bring us. May he banish from the souls of men whatever might endanger peace. May he transform all men into witnesses of truth, justice and brotherly love. May he illumine with his light the minds of rulers, so that, besides caring for the proper material welfare of their peoples, they may also guarantee them the fairest gift of peace.

Finally, may Christ inflame the desires of all men to break through the barriers which divide them, to strengthen the bonds of mutual love, to learn to understand one another, and to pardon those who have done them wrong. Through his power and inspiration may all peoples welcome each other to their hearts as brothers, and may the peace they long for ever flower and ever reign among them.[19]

—St. John XXIII

CARE FOR GOD'S CREATION

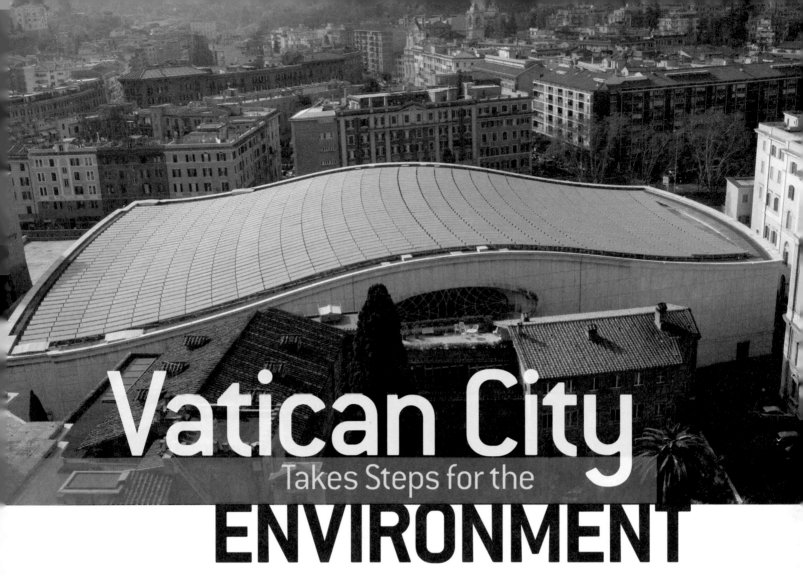

Vatican City
Takes Steps for the
ENVIRONMENT

The Catholic Church has long taught that it is important to respect God's creation. This is more than just lip service. Vatican City, the smallest country in the world, with about eight hundred inhabitants in a one-fifth square mile area, has made great strides in "going green."

Pope Benedict XVI, who has been called the "green" pope, began weighing in on environmental issues early in his papacy. In addition to calling all Catholics and all people to protect the environment, he introduced environment-friendly initiatives at the Vatican. In 2008, the roof of the Paul VI Audience Hall was covered with solar panels. This alternative energy source is enough to power the lighting, heating, and cooling of the entire building year-round. Pope Benedict also replaced the iconic "popemobile" with a model with a motor that runs on green gas.

Even more, Vatican City is the only "carbon neutral" country in the world. This was accomplished by planting a thirty-seven-acre forest in Hungary that will absorb as much carbon dioxide as Vatican City produces through its energy use.

In more recent times, Pope Francis has spoken for protection of the environment. At the World Peace Day in 2014 he said, "Even if nature is at our disposition, all too often we do not respect it or consider it a gracious gift which we must care for and set at the service of our brothers and sisters, including future generations."

Photo: The roof of the Paul VI Audience Hall in Vatican City is covered with 2,400 photovoltaic cells.

FOCUS QUESTION

How are you a steward of GOD'S CREATION ?

Chapter Overview

INTRODUCTION
The Goodness of God's Creation

MAIN IDEA

All that God created is good. However, because of sin, humankind's relationship with the created world has been altered. This relationship can be restored only through conversion and the redemptive actions of Jesus Christ.

Have you ever stopped to look at the wonder of the created world? Has what you have seen led you to contemplate its Creator? Does it anger you when the beautiful world God created is abused and destroyed? What about all of the people, often the poor, who are affected by environmental disasters? These questions are an essential part of understanding the theme of Catholic social teaching "care for God's creation."

In Genesis, God gave Adam and Eve dominion over creation. Even though the earth is not your eternal home (that would be *Heaven*), the created world is God's gift for humans to use. In the case of creation, when one misuses God's creation, it demonstrates a lack of honor to the Creator.

Contemporary thinkers often present two different views for how care for creation should be lived out. These perspectives are worth stating before a Christian understanding of care for the environment is explored.

The first view focuses on the inherent worth of all living things and stresses that all living species, including humans, are interdependent. However, this model of creation holds that humans are not superior to other living things, nor masters of them. Rather, it holds that humans are simply part of creation and codependent on it.

NOTE TAKING

Identifying Supporting Details. Make a flow chart like the one below to help you remember each Christian teaching on the environment described in this section. Write one summary phrase and draw one sketch for each teaching.

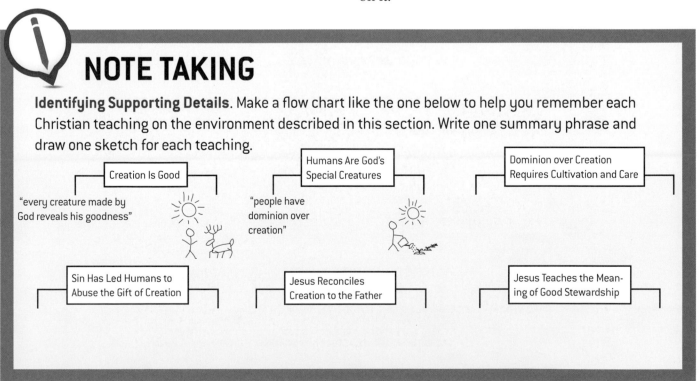

A second ecological view holds that both nonhuman and human ecosystems have an equal right to flourish in all their richness and diversity. According to this view, humans are not to be preferred over nonhuman creatures. In fact, humans are seen as the major offenders against the natural world. The solution to the problem is to decrease human population so humans will not further destroy the nonhuman world.

These and other modern theories about the environment often criticize the Judeo-Christian understanding of creation and the environment. Many criticize Scripture-based religions and claim that because these religions believe that humans are the pinnacle of God's creation and stewards of all other living things, therefore, these religions have contributed or caused current problems in the environment with a "subdue the earth" mentality.

These views are not accurate. Furthermore, the Bible and Church teaching reveal that it is *human sinfulness* that has alienated humans from God. Sin and alienation have led to the serious abuses that have created today's environmental crisis.

Some main points of the Church's rightful understanding of creation, the environment, and the role of humans in caring for creation follow. These understandings often find their roots in Scripture, from the accounts of creation in the Book of Genesis to Jesus' teachings in the Gospels.

Creation Is Good

A recurring refrain in the Book of Genesis is God's declaration that all creation is good: "God looked at everything he had made, and he found it very good" (Gn 1:31). In his wisdom and power, every creature that God made reveals his goodness. This includes the heavens and the earth, the sun and the moon, the land and the sea, fish and birds, animals, and especially human beings. All creation is a gift from God. All creatures reveal something about the loving Creator who made them and keeps them in existence.

Humans Are God's Special Creatures

God gave his gift of creation to humans. Humans are the summit of God's creation because God made human beings in his image and likeness. People are to have dominion over the earth and all of its resources. However, dominion over the earth does not mean exploiting it. Rather, it entails a special responsibility to care for, and protect, the earth and its resources. When God placed Adam and Eve in the Garden of Eden, he told them "to cultivate and care for it" (Gn 2:15).

Dominion over Creation Requires Cultivation and Care

God alone has sovereignty over the earth; people are the earth's stewards. This dominion, or control, over creation involves cultivation and care and requires humans to preserve "the beauty, diversity, and integrity of nature, as well as . . . fostering its productivity."[1] People may not do anything to harm God's gift of creation. As St. John Paul II wrote:

> One cannot use with impunity the different categories of beings, whether living or inanimate—animals, plants, the natural elements—simply as one wishes, according to one's own economic needs. On the contrary, one must take into account the nature of each being and of its mutual connection in an ordered system, which is precisely the cosmos. (*Sollicitudo Rei Socialis*, §34)

Sin Has Led Humans to Abuse the Gift of Creation

Pride, selfishness, materialism, consumerism, and other sins flowing from Original Sin have led humanity to rebel against God and neglect or misuse his beautiful creation.

The prophet Hosea wrote that when humans abandon God and act unjustly, then all of nature suffers:

> Hear the word of the Lord, O people of Israel,
> for the Lord has a grievance
>   against the inhabitants of the land:
> There is no fidelity, no mercy,
>   no knowledge of God in the land.
> False swearing, lying, murder, stealing
>   and adultery!
>   in their lawlessness, bloodshed
>   follows bloodshed.
> Therefore the land mourns,
>   and everything that dwells in it languishes:
> The beasts of the field,
>   the birds of the air,
>   and even the fish of the sea perish. (Hos 4:1–3)

Sin leads to disorder in all of creation. If you are not at peace with God, you cannot be at peace with God's creation.

The prophets urged the Israelites to be attentive to nature and their obligation to use it for the good of all. For example, they instructed the people to rest the land every seven years, taking care to restore the balance between the land and the people, and to restore God's justice, especially by looking out for the needs of the poor. However, the people repeatedly disregarded these instructions, and the minority became rich. The rich dispossessed the poor and exhausted the land. The prophets warned of a coming Day of Judgment. But they also told of a day when humans and nature would be renewed and made whole again by God's Spirit.

Jesus Reconciles Creation to the Father

Through his Passion, Death, Resurrection, and Ascension, Jesus overcame what separates people from God

and one another, and he has overcome the disharmony between creation and human beings, part of the effects of Original Sin. Through Christ Jesus, the Father reconciled

> all things for him,
> making peace by the blood of his cross
> [through him], whether those on earth or
> those in heaven. (Col 1:19–20)

Through the gift of his Holy Spirit, God gives all people the power to renew the earth, to serve each other, and to respect all the gift of creation.

Jesus Teaches the Meaning of Good Stewardship

Jesus showed his closeness to, and love of, creation during his time on earth. He compared God to a loving shepherd who sought out his lost sheep, and described himself as the Good Shepherd. He also spoke of the lilies of the field and the birds of the air to encourage all to trust God and to stop worrying about material possessions. Jesus also used images from nature in his parables, such as wheat growing, farmers sowing, and vineyard workers caring for their vines. All of these images are meant to teach that humans are to be good stewards of God's beautiful creation.

Jesus spoke directly about stewardship in the parable of the Ten Gold Coins (cf. Lk 19:11–17). In the parable, a rich noble entrusted his fortune to ten of his servants and instructed them to invest it on his behalf. On his return, the noble praised and rewarded those who invested the money and earned him a profit; he punished the servant who buried the money out of fear. When the meaning of the parable is applied to the environment the compelling conclusion is that the resources of the earth must be used wisely and for the good of all people, both in the current generation and for future generations.

THE BEAUTY OF CREATION IN SCRIPTURE

The psalms acknowledge God as Creator. Read the following psalms and complete the writing tasks that follow.

PSALM 8
GOD'S MAJESTY AND HUMAN DIGNITY

1. What does this psalm reveal about God's intention?

PSALM 104
PRAISE OF GOD THE CREATOR

2. Write two verses from the psalm that inspire your view of creation.

PSALM 148
ALL CREATION IS CALLED TO PRAISE GOD

3. Write a one-paragraph summary of this psalm.

In addition, no one should hoard his or her gifts. In another parable on stewardship, Jesus warned:

> Much will be required of the person entrusted with much, and still more will be demanded of the person entrusted with more. (Lk 12:48)

Pope Benedict XVI compared the renewal of the doctrine of creation with "a new understanding of the inseparability of creation and Redemption."[2] In other words, you cannot look *just* at the story of creation to understand the glory of God. Instead, it must be seen within the entire context of Salvation History. Indeed, it is only in, and through, Christ that one has access to the graces necessary to restore humanity's relationship with creation and the environment itself.

SECTION ASSESSMENT

NOTE TAKING

Briefly study the notes you made for this section, including the sketches. Then close your notes and complete the following items from memory.

1. Discuss three truths the Bible reveals about God's creation.
2. What role do humans play in creation?
3. From a scriptural point of view, what is the root of the ecological crisis?

COMPREHENSION

4. Name and briefly summarize the theme of Catholic social teaching discussed in this chapter.

CRITICAL THINKING

5. How do the two contemporary views of the environment mentioned in this section contradict the Church's understanding of the environment?

SECTION 1
The Scope of Modern Environmental Issues

MAIN IDEA
Current environmental issues—many with origins in the nineteenth century—are related to other social concerns, such as the protection of human life, poverty, and consumerism. The virtue of solidarity is essential to protecting the environment.

From a historical perspective, concern about the environment is a relatively recent phenomenon. In the nineteenth century, for example, postcards showcasing American achievements often featured industrial factories belching dark smoke into the air. These smokestacks were a point of pride because they showed that a particular city was prospering economically. In this time period and beyond, people believed that the earth could easily absorb industrial by-products and that such pollution was a small price to pay for economic progress.

The environment today shows the effects of this attitude. Industrialization spread from North America and Europe to many countries around the world. It became clear that the earth's growing population could not afford to waste any of the earth's valuable resources. With industrialization came wealth and disposable income. Items like cars—owned by a majority of employed adults—contributed greatly to the smog problem in many cities throughout the world.

More recently, individuals and nations have awakened to the ecological crisis that has resulted from such attitudes. St. John Paul II offered the reminder that

> We cannot interfere in one area of the ecosystem without paying due attention both to the consequences of such interference in other areas and to the well-being of future generations. (*The Ecological Crisis: A Common Responsibility*, §6)

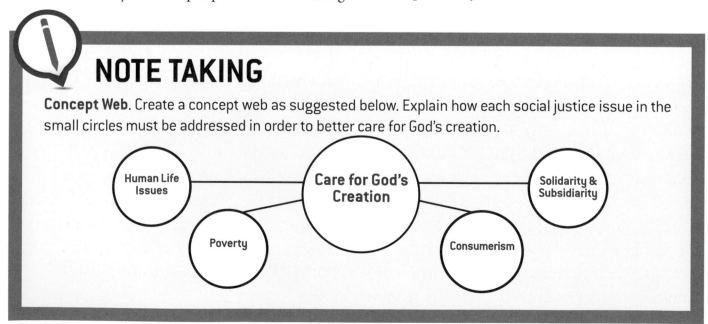

NOTE TAKING

Concept Web. Create a concept web as suggested below. Explain how each social justice issue in the small circles must be addressed in order to better care for God's creation.

- Human Life Issues
- Poverty
- Care for God's Creation
- Consumerism
- Solidarity & Subsidiarity

Food distribution to needy children takes place at a camp for victims of the 2010 earthquake in Haiti.

At the root of the ecological crisis, fundamentally a moral problem, is a profound disrespect for life. Economic interests have too often taken precedence over human dignity. The exploitation of natural resources and the destruction of animal and plant life have contributed immensely to the ecological imbalances the world is experiencing today. A society that will easily dispose of God's good earth will also find disposing of people easy as well. This is why the Church shows so much concern about the connection between respect for the dignity of people (especially the poor) and respect for the environment.

The Church is clear that preservation of the environment and sustainable development are of "grave concern for the entire human family." As Pope Benedict XVI taught: "The consequences of disregard for the environment cannot be limited to an immediate area or populous because they always harm human coexistence, and thus betray human dignity and violate the rights of citizens who desire to live in a safe environment."[3] Protection of God's creation is linked with other social justice concerns including human life issues, poverty, and the struggle with consumerism. The virtue of solidarity and the principle of subsidiarity are essential elements in the response to environmental problems. The following sections (beginning on page 290) look more closely at each of these issues.

THE ENVIRONMENTAL REALITY TODAY

The scope of environmental problems the world faces is expansive and complex.

CLEAN WATER IS ESSENTIAL TO LIFE.

Some 800 million people do not have access to clean water.

That means **1 out of 10** people drink or use polluted water.

Nearly **3.4 million** people die each year from a water-related disease.[4]

AIR POLLUTION IS A MAJOR ENVIRONMENTAL RISK TO HUMAN HEALTH.

Air pollution is responsible for **2 million** premature deaths every year.[5]

Several of India's cities have a high rate of outdoor pollution, and indoor pollution takes 500,000 lives every year in the country.

Indoor air pollution results from burning wood, coal, and animal dung as fuel.

Nearly 70 % of the homes in rural India do not have any type of ventilation.[6]

Outdoor air pollution has both serious and deadly effects.

Air pollution also affects the way children learn.

The Environmental Defense Fund (EDF) reports that 13,000 Americans die prematurely and unnecessarily every year. Half of all coal-burning power plants lack basic, readily available pollution control technologies.

The EDF claims that if there had *not* been a ban in the United States on leaded gas 10 years ago, 300,000 more children would have IQ scores below 70.[7]

LOW-INCOME COMMUNITIES SUFFER MORE FROM ENVIRONMENTAL CONTAMINATION THAN DO THEIR HIGHER-INCOME COUNTERPARTS.

Toxic-waste incinerators, chemical plants, and solid-waste dumps are frequently located in low-income neighborhoods.

This is often the result of the relative political powerlessness of the poor.

DEFORESTATION IS THREATENING TO ALL LIFE ON EARTH.

Forests are the largest storehouses of carbon on earth and are the third biggest source of carbon emissions (after coal and oil), when harvested (see photo on page 286).

Climate change affects forests by drying them out, making them more susceptible to fires and more vulnerable to disease and pests.

Threatening forests means threatening the diversity of plant and animal life that live within them.[8]

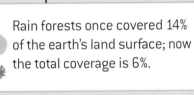

14%

6%

Rain forests once covered 14% of the earth's land surface; now the total coverage is 6%.

If rain forests disappear in fewer than 40 years—as some scientists think—almost 50% of the world's species of plants, animals, and microorganisms will be destroyed or threatened.[9]

BIODIVERSITY IS AN IMPORTANT PART OF THE EARTH'S BALANCE.

1 in every 8 plant species is at risk of extinction.

Almost **25%** of the world's **mammals** and **11%** of **bird species** are threatened.

The United Nations proposes that as long as deforestation, land and water degradation, and monoculture cropping continue to increase, the threats to biodiversity will continue to grow.[10]

Pope Benedict XVI explained that the modern results of humans not treating the environment as a gift from God include climate change, pollution, and deforestation. He emphasized the particular tragedy when these environmental issues affect groups of people: "Can we remain impassive in the face of actual and potential conflicts involving access to natural resources? All these are issues with a profound impact on the exercise of human rights, such as the right to life, food, health, and development."[11]

The Link between the Environment and Human Life Issues

Any discussion of protecting the environment must begin with consideration for the protection of the human person. When people are valued, so too is the environment. Similarly, when human dignity is at risk, so too is the rest of God's creation. Pope Benedict explains: "Our duties toward the environment flow from our duties toward the person, considered both individually and in relation to others."[12]

Common sense would dictate that it is important to protect endangered species. And yet, protection of the human person, especially the most vulnerable, will always have a place of higher priority. The link is undeniable. For example, consider the issue of abortion and our call to protect the unborn, as explained by the United States Conference of Catholic Bishops:

> We must care for all God's creatures, especially the most vulnerable. How, then, can we protect endangered species and at the same time be callous to the unborn, the elderly, or disabled persons? Is not abortion also a sin against creation? If we turn our backs on our own unborn children, can we truly expect that nature will receive respectful treatment at our hands? The care of the earth will not be advanced by the destruction of human life at any stage of development.

As St. John Paul II has said, "protecting the environment is first of all the right to live and the protection of life" (October 16, 1991, homily at Quiaba, Mato Grosso, Brazil).

St. John Paul II and Pope Benedict XVI also spoke about a "human ecology," in which the human person is honored and revered within God's creation. What they meant by this term is that when people understand the nature of themselves and their relationship with God—then, the proper view of environmental ecology could occur.

Similarly, when Pope Francis spoke of a "culture of waste," he spoke of a mentality in which human life is no longer perceived as being of primary value, especially if it is seen as not useful, as in the case of the unborn or the elderly. Such a worldview connects with the issue of the environment, in that in a "culture of waste" the goods of creation are just used and disposed of, rather than protected and valued.

Environmental Offenses and the Poor

Environmental problems often affect the poor more than other members of society. For example, in the nuclear plant accident at Chernobyl in 1986, the poor

The damaged nuclear reactor at the Chernobyl plant in northern Ukraine. Chernobyl was the site of one of the worst nuclear accidents in history in April 1986.

The United States Catholic Bishops ask that "the poor and vulnerable at home and abroad be accorded a special and urgent priority in all efforts to care for our environment."

and working people suffered the worst contamination, in part because they could not afford to abandon their homes and restart their lives outside of the zone with high radiation. Pope Benedict XVI called people who are forced to leave their homes and possessions behind due to environmental degradation "environmental refugees." As societies begin to respond to environmental issues, the needs of the poor must not be neglected. Nor should the costs of ecological reform be at the expense of working people. The *Compendium of the Social Doctrine of the Church* explains:

> The present environmental crisis affects those who are poorest in a particular way, whether they live in those lands subject to erosion and desertification, are involved in armed conflicts or subject to forced immigration, or because they do not have the economic and technological means to protect themselves from other calamities. (§482)

Societal injustice also often contributes to environmental destruction. For example, rural poverty and unjust land distribution can lead to subsistence farming and subsequent soil exhaustion. Similarly, as farmers clear new land for crops or grazing, unchecked deforestation can result. Poor countries in heavy debt

to the rich nations often stop raising crops to feed their own citizens in order to create new export products to help relieve their debt. These examples are built into the structures of society.

Also, the poorer areas of the United States tend to be the locations for such hazards as toxic waste dumps and polluting coal plants, validating what the United States Catholic Bishops said in regard to this, that "in most countries today, including our own, it is the poor and the powerless who most directly bear the burden of current environmental carelessness."[13]

The Environment and Consumerism

Caring for God's creation is not *just* about "cleaning up the environment." Instead, on a more profound level, it is about personal conversion. And one of the most significant areas in need of conversion is the consumerist mentality.

As you will recall from Chapter 7, consumerism is a social and economic worldview that encourages the purchase of goods in ever greater amounts. It is the cycle of buying and disposing of goods. Consumerism is in opposition to the poverty of spirit and simplicity of life that the Christian is called to. In *Centesimus Annus,* St. John Paul II explained consumerism this way: "In his desire to have and to enjoy rather than to be and to grow, man consumes the resources of the earth and his own life in an excessive and disordered way" (§37). This excessive and disordered use of the earth's resources contributes to its degradation. In fact, the biggest factor contributing to environmental destruction is *overconsumption* by developed nations. This stands in stark contrast to the argument or fear of some individuals or organizations that the earth is threatened by overpopulation. Population growth, especially in developing countries, can be supported through sustainable development strategies.

The Church addresses the population issue in light of the values of respect for life, just economic and social structures, care for the environment, and the responsibility of parents to cooperate with God in relation to the number and natural spacing of births. The Church opposes any coercive method of population control. "Respect for nature ought to encourage policies that promote natural family planning and true responsible parenthood."[14]

The Environment and Solidarity and Subsidiarity

Environmental issues are also linked to the virtue of solidarity. For example, consider that pollution from one country often affects people in other parts of the world.

The virtue of solidarity commits nations and individuals to work for the common good, to sacrifice for the sake of others, rather than simply to further their own interests. St. John Paul II warned:

> The ecological crisis reveals the urgent moral need for a new solidarity, especially in relations between the developing nations and those that are highly industrialized. . . . This need presents new opportunities for strengthening cooperative and peaceful relations among states. (*The Ecological Crisis: A Common Responsibility*, §10)

Industrialized and developed nations must recognize the harm they themselves have caused to the environment and must take responsibility for developing and implementing solutions. Further, modern society, collectively and individually, is called to examine its own lifestyle. "Simplicity, moderation and discipline, as well as a spirit of sacrifice, must become a part of everyday life, lest all suffer the negative consequences of the careless habits of a few."[15]

Solidarity is always guided by the principle of subsidiarity. Everyone must work toward proper stewardship of the earth on his or her appropriate level. Although the government can plan an important role in making the necessary changes, it is not the only group responsible. The task of protecting the environment must begin with individuals. Although governments may have a certain responsibility with environmental protection initiatives, so too do other private organizations and the media.

SECTION ASSESSMENT

NOTE TAKING

Use your notes from the concept web to help you answer the following questions.

1. How are human life issues related to environmental issues?
2. How does a consumerist mind-set lead to disrespect of creation?
3. Explain how overconsumption, rather than population growth, is a more serious threat to the environment.

COMPREHENSION

4. Why should respect for human life be a priority when dealing with environmental issues?
5. What did Pope Benedict XVI mean by the term "human ecology"?
6. What are some ways environmental degradation affects the poor?
7. Why is the issue of solidarity important in protecting the environment?

APPLICATION

8. Pope Benedict XVI described "environmental refugees" as people forced to forsake their natural surroundings and "often their possessions as well." Who are environmental refugees today (1) in the world and (2) in your nation? Explain their circumstances.

SECTION 2

The Environment and Other Social Concerns

MAIN IDEA
The world is not your own. It has been entrusted to you by God to care for. You are called to be a steward and protector of creation.

God placed humans at the summit of all his creation. Because of this, men and women have a privileged position in caring for the environment, as *stewards* of the environment. A steward is one who takes care of something as his own, when ultimately it is not. You are a steward of any gifts you have been given in this life—money, family, talents, and more. In regard to the environment, the world is ultimately God's, but he has given you the opportunity to "cultivate and care for" it with others (Gn 2:15).

God's dominion or control over creation requires humans to preserve "the beauty, diversity, and integrity of nature, as well as . . . fostering its productivity."[16] God alone has sovereignty over the earth; people are the earth's stewards. People may not do anything to harm God's gift of creation.

In his March 19, 2013, homily, Pope Francis spoke about the need to look to the example of St. Joseph, the foster father of Jesus who protected his family. He said you too are to be "protectors" of God's creation. This means:

- respecting each of God's creatures;

- respecting the environment in which you live;

NOTE TAKING

Summarizing Main Ideas. Create a concept web like the one below. In each circle, summarize what the text says about stewardship for each term.

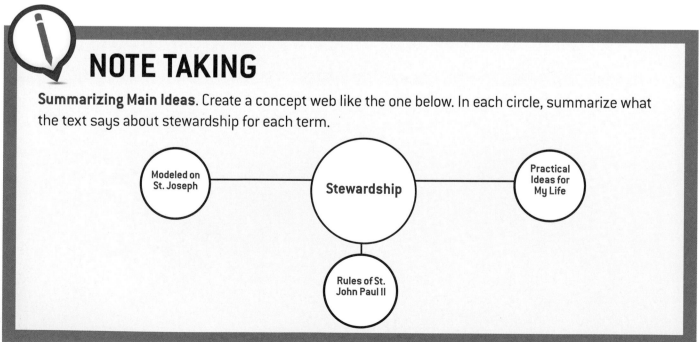

- protecting people by showing loving concern for each and every person, especially children, the elderly, those in need;

- caring for one another in your family;

- building sincere relationships in which you protect one another in trust, respect, and goodness.

Pope Francis summarized what it means to be protectors:

> To protect the whole of creation, to protect each person, especially the poorest, to protect ourselves: this is a service . . . to which all of us are called, so that the star of hope will shine brightly. Let us protect with love all that God has given us!

Humans Are the Guiding Principle of Stewardship

Respect for human dignity should always be at the heart of the practice of stewardship. For example, recall the principle of the universal destination of goods (pages 191–193). You know that it is not the resources themselves that have priority; it is the people for whom the resources of the earth are intended. Thus, "under the leadership of justice and in the company of charity, created goods should be in abundance for all in like manner."[17]

Likewise, nature will never be more important than the human person. That is not to say that natural resources should be used erratically or without concern; on the contrary, protecting the natural world in the end benefits the human person. And yet, this protection should never be to the detriment of the person.

Rules for Stewardship

As a summary for good stewardship, consider these rules for the environment offered by St. John Paul II:[18]

- *You can use the earth's resources—including* animals, plants, and sources of energy—*but you can't do so haphazardly* without any effort to replenish them and maintain the natural balance of resources.

- *You must look out for future generations*, who will also have to use natural resources; and thus, the current use of resources should not be so short-sighted so as to abuse the created earth, rendering it unusable for the future. Some natural resources are limited; some are not, as it is said, renewable. Using them as if they were inexhaustible, with

STEWARDSHIP of the ENVIRONMENT in YOUR DAILY LIFE

At the heart of being a good steward of God's creation is acknowledging that all that you have ultimately is not your own. However, there are simple, practical ways in which you can live out this stewardship. Read the accompanying questions and add some ideas of your own.

1. *Save energy.* Turn off lights and other electrical appliances when you're not using them. Walk when possible. If you have a car, make sure it is tuned up. Carpool.

   • What are other things you can do to save energy?

2. *Recycle.* Recycle paper, plastic, glass, and other recyclable materials through your local community. Whenever possible, avoid buying products in nonrecyclable packaging, or Styrofoam products, which do not decompose and create landfill problems. Cut back on using disposable products. Though convenient, paper napkins and towels and disposable plates and cups can be wasteful.

   • Name some ways you can increase your own or your family's current level of recycling, or ways you can reduce waste.

3. *Don't litter.* Whether you're in your neighborhood or enjoying a day in the mountains or at the beach, dispose of garbage in appropriate receptacles. And, of course, recycle whenever possible. Also, when feasible, take time to clean up litter left by others.

   • What are some opportunities to participate in a school or neighborhood clean-up campaign?

4. *Plant a vegetable garden.* Growing your own food will keep you close to nature and provide a healthy food source. After you've raised some produce, donate part of your harvest to a local food bank.

   • What are some ways you can support local produce growers in your area?

5. *Simplify your lifestyle by consuming less.* Buy things because you need them, not simply for their status value.

   • What are three personal items that you might donate to an agency that helps the poor?

6. *Join a community clean-up group.* Also consider other ways you can take part in clean-up or conservation efforts.

   • Conduct an online search to identify agencies in your area that support environmental responsibility. Name at least three.

7. *Write to local politicians and encourage them to pass and enforce laws that protect the environment.* In addition, keep informed about the positions on the environment taken by your elected officials.

   • How can you raise awareness of the record of local and national elected officials on environmental issues among your peers?

8. *Pray.* At Mass, praise and thank God for his goodness and the beauty of his creation. Pray for children (including the unborn) and for the poor because they are at the greatest risk for environmental hazards and suffer the most from environmental destruction. Pray for a spirit of conversion away from consumerism that contributes to ecological waste.

   • How can your environmental action be animated by a spirit of ongoing prayer?

absolute dominion, seriously endangers their availability not only for the present generation, but above all, for generations to come.

- *You must remain vigilant against unchecked industrialization.* Certain types of manufacturing produce pollution that not only hurts the created world, but even more affects the health and well-being of humans. The direct or indirect result of industrialization is, ever more frequently, the pollution of the environment, with serious consequences for the health of the population.

Being a steward, or protector, of God's creation is a profound responsibility. Honoring this responsibility shows a great reverence for the Creator. It also comes with great reward, including the use of the earth's resources, sustenance, and pleasure.

SECTION ASSESSMENT

NOTE TAKING

Use the notes you recorded in your concept web to help you answer the following questions.

1. What does it mean to be a "steward" of the environment?
2. What are St. John Paul II's three rules for stewardship?
3. How is St. Joseph a model of stewardship?

COMPREHENSION

4. What does it mean to be "protectors" of God's creation?

CRITICAL THINKING

5. Explain the meaning of the statement: "Humans are the guiding principle of stewardship."
6. Describe one way not named in this section that you can be a steward of the environment in your daily life.

SECTION 3
The Ten Commandments for the Environment

MAIN IDEA
The Church's teaching on the environment can be summarized in ten "commandments" or guidelines that emphasize the primacy of the human person and the importance of creation leading one back to God.

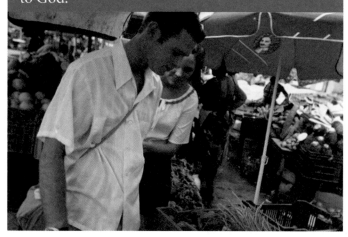

In your study of Catholic social teaching, at first you may not have connected the themes of social encyclicals beginning with *Rerum Novarum* in 1891 with environmental issues. However, if you retrace your perspective of care for the environment to its first principle of care and protection of human dignity, you can see that many of the statements of modern Catholic social teaching do focus on environmental themes.

Any of the encyclicals that address industrialization, the rights of workers, and consumerism also have an environmental focus. The Second Vatican Council documents—especially *Gaudium et Spes*—explicitly addressed a broad range of social issues and reemphasized the dignity of every human individual. St. John Paul II expanded on this work in *Laborem Exercens* and laid the foundation for explicit teaching on ecological concerns by connecting human work with the work of creation. His 1988 encyclical *Sollicitudo Rei Socialis*, marking the twentieth anniversary of Pope Paul VI's encyclical *Populorum Progressio* ("The Development of Peoples"), connected human dignity and environmental protection with personal morality. His

NOTE TAKING

Summarizing Ideas and Identifying Examples. Create a chart like the one below. For each commandment of the environment, summarize it in your own words and think of an example to describe it. The first has been done for you

Commandment	Summary	Example
1	God made the human person to be superior among creatures. Christ shows this reality most perfectly.	Human life cannot be destroyed, even to protect the environment.
2		
3		
4		
5		
6		
7		
8		
9		
10		

three rules for the environment were addressed in the previous section on pages 295 and 297.

This section examines the so-called Ten Commandments for the Environment. Although these ten principles are commonly associated with Pope Benedict XVI, they were actually presented by Bishop Giampaolo Crepaldi, the secretary of the Pontifical Council for Justice and Peace, at the 2005 Congress on "Ethics and the Environment" in Rome. They are drawn from the *Compendium of the Social Doctrine of the Church*.[19] A summary of the ten principles follows.

1. You Must Cooperate with All of Creation

The human being, created in God's image, is placed above all earthly creatures. In turn, you must use and care for creation in a responsible way in cooperation with the divine plan of Redemption.

God is both Creator and Redeemer. The very God who made the earth and all within it actually became man to reconcile the world to himself. All life has come

Though humans are the pinnacle of all creation, all elements of creation are important.

from God, and humans are called to a relationship with him. Humans are positioned as the most important part of the created world, because they are made in God's image and likeness. However, all elements of creation are important; God made all good, and through his saving actions he has renewed the earth (Ps 104:30). Though the earth is not your ultimate home, the fact that God created it and lived here is of great consequence. The world that God created and walked upon must be treated with great care.

2. You Must Strike a Balance between Materialism and Nature

Nature must not be reduced to a utilitarian object of manipulation, nor absolutized or placed above human dignity.

The created world is a *gift* to humans. Humans have *dominion* over the created world; however, this dominion entails a responsibility to care for and cultivate the earth and its resources.

God's command to "fill the earth and subdue it" (Gn 1:28) is a command of responsibility more than a delegation of authority. Pope Benedict XVI pointed out in a meeting with Italian clergy in 2008 that "the task of 'subduing' was never intended as an order to enslave creation but rather as the task of being guardians of creation and developing its gifts."

3. You Must Consider the Entire Planet in Any Environmental Questions

The question of the environment entails the whole planet, as it is a collective good. Your responsibility toward ecology extends to future generations.

Remembering the virtue of solidarity, you are called to move *beyond* the mentality of, "well, if this particular problem doesn't affect me directly right now, then I will not concern myself with it." Instead, you need to remember that you are united with humanity of both the present and the future. Such a union is rooted in the common good: if even one person suffers needlessly, then it hurts what is commonly good for all. *You* are personally responsible for upholding this and all themes of Catholic social teaching.

Pope Benedict XVI linked caring for the environment with working toward peace among all the earth's people. He said,

All this means that humanity, if it truly desires peace, must be increasingly conscious of the links between natural ecology, or respect for nature, and human ecology. Experience shows that *disregard for the environment always harms human coexistence*, and vice versa. It becomes more and more evident that there is an inseparable link between peace with creation and peace among men. (World Day of Peace Message, 2007)

Justice and peace are inseparable; stewardship of the earth is indeed part of justice for all.

4. You Must Place Human Rights ahead of Scientific Advances

In dealing with environmental problems, ethics and human dignity should come before science and technology.

In the modern world, technological advances are taking place at a remarkable rate. Many serve the human person and the common good. Sometimes, however, industrial advancement is to the detriment of the human person.

The Church does not oppose scientific advancements and discoveries. She teaches, instead, that these advances must not jeopardize the good of creation or of the human person, and that when these are the effects of scientific advancement, then scientific advancement has gone too far. One example of such excessive advancement is the genetic modification of agricultural crops, which has been linked to a negative impact on the environment and poses many unanswered questions with regard to the impact on human health.

5. You Must Remember That Nature Is Not a Divine Reality, but a Gift from God

Nature is not a sacred or divine reality, removed from human intervention. Thus, human intervention that modifies some characteristics of living things is not wrong, as long as it respects their place in their particular ecosystem.

The natural world is *not* divine in and of itself. There is no such thing as "Mother Earth" in a divine sense. Certainly, the beauty of the earth reflects God's beauty.

This commandment is another reminder that humans are entrusted as stewards of God's creation.

Recent times have provided examples that the Church has made stewardship a priority in her own activities. For example, at World Youth Day in Sydney, Australia, in 2008, Pope Benedict XVI insisted that the environmental impact of all the pilgrims would be as limited as possible. These efforts included walking when possible, instead of using public transportation, timers on the showers to reduce wasted water, and using reusable batteries in their flashlights. The result was the lowest polluting crowd per capita for a group in Sydney.[20]

These teens began their own recycling campaign at their high school.

6. You Must Help Balance Development with Preservation

The politics of development must be coordinated with the politics of ecology, and every environmental cost in development projects must be weighed carefully.

The Church teaches that the economy should *serve* the human person and the common good while also maintaining the integrity of the natural world. This can be a difficult guideline to put into practice in the everyday world. It takes prudential decisions on a case-by-case basis. For example, cutting down the rainforest can be detrimental to the ecological balance of the environment. And yet, often this is the only source of income for the very poor in developing countries. What is the right decision in this case? It takes wisdom and prudence to make these determinations.

7. You Must Share the Goods of the World with All

Ending global poverty is related to the environmental question, remembering that the goods of the earth must be shared equitably.

Of the many environmental issues that affect the poor, one that is of utmost importance is the lack of clean, drinkable water available worldwide. Recall that recent estimates show that 780 million people lack access to clean water. That's more than two-and-a-half times the population of the United States. Each year 3.4 million people die due to a water-related disease; 99 percent of these deaths occur in developing countries.[21]

In many parts of the world, drought and its resulting water shortages is a recurring problem. Eastern Africa is an area that typically faces drought due to the lack of rainfall. For example, in 2011, more than 4.5 million people in Ethiopia faced severe hunger due to the lack or water. Farmers were forced to move their livestock up to six miles per day in search of water. Many of their herds died of starvation.

You may wonder what is possible in situations like this where the land is dry and barren. Water is a renewable resource. Ensuring access to water for the poor requires human ingenuity and scientific help. "There is a solution to this problem," said Bekele Abaire, a water and sanitation program manager for Catholic Relief Services. "The challenge is that the water runs below the surface in underground caverns as deep as 1,000 feet. The water is difficult but not impossible to access."

In recent years, Catholic Relief Services has brought in rigs to drill wells; there are twenty-eight such wells in Ethiopia that remain operational. Each well was built to serve 5,000 people. "But we're finding that the need is so severe that up to 10,000 are now flocking to these water points," said Abaire. In Ethiopia and in developing nations around the world, much more work needs to be done.

8. You Must Collaborate with Governments to Protect the Environment

The right to a safe environment needs to be protected through international cooperation and accords.

The principle of the universal destination of goods can only be upheld if it is practiced on an international basis. Also, national governments must work together to pass international laws and treaties to protect the environment. This has already been done in many cases; for example, there have long been international regulations that prohibit whaling, and laws regulating ozone-depleting chemicals are also shared between nations.

CATHOLIC RESPONSE TO AN ENVIRONMENTAL DISASTER

An oil rig explosion in April of 2010 in the Gulf of Mexico caused what was then the largest oil spill in US history. The news media presented heart-wrenching pictures of oil-soaked birds and other wildlife. The Gulf waters were closed to fishing. Many people whose livelihoods depended on the fishing and tourism industries suffered financial hardship because of the oil spill.

The Church responded to this crisis in several ways. Catholic Charities USA responded to the immediate needs of unemployed workers. Meanwhile, the United States Conference of Catholic Bishops called on Catholics to offer their prayers for the people and all of God's creation affected by the oil spill and to support those affected by the spill through generous financial contributions.

Catholic Charities USA also responded at the national level by bringing people's needs to the attention of Congress. Fr. Larry Snyder, Catholic Charities USA president, testified at a House Ways and Means Subcommittee on Oversight to urge the federal government to help individuals and families afflicted by the oil spill. He emphasized that many of the same people who had been traumatized by Hurricane Katrina and other storms were being affected by the spill.

Fr. Snyder made several recommendations to the committee, for both immediate and long-term assistance. He suggested that the federal government declare the Gulf region a national disaster area in order to free funds to serve families better. He also asked that the government better plan for possible future disasters by:

- developing a new unemployment assistance program;
- working on long-term recovery;
- improving coordination among federal agencies;
- providing tax relief for those affected by the disaster;
- offering loans to sustain non-profits and small businesses;
- studying the long-term health impact of the disaster.

Downsizing by donating unneeded clothing and goods helps to combat overconsumption, one of the main causes of environmental damage.

these goods that contributes to environmental degradation.

Pope Benedict XVI said that, while it is important to discover techniques that would prevent environmental harm (including alternative forms of energy), all this won't be enough if people don't find a new style of life, a discipline which is made up in part of renunciations: a discipline of recognition of others, to whom creation belongs just as much as those who can make use of it more easily; a discipline of responsibility to the future for others. It's a question of responsibility before God, who is Judge. God is Redeemer as well, but nonetheless also your Judge (Pope Benedict's Question and Answer with Priests in Northern Italy, 2008).

9. You Must Adopt a Lifestyle of Sobriety, Temperance, and Self-Discipline

Environmental protection requires a change in lifestyle that reflects moderation and self-control, on a personal and social level. That means moving away from the mind-set of consumerism.

Caring for the environment is a question of responsibility. Each and every person has the responsibility to live a more simple life of moderation, in order to make sure the world's resources can be available to those who really need it.

It is crucial to understand that there is nothing wrong with enjoying the goods of creation. In fact, eating a delicious meal from the fruits of the earth or wearing a nice piece of clothing woven from natural fibers or using natural gas to heat your home are all acts that *can* be an opportunity of gratitude and praise of the Creator. Rather, it is the *over*consumption of

10. You Must Always Keep a Spirit of Gratefulness for God's Gift of Creation

Environmental issues call for a spiritual response, inspired by the belief that creation is a gift that God has entrusted to your loving care. A person's attitude toward nature should be one of gratitude to the God who has created it and supports it.

This tenth commandment, or principle, for the environment is a reminder that creation is good, *because of the Creator*. God is both the origin and destiny of the whole world. This is not just a lofty sentiment, but rather the eternal truth that should animate discussions and actions for the environment.

As the Psalmist proclaims:

How varied are your works, LORD!

In wisdom you have wrought them all;

the earth is full of your creatures.
Look at the sea, great and wide!
    It teems with countless beings,
        living things both large and small. . . .
All of these look to you
    to give them food in due time.
When you give it to them, they gather;
    when you open your hand, they are well filled.

When you hide your face, they are lost.
    When you take away their breath, they perish
        and return to the dust from which they came.
When you send forth your breath, they are created
    and you renew the face of the earth.
(Ps 104:24–25, 27–30)

SECTION ASSESSMENT

NOTE TAKING

Use the summary statements and examples of the ten commandments for the environment you listed in your chart to help you complete the following items.

1. Explain the balance between materialism and nature.
2. Why is creation inherently *good*?
3. What must economic development always keep in mind?
4. Share an example showing why it is necessary for national governments to collaborate with one another on environmental issues.

COMPREHENSION

5. Describe two ways the Church responded to the oil spill in the Gulf of Mexico.
6. Why is it not appropriate to refer to the earth or creation as "Mother Earth"?
7. Give an example of why the poor are frequently the most affected by environmental problems.
8. When does enjoying the goods of creation become wrong or sinful?

CRITICAL THINKING

9. What does God's command to "subdue the earth" mean in how you are to live your life?
10. Contrast the view of nature as a gift from God with nature as divine itself.

Section Summaries

Focus Question

How are you a steward of God's creation?

Complete one of the following:

Read paragraphs 466, 481–482, and 486–487 from the *Compendium of the Social Doctrine of the Church*. It is available at www.vatican.va. Summarize these paragraphs in one or two paragraphs.

Photograph some favorite nature scenes. Then, take contrasting photos of places ruined or disfigured by human activity and misuse. Create a multimedia presentation to depict the contrast between God's beauty and human folly.

Pick one of the evidences of assault on the environment from the feature "The Environmental Reality Today" (pages 288–289). Research this issue. Write a one-page report that updates the statistics from the feature and details new efforts being made to correct this environmental problem.

INTRODUCTION (PAGES 281–285)

The Goodness of God's Creation

God's truth, beauty, and goodness are seen in creation. And yet, your relationship with the created world has been altered by sin. Christ came to reconcile the world to himself, and thus, in him, your relationship with creation.

Write a prayer that praises God for the beauty of his creation. You might want to accompany the prayer with an illustration or other art.

SECTION 1 (PAGES 286–293)

The Scope of Modern Environmental Issues

Like many issues of social justice, caring for God's creation is not an isolated act. It is related to respecting the dignity of the human person, the preferential option for the poor, the avoidance of a consumerist mentality, and the virtues of solidarity and subsidiarity.

Research Catholic Relief Services' initiatives to provide clean water and sanitation to develping countries. Report your findings to the class.

SECTION 2 (PAGES 294–297)

The Environment and Other Social Concerns

The goodness of the created world is under assault from improper use of natural resources. Humans are not the only part of the natural world, but they are the most important part. Humanity is called to stewardship of the environment. Being a steward means being able to use the created goods of the world, but also requires being a protector of creation.

 Research and report on environmental clean-up volunteer opportunities in your local community. Often, local parks, rivers, lakes, and other places have days in which people nearby can help pick up litter or clean up graffiti.

SECTION 3 (PAGES 298–305)

The Ten Commandments for the Environment

To summarize the Church's teaching on the environment, Bishop Giampaolo Crepaldi proposed the ten commandments, or guidelines, for Catholics and the environment based on the teachings in the *Compendium of the Social Doctrine of the Church*. They focus on the reality that creation is a *gift* God has given to humans, who have been entrusted with its care.

 Pick one of the commandments of the environment and prepare an action plan for implementing it in your own life.

Chapter Assignments

1. Learn and Act

 The United States Conference of Catholic Bishops offer four broad suggestions for ensuring a safe and healthy environment. A synopsis of their recommended steps follows:

- Survey groups and organizations in your community working on issues related to the environment;

- Chart news coverage pertaining to the environment (e.g., incidences of asthma, childhood cancer, children's exposure to lead, pesticide use in public areas like parks and school facilities, housing and building code violations);

- Make your understanding and concerns about the health of the environment and the health of children known to your community, state, and national leaders;

- Create a coalition of key individuals and groups in your community regarding the environment.

Work with a group of peers and adults, both within your school community and outside of it, to develop a detailed plan for addressing an environmental concern. Write a three-page report detailing your plan, including how the steps above will be incorporated. Include a timetable for how the plan will be enacted.

See the USCCB website for more information: http://www.usccb.org/issues-and-action/human-life-and-dignity/environment/what-can-you-do-to-ensure-a-safe-and-healthy-environment.cfm.

2. Research an Ecological Issue

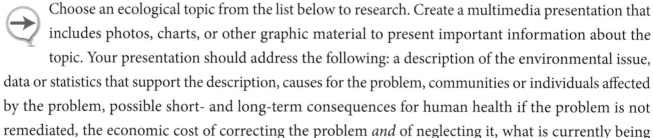 Choose an ecological topic from the list below to research. Create a multimedia presentation that includes photos, charts, or other graphic material to present important information about the topic. Your presentation should address the following: a description of the environmental issue, data or statistics that support the description, causes for the problem, communities or individuals affected by the problem, possible short- and long-term consequences for human health if the problem is not remediated, the economic cost of correcting the problem *and* of neglecting it, what is currently being done to address the problem, and what more needs to be done.

In addition, your presentation should include a call to action for your peers, encouraging them to take specific steps to respond to the problem. Remember, too, that your presentation should reflect a Catholic perspective on the environment.

Choose from the following topics:

- water pollution

- air pollution

- deforestation

- global warming

- ozone depletion

- dangers in the use of pesticides

- toxic waste disposal

- endangered species

3. Archaeological Display

 Set up an "archaeological display" of ten items that you feel will be obsolete or extinct by the turn of the century—that is, by 2100.

For each item, write a description of the item and how it went extinct. For example,

- Display an empty can of motor oil. Explain how cars used to burn a nonrenewable energy source that caused pollution. Tell what replaced the gas-powered automobile.

- Display the console of a gaming system with some game cartridges. Explain a new concept in gaming for children and teens.

Share ideas for many other items that might be used for packaging, transportation, communication, and education.

Finally, write two paragraphs explaining how the earth will be more ecologically friendly in 2100 than it is today. Include references to Catholic teaching on stewardship.

Faithful Disciple

St. Francis of Assisi

St. Francis Speaking to the Birds *by Giotto, ca. 1296*

In 1979, St. John Paul II named St. Francis of Assisi the patron saint of ecology. This simple man is one of the most popular Christian saints.

St. Francis's mother had him baptized John (Giovanni) after St. John the Baptist. However, when his absent father Peter Bernardone found out, he changed the baby's name to Francesco ("Frenchman") to reflect the father's love for France. Peter did not want his son dedicated to religion. His dream for St. Francis was that he would come to admire his own worldly ways—that of a cloth merchant and lover of France.

During his youth, Francis lived a carefree life of self-indulgence. He longed to be a noble and, in his own mind, achieved some glory when he was imprisoned after a petty war with a neighboring town. After a year-long imprisonment, Francis returned to his former life but longed for even greater glory. He joined in the efforts of a local war, but not a day's ride from Assisi he had a powerful dream in which God revealed to him that he was seeking glory in the wrong place. Francis returned home to mocking villagers and to an angry father who felt St. Francis wasted money on armor for a battle he would never fight.

Francis turned to prayer and shed tears over his former, dissolute life. A turning point came when Francis kissed the hand of a leper, someone whose physical appearance disgusted him. When the leper returned his kiss of peace, Francis felt an indescribable joy. When he began to ride off and turned to look back at the leper, Francis saw that the leper had disappeared. He interpreted this as a sign from God.

Soon after, Francis was praying at San Damiano church and heard a voice from the cross say, "Francis, go rebuild my Church, which you see is falling into ruins." At first he took these words literally and he set out to repair the ancient church at San Damiano, paying for the repairs from the proceeds of some of his father's goods. His father thought his son a madman and took him to the local bishop to disinherit him. In response, Francis renounced his father's wealth, even stripping off the clothes his father had given him. From that day on, Francis begged for his food, preached, and joyfully sang about God's goodness.

Not long after this, in 1209, Francis heard a sermon that changed his life even more dramatically. The sermon was about the commissioning of the disciples (see Matthew 10:5–15), in which Jesus instructed his followers to go forth and proclaim the kingdom without taking "gold or silver or copper for your belts; no sack for the journey, or a second tunic, or sandals, or walking stick" (verses 9–10). Francis was inspired to devote his life to this life of poverty and complete dependence on God.

Francis sought permission from Pope Innocent II to found a new religious order. Although the pope at first had doubts, in April 1210 he approved the founding of the Franciscan Order, a mendicant order, whose members begged for their sustenance as they joyfully proclaimed the Gospel. St. Francis and his brothers preached in the streets and had no possessions.

St. Francis's love embraced all of nature as part of God's creation, and preached that all of God's creatures had an ability and duty to praise him, and that humankind had a duty to protect God's creation. Many stories about St. Francis tell of his love for God's creatures. In one, St. Francis preached to the birds and told them to thank God for how he clothed them, for their freedom, and for God's care. The story tells how the birds quieted down when St. Francis was with them and only flew off when he gave them permission to do so.

Another famous story tells about Francis's taming of a wolf that had been attacking a town, devouring human beings for food. When the outraged citizens wanted to kill the wolf, St. Francis spoke to the wolf and ordered him not to kill any more humans. The wolf obeyed and, before long, became a pet who was well fed by the townsfolk.

St. Francis found God in all things: in sunrises and sunsets, in the smile of a baby, in a sparrow winging its way across an open field, in a gentle babbling brook, in grass growing, in leaves falling. He taught his followers to praise and thank God for all his creation and all his gifts. His example encourages people today to care for, and respect, God's precious creation.

To finish St. Francis's story: In his lifetime, his ever-growing order experienced dissension. Some friars argued for more organization. They decided it was impractical for such a large order not to own goods. St. Francis saw that times were changing and eventually surrendered his leadership role. He and a few followers retired to a mountain retreat at La Alvernia, where St. Francis suffered much in his last years.

St. Francis's profound devotion to the suffering Lord led to his receiving the stigmata, the five wounds of Christ. His austere life had led to blindness and suffering, but toward the end of his life, he composed the beautiful "Canticle of the Sun," a hymn praising God for his awesome creation. St. Francis died on October 4, 1226, at the age of forty-five.

 ## Reading Comprehension

1. How did St. Francis seek glory in the wrong places in his youth?
2. What effect did the sermon about the commissioning of the disciples have on St. Francis?
3. What did St. Francis teach about the created world?
4. What did St. Francis receive at the end of his life?

 ## Writing Task

- What possession, interest, activity, or relationship would you find most difficult to give up for the Lord? Why?

Explaining the Faith

If Catholics are supposed to care for God's creation, is it permissible to eat meat?

Yes. Animals are to be treated well in that they are part of God's created world; however, because God has given man dominion over creation, one may use animals for food, clothing, labor, and transportation. Scientific experimentation on animals is also acceptable if it remains within reasonable limits and contributes to caring for or saving human lives (see *CCC*, 2417).

At times people falsely anthropomorphize animals; that is, give human attributes to them. Remember that humans are markedly different from animals, notably in that humans have an immortal soul, which includes having an intellect and a will. And thus, it is permissible to utilize animals for humans' benefit, but, as with all of God's creation, one may never misuse them, such as through torture. Again, *using* a gift like creation is vastly different from *abusing* it. This is the crux of this theme.

Further Research

- Read paragraphs 2415–2418 from the *Catechism of the Catholic Church*. Explain the meaning of the statement "One can love animals; one should not direct to them the affection due only to persons" (*CCC*, 2418) in light of these four paragraphs.

Prayer
Canticle of the Sun

O most High, almighty, good Lord God,
   to you belong praise, glory, honor, and all
   blessing!
Praised be my Lord God with all creatures;
   and especially our brother the sun,
   which brings us the day and the light;
   fair is he, and shining with a very great
   splendor:
   O Lord, he signifies you to us!
Praised be my Lord for our sister the moon,
   and for the stars,
   which God has set clear and lovely in heaven.
Praised be my Lord for our brother the wind,
   and for air and cloud, calms and all weather,
   by which you uphold in life all creatures.
Praised be my Lord for our sister water,
   which is very serviceable to us,
   and humble, and precious, and clean.
Praised be my Lord for brother fire,
   through which you give us light in the
   darkness;
   and he is bright, and pleasant, and very
   mighty,
   and strong.

Praised be my Lord for our sister the Earth,
   which sustains us and keeps us,
   and yields diverse fruits, and flowers of many
   colors, and grass.
Praised be my Lord for all those who pardon
   one another for God's love's sake,
   and who endure weakness and tribulation;
   blessed are they who peaceably shall endure,
   for you, O most High, shall give them a
   crown!
Praised be my Lord for our sister,
   the death of the body, from which no one
   escapes,
   Woe to him who died in mortal sin!
   Blessed are they who are found walking
   by your most holy will,
   for the second death shall have no
   power to do them harm.
Praise you, and bless you the Lord
   and give thanks to God, and serve God with
   great humility.

—St. Francis of Assisi

Beliefs

Apostles' Creed

I believe in God,
the Father almighty,
Creator of heaven and earth,
and in Jesus Christ, his only Son, our Lord,
who was conceived by the Holy Spirit
born of the Virgin Mary,
suffered under Pontius Pilate,
was crucified, died and was buried;
he descended into hell;
on the third day he rose again from the dead;
he ascended into heaven,
and is seated at the right hand of God the Father
    almighty;
from there he will come to judge the living and
    the dead.

I believe in the Holy Spirit,
the holy catholic Church,
the communion of saints,
the forgiveness of sins,
the resurrection of the body,
and life everlasting. Amen.

Nicene Creed

I believe in one God,
the Father almighty,
maker of heaven and earth,
of all things visible and invisible.

I believe in one Lord Jesus Christ,
the Only Begotten Son of God,
born of the Father before all ages.
God from God, Light from Light,
true God from true God,
begotten, not made, consubstantial with the Father;
through him all things were made.
For us men and for our salvation
he came down from heaven,
and by the Holy Spirit was incarnate of the Virgin
    Mary, and became man.
For our sake he was crucified under Pontius Pilate,
he suffered death and was buried,
and rose again on the third day
in accordance with the Scriptures.
He ascended into heaven
and is seated at the right hand of the Father.
He will come again in glory
to judge the living and the dead
and his kingdom will have no end.

I believe in the Holy Spirit, the Lord, the giver of
    life,
who proceeds from the Father and the Son,
who with the Father and the Son is adored and
    glorified,
who has spoken through the prophets.

I believe in one, holy, catholic, and apostolic
    Church.
I confess one Baptism for the forgiveness of sins
and I look forward to the resurrection of the dead
and the life of the world to come. Amen.

Moral Life

The Ten Commandments

The Ten Commandments are a main source for Christian morality. God revealed the Ten Commandments to Moses. Jesus himself acknowledged them. He told the rich young man, "If you wish to enter into life, keep the commandments" (Mt 19:17). Since the time of St. Augustine in the fourth century, the Ten Commandments have been used as a source for teaching baptismal candidates. See pages 316–318 for a list and reflections on the The Ten Commandments.

The Beatitudes

The word *beatitude* means "happiness." Jesus preached the Beatitudes in his Sermon on the Mount. See page 325 for a list and reflections on the Beatitudes.

Cardinal Virtues

Habits that help in leading moral lives that are acquired by human effort are known as moral or human virtues. Four of these are the cardinal virtues. They form the hinge that connects all the others.

- *Prudence*: the virtue that inclines you to lead a good, ethical, and moral life.

- *Justice*: the virtue that offers you the firm will to give God and others their due.

- *Fortitude*: the virtue that ensures you have "firmness in difficulties and constancy in the pursuit of the good" (CCC, 1808).

- *Temperance*: the virtue that regulates your attraction to pleasure and helps you use God's created good in a balanced way.

Theological Virtues

The theological virtues are the foundation for a moral life. They are related directly to God.

- *Faith*: the virtue that is your acknowledgment of and allegiance to God.

- *Hope*: the virtue by which you desire Heaven and eternal life as your happiness.

- *Love*: the virtue by which you show charity or love to God above all things for his own sake and love your neighbor as yourself for the love of God.

Corporal (Bodily) Works of Mercy

1. Feed the hungry.
2. Give drink to the thirsty.
3. Clothe the naked.
4. Visit the imprisoned.
5. Shelter the homeless.
6. Visit the sick.
7. Bury the dead.

Spiritual Works of Mercy

1. Counsel the doubtful.
2. Instruct the ignorant.
3. Admonish the sinner.
4. Comfort the sorrowful.
5. Forgive all injuries.
6. Bear wrongs patiently.
7. Pray for the living and the dead.

Precepts of the Church

1. You shall attend Mass on Sundays and on holy days of obligation and rest from servile labor.

2. You shall confess your sins at least once a year.

3. You shall receive the Sacrament of Eucharist at least during the Easter season.

4. You shall observe the days of fasting and abstinence established by the Church.

5. You shall help to provide for the needs of the Church.

Sin and the Sacrament of Penance

Types of Sins

Sin is an offense against God.

Mortal sin is the most serious kind of sin. Mortal sin destroys or kills a person's relationship with God. To be a mortal sin, three conditions must exist:

- The moral object must be of grave or serious matter. Grave matter is specified in the Ten Commandments (e.g., do not kill, do not commit adultery, do not steal, etc.).

- The person must have full knowledge of the gravity of the sinful action.

- The person must completely consent to the action. It must be a personal choice.

Venial sin is less serious sin. Examples of venial sins are petty jealousy, disobedience, and "borrowing" a small amount of money from a parent without the intention of repaying it. Venial sins, when not repented, can lead a person to commit mortal sins.

Vices are bad habits linked to sins. The seven capital vices are pride, avarice, envy, wrath, lust, gluttony, and sloth.

The Effects of the Sacrament of Penance

The Sacrament of Penance brings about forgiveness of sins, which in turn makes communion with God possible. "The whole power of the sacrament of Penance consists in restoring us to God's grace and joining us with him in an intimate friendship" (*Roman Catechism*, II, V, 18, quoted in *CCC*, 1468). The sacrament also brings about reconciliation with the Church, bringing the sinner again into communion with all members of Christ's Mystical Body. Catholics are required to confess to a priest in the Sacrament of Penance all unconfessed grave or mortal sins they remember after carefully examining their conscience. It is recommended to confess venial sins.

A penitent may confess his or her sins anonymously or face-to-face with the priest.

Examination of Conscience Based on the Ten Commandments

Before celebrating the Sacrament of Penance, it is important for both the celebrant and the penitent to prepare. As the *Rite of Penance* explains, the confessor "should call upon the Holy Spirit so that he may receive enlightenment and charity" (Intro, *Rite of Penance*, 15). You, as penitent, also have preparation to do. You should make time for an honest examination of conscience so that we can acknowledge any sins that have been committed since the last confession and pray for God's mercy.

Here is a sample examination of conscience based on the Ten Commandments (adapted from the *Rite of Penance*, pp. 441–445) you may wish to use:

I. I am the Lord your God: you shall not have strange gods before me.

- Is my heart set on God, so that I really love him above all things and am faithful to his commandments, as a child loves a parent? Or am I more concerned about the things of this world? Have I a right intention in what I do? Is my faith in God firm and secure?

- Am I wholehearted in accepting the Church's teachings? Have I been careful to grow in my understanding of the faith, to hear God's Word, to listen to instructions on the faith, to avoid dangers to faith?

- Have I been always strong and fearless in professing my faith in God and the Church? Have I been willing to be known as a Christian in private and public life?

- Have I prayed morning and evening? When I pray, do I really raise my mind and heart to God, or is it a matter of words only? Do I offer God my difficulties, my joys, and my sorrows? Do I turn to God in time of temptation?

II. You shall not take the name of the Lord your God in vain.

- Have I love and reverence for God's name?

- Have I offended God in blasphemy, swearing falsely, or taking his name in vain?

- Have I shown disrespect for the Blessed Virgin Mary and the saints?

III. Remember to keep holy the Lord's Day.

- Do I keep Sundays and feast days holy by taking a full part, with attention and devotion, in the liturgy, and especially in the Mass? Have I fulfilled the precept of annual confession and of Communion during the Easter season?

- Are there false gods I worship by giving them greater attention and deeper trust than I give to God—including money, superstition, or occult practices?

IV. Honor your father and your mother.

- In my family life, have I contributed to the well-being and happiness of the rest of the family by patience and genuine love? Have I been obedient to my parents, showing them proper respect and giving them help in their spiritual and material needs?

- Have I obeyed legitimate authority and given it due respect?

- If I am given a position of responsibility or authority, do I use this for my own advantage, or for the good of others, in a spirit of service?

V. You shall not kill.

- Have I done violence to others by causing damage to life or limb, reputation, honor, or material possessions? Have I involved them in loss?

- Have I been responsible for advising an abortion or procuring one?

- Have I kept up hatred for others? Am I estranged from others through quarrels, hatred, insults, or anger?

- If I have been injured, have I been ready to make peace for the love of Christ and to forgive, or do I harbor hatred and the desire for revenge?

VI. You shall not commit adultery.

IX. You shall not covet your neighbor's wife.

- Do I have a genuine love for my neighbors? Or do I use others for my own ends or treat them badly?

- Have I given grave scandal by my words or actions?

- Have I imposed my will on others, without respecting their freedom and rights?

- Have I kept my senses and body pure and chaste? Have I dishonored my body by fornication, impure acts, unworthy conversation or unchaste thoughts, evil desires, or actions? Have I indulged in reading, conversation, Internet sites, and entertainment that offend against Christian and human decency? Have I encouraged others to sin by my own failure to maintain these standards?

VII. You shall not steal.

X. You shall not covet your neighbor's goods.

- Do I share my possessions with the less fortunate? Do I do my best to help the victims of oppression, misfortune, and poverty? Or do I look down on my neighbor, especially the poor, the sick, the elderly, strangers, and people of other races?

- Do I share in the apostolic and charitable works of the Church and in the life of my parish? Have I helped meet the needs of the Church and of the world and prayed for unity in the Church, for the spread of the Gospel among the nations, for peace and justice, etc.?

- Am I concerned for the good and prosperity of the human community in which I live, or do I spend my life caring only for myself? Do I share to the best of my ability in the work of promoting justice, morality, harmony, and love in human relations?

- In my work, am I just, hardworking, honest, and loving? Have I been faithful to my promises?

- Have I stolen the property of others? Have I desired the property of others unjustly and inordinately?

Have I damaged it? Have I made restitution of other people's property and made good their loss?

VIII. You shall not bear false witness against your neighbor.

- Have I been truthful and fair, or have I injured others by deceit, slander, rash judgment, or the violation of a secret?

- Have I refused to testify to the innocence of another because of selfishness?

After examining your conscience, sincerely tell God you are sorry for your sins. Ask God for forgiveness and for the grace you will need to change what needs changing in your life. Promise God you will try to live according to his will for you. You are ready to celebrate the Sacrament of Penance.

How to Go to Confession

1. Approach the area for confession. Wait an appropriate distance until it is your turn.

2. Make the Sign of the Cross with the priest and say, "Bless me, Father, for I have sinned." He may say: "May God, who has enlightened every heart, help you to know your sins and trust his mercy." You reply: "Amen." Indicate the last time you went to Confession; for example, say, "It's been _____ since my last Confession."

3. Confess your sins to the priest. Simply and directly talk to him about the areas of sinfulness in your life that need God's healing touch.

4. The priest will ask you to pray an Act of Contrition. Pray an Act of Contrition you have committed to memory, for example:

O my God,
    I am heartily sorry for having offended you.

After you confess your sins, the priest extends his hand and prays the Church's prayer of absolution.

I detest all my sins because I dread the loss of Heaven

and the pains of hell.

But most of all because they offend you, my God,

Who are all good and deserving of all my love.

I firmly resolve,

with the help of your grace to sin no more

and to avoid the near occasions of sin.

Amen.

Or, say something in your own words, like: "Dear God, I am sorry for my sins. I ask for your forgiveness, and I promise to do better in the future."

5. The priest will talk to you about your life, encourage you to be more faithful to God in the future, and help you decide what to do to make up for your sins—your penance.

6. The priest will then extend his hands over your head and pray the Church's official prayer of absolution:

God, the Father of mercies, through the death and resurrection of his Son, has reconciled the world to himself and sent the Holy Spirit among us for the forgiveness of sins; through the ministry of the Church may God give you pardon and peace, and I absolve you from your sins in the name of the Father, and of the Son, and of the Holy Spirit.

You respond: "Amen."

9. The priest will wish you peace. Thank him and leave.

10. Go to a quiet place in church and pray your prayer of penance. Then spend time quietly thanking God for the gift of forgiveness.

Catholic Social Teaching

and Historic Milestones

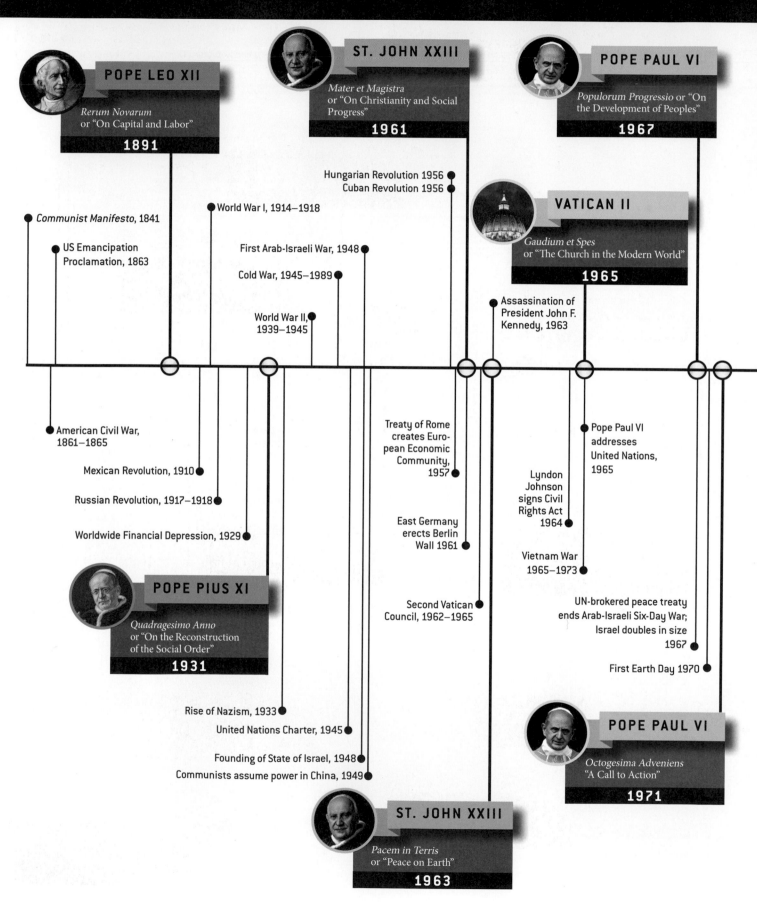

POPE LEO XII

Rerum Novarum or "On Capital and Labor"

1891

ST. JOHN XXIII

Mater et Magistra or "On Christianity and Social Progress"

1961

POPE PAUL VI

Populorum Progressio or "On the Development of Peoples"

1967

VATICAN II

Gaudium et Spes or "The Church in the Modern World"

1965

Hungarian Revolution 1956
Cuban Revolution 1956

Communist *Manifesto*, 1841

World War I, 1914–1918

US Emancipation Proclamation, 1863

First Arab-Israeli War, 1948

Cold War, 1945–1989

Assassination of President John F. Kennedy, 1963

World War II, 1939–1945

American Civil War, 1861–1865

Treaty of Rome creates European Economic Community, 1957

Pope Paul VI addresses United Nations, 1965

Mexican Revolution, 1910

Lyndon Johnson signs Civil Rights Act 1964

Russian Revolution, 1917–1918

East Germany erects Berlin Wall 1961

Worldwide Financial Depression, 1929

Vietnam War 1965–1973

UN-brokered peace treaty ends Arab-Israeli Six-Day War; Israel doubles in size 1967

First Earth Day 1970

POPE PIUS XI

Quadragesimo Anno or "On the Reconstruction of the Social Order"

1931

Second Vatican Council, 1962–1965

Rise of Nazism, 1933

United Nations Charter, 1945

Founding of State of Israel, 1948

Communists assume power in China, 1949

POPE PAUL VI

Octogesima Adveniens "A Call to Action"

1971

ST. JOHN XXIII

Pacem in Terris or "Peace on Earth"

1963

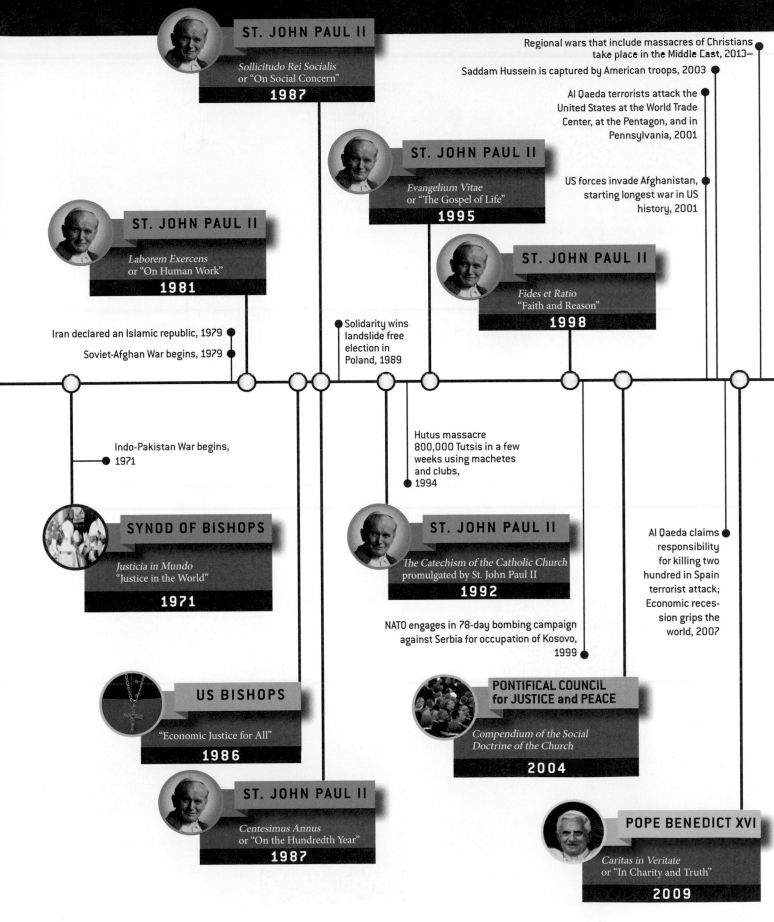

ST. JOHN PAUL II

Sollicitudo Rei Socialis
or "On Social Concern"

1987

Regional wars that include massacres of Christians
take place in the Middle East, 2013–

Saddam Hussein is captured by American troops, 2003

Al Qaeda terrorists attack the
United States at the World Trade
Center, at the Pentagon, and in
Pennsylvania, 2001

ST. JOHN PAUL II

Evangelium Vitae
or "The Gospel of Life"

1995

US forces invade Afghanistan,
starting longest war in US
history, 2001

ST. JOHN PAUL II

Laborem Exercens
or "On Human Work"

1981

ST. JOHN PAUL II

Fides et Ratio
"Faith and Reason"

1998

Iran declared an Islamic republic, 1979

Soviet-Afghan War begins, 1979

Solidarity wins
landslide free
election in
Poland, 1989

Indo-Pakistan War begins,
1971

Hutus massacre
800,000 Tutsis in a few
weeks using machetes
and clubs,
1994

SYNOD OF BISHOPS

Justicia in Mundo
"Justice in the World"

1971

ST. JOHN PAUL II

The Catechism of the Catholic Church
promulgated by St. John Paul II

1992

Al Qaeda claims
responsibility
for killing two
hundred in Spain
terrorist attack;
Economic reces-
sion grips the
world, 2007

NATO engages in 78-day bombing campaign
against Serbia for occupation of Kosovo,
1999

US BISHOPS

"Economic Justice for All"

1986

**PONTIFICAL COUNCIL
for JUSTICE and PEACE**

*Compendium of the Social
Doctrine of the Church*

2004

ST. JOHN PAUL II

Centesimus Annus
or "On the Hundredth Year"

1987

POPE BENEDICT XVI

Caritas in Veritate
or "In Charity and Truth"

2009

Epilogue: Discipleship

Throughout this course you have examined the implications of what it means to be a *social* being. You now know that no person is truly ever isolated; your very nature bespeaks a communion with others. Ultimately, this mirrors the inner life of the Trinity. Sadly, however, you have seen that within relationships with others, often injustices and other difficulties can emerge. The Church in her wisdom guides you in how to manage these adversities and live a full humanity, always aimed at the common good.

Catholic social teaching is not some abstract concept for theologians to discuss or politicians to debate; rather, it is a concrete reality that should guide your life and the lives of others. And thus, you are brought to the question: What does all of this have

Daily choices to care for and converse with those who need you are part of your task as a disciple of Christ.

to do with *me*? You have seen hints to your personal role within Catholic social teaching; now it is time to look more specifically at your calling to transform the world, one social relationship at a time.

Encountering Christ

A newspaper once asked the famous Catholic author, G. K. Chesterton, "What's wrong with the world?" He responded: "I am." That simple notion is actually quite profound. You can point fingers at others—the government, corporations, etc.—but, any true change has to

begin with you. Jesus has called you to be his **disciple**. This is not an optional request for the person serious about living out their Catholic faith and transforming the social order.

Foremost, it begins with your relationship with Christ and how you live this relationship in your daily life. In order to be his disciple, you must take up your cross and follow him (Mt 6:24). However, being a disciple is more than *just* following Christ; rather, you are to conform your life to his very self. The *Catechism of the Catholic Church* teaches, "Christ enables us to live in him all that he himself lived, and he lives it in us" (*CCC*, 521). And St. Paul proclaims, "I have been crucified with Christ; yet I live, no longer I, but Christ lives in me" (Gal 2:19–20).

> **disciple** A follower of Jesus Christ. The word disciple comes from a Latin word that means "learner."

The brokenness of the world is a sign of the effects of Original Sin, and thus points to the need for Redemption. At the root of all social problems is a need for Christ, because he is the answer to *every* human longing. By virtue of your reception of the Sacraments of Christian Initiation, you have the common calling to be holy and to evangelize the world. Essentially, you are to permeate the world around you with the truth and beauty of Christ, both in your words and example. However, you cannot bring Christ to the world without first encountering him yourself. In order to be an evangelizing disciple, you must commit yourself to God, no matter the cost. You must cultivate your gifts and talents for the service of the Kingdom of God.

This encountering of Christ happens foremost in the sacraments, through which you can receive the very presence of Christ. Pope Benedict XVI spoke about the importance of receiving the Eucharist, in order that one might turn away from individualism to serve others in the social life, especially the most vulnerable. The Eucharist, he said, "leads to the rediscovery of gratuitousness, the centrality of relationships, beginning with the family, with a particular care for binding the wounds of the broken."[1]

Encountering Culture

Whether you realize it or not, you are part of a certain **culture**. In fact, you are probably part of many different cultures—your American culture, the teen culture, the culture of your region, your family, your ancestors, and so forth. Cardinal Avery Dulles explained how culture can be even more significant than political and economic societies:

> The political and economic orders, important though they obviously are, do not exhaust the reality of human life and human society. They deal only with particular aspects of life in community. More fundamental than either is the

Cardinal Avery Dulles

order of culture, which deals with the meaning and goal of human existence in its full range. Culture shapes and expresses our ideas and attitudes regarding all the typical human experiences, and in so doing touches on the transcendent mystery that engulfs us and draws us to itself. ("God's Gift of Freedom Must be Used to Choose the Good," *Acton Institute*, November, 2011*)*

Part of being a disciple of Jesus Christ is influencing your particular culture. God himself entered a

> **culture** The personality of a society. As understood in Catholic social philosophy, culture is the totality of a people's traditions (what they believe), attitudes (what they desire), customs (what they do), and institutions (how they live).

culture in the person of Jesus Christ, and the Church has for ages spoken to the various cultures in which she lived.

Regarding the modern world, as you learned in Chapter 3, St. John Paul II defined the dramatic conflict between the "culture of life"—one that respects the dignity of the human person—and the "culture of death"—one that denies the dignity of the human person.[2] He warned that the world is being infiltrated by the "culture of death." This is apparent with such literal examples as widespread abortion, war, and famine. However, the "culture of death" can also be seen through such tragedies as broken families; music, television, and movies that degrade human dignity and basic moral values; the loneliness that is associated with greed and consumerism; and the widespread acceptance of immoral lifestyles like same-sex unions and cohabitation.

As a disciple in the modern world, you have the choice *every day* whether to live the "culture of life" or the "culture of death." You have the obligation for your own generation, and generations to come, to embrace the power of the Cross so as to build a "culture of life" in your particular societies. Part of this is realizing that your faith should infiltrate every aspect of your lives— your families, your friendships, your school life, your jobs, and so on. Each of your social interactions can be a means to build up the "culture of life," or they can lead to its degradation.

One of the biggest struggles in this pursuit to positively build up the culture is the fight against secularism, in which faith is separated from the other aspects of life and society. In secularism, one's faith becomes something that just happens on Sunday or in the privacy of home, instead of being a part of *every* aspect of the person's life. The Second Vatican Council's *Gaudium et Spes* warned that "one of the gravest errors of our time is the dichotomy between the faith which many profess and the practice of their daily lives" (§43).

Your social relationships can either build up life or destroy it.

It is important to note that not every aspect of the modern culture is evil. Rather, the Church sees what is good and allows it to be renewed in Christ, so that society may be transformed into one that upholds human dignity. *Gaudium et Spes* continued: "In this way the Church carries out its mission and in that very act it stimulates and advances human and civil culture, as well as contributing by its activity, including liturgical activity, to man's interior freedom."[3]

THE
BEATITUDES
and DISCIPLESHIP

RELATED TO THE THEME OF DISCIPLESHIP, THE BEATITUDES OFFER AN ESSENTIAL BLUEPRINT FOR THE CHRISTIAN LIFE. THESE FAMOUS EXHORTATIONS OF CHRIST ARE AT THE ROOT OF DISCIPLESHIP. WHILE THE BEATITUDES HAVE IMPLICATIONS FOR A PERSON'S OWN PERSONAL AND SPIRITUAL LIVES, THEY ALSO HAVE A SOCIAL DIMENSION. THE UNITED STATES CATHOLIC BISHOPS EXPLAINED THIS SOCIAL ASPECT:*

BLESSED ARE THE POOR IN SPIRIT, FOR THEIRS IS THE KINGDOM OF HEAVEN.

Work to choose a lifestyle that benefits those most in need; otherwise, your life may tend toward materialism, selfishness, and exploitation of others.

BLESSED ARE THOSE WHO MOURN, FOR THEY SHALL BE COMFORTED.

Be compassionate to those in pain. You cannot cease caring for the living and defenseless.

BLESSED ARE THE MEEK, FOR THEY SHALL INHERIT THE EARTH.

Develop self-discipline in the face of evil, which includes gentleness and unselfishness. Work to overcome violence, arrogance, and disrespect toward others.

BLESSED ARE THE MERCIFUL, FOR THEY SHALL OBTAIN MERCY.

Forgive one another and be quick to ask forgiveness. Don't hold grudges, for that only brings growth in bitterness.

BLESSED ARE THOSE WHO HUNGER AND THIRST FOR RIGHTEOUSNESS, FOR THEY SHALL BE SATISFIED.

Develop a social conscience, in which you are outraged at injustices. You cannot be indifferent to the mistreatment of others.

BLESSED ARE THE PURE IN HEART, FOR THEY SHALL SEE GOD.

Work on the virtues of modesty and chastity to combat the many expressions of lust in yourself and your society.

BLESSED ARE THE PEACEMAKERS, FOR THEY SHALL BE CALLED SONS OF GOD.

Understand that only in God's will can you find peace. Avoid being a divider, troublemaker, or warmonger. Rather, perform works of peace.

BLESSED ARE YOU WHEN MEN REVILE YOU AND PERSECUTE YOU AND UTTER ALL KINDS OF EVIL AGAINST YOU FALSELY ON MY ACCOUNT. REJOICE AND BE GLAD, FOR YOUR REWARD IS GREAT IN HEAVEN.

Always witness to Jesus and the Church, even unto death. Root out all cowardice and moral compromise in our lives.

Living the Themes of Catholic Social Teaching

This course examined Catholic social teaching through the lens of the seven themes presented by the United States Catholic Bishops. Hopefully, there have been certain issues that particularly struck you and challenged you. Here are some concrete actions you can take to live out each of the seven themes as a disciple of Jesus Christ in the modern world.

1. Life and Dignity of the Human Person (Chapter 3)

- Always have a profound respect for every person you meet. This includes valuing your *own* dignity and worth.

- Work to fight unjust laws that deny the dignity of all human life, such as laws that allow abortion or the unjust use of the death penalty.

- Start a pro-life club at your school, in which you keep up-to-date on human life issues and raise awareness of them within your school and the wider community.

- Volunteer at a crisis pregnancy center that aids women contemplating abortion.

Search out organizations that support pro-life responses at all times of the life spectrum.

2. Call to Family, Community, and Participation (Chapter 4)

- Live a life of chastity, in which you view others as persons to be valued, not means to your own gratification. This includes dressing modestly and avoiding occasions of sin that would lead you to impurity. For married couples, this includes being faithful to one's spouse and being open to life by not using artificial means of contraception.

- Work to support laws that uphold marriage as a lifelong commitment between a man and a woman that is open to life.

3. Rights and Responsibilities (Chapter 5)

- Always remember the balance between appreciating your human rights and taking responsibility for duties associated with these rights. This involves avoiding the attitude of, "well, someone *else* will take care of that problem." Very often, you *are* that someone else.

- Become involved in your parishes, neighborhoods, and cities. Volunteer for organizations in your area that work to uphold the dignity of the human person. This could mean supporting political candidates who support the tenets of Catholic social teaching. It especially means using the power of your vote to help elect officials and enact policies that are in accord with the dignity of the human person and the common good.

4. Option for the Poor and Vulnerable (Chapter 6)

- Seek out the poor in your own life. Keep in mind that poverty doesn't just mean lacking material goods; it also can be the poverty of loneliness, abuse, or ignorance. Serving the poor starts in your own home, school, and neighborhood. Perhaps this means tutoring a struggling classmate, comforting a family member going through a difficult time, sitting with the person who is always alone in the lunchroom, gently telling an unaware friend aspects of his or her lifestyle are sinful, or visiting a local nursing home to spend time with the elderly.

- Live a grateful life marked by poverty of spirit, in which you recognize that all you are, and all you have, ultimately comes from God.

- Work to fight poverty in the United States and worldwide through collecting food for food banks, supporting missionaries monetarily and prayerfully, volunteering at a homeless shelter or soup kitchen, becoming involved in outreach programs for teens on the street, or helping build homes for the less fortunate.

5. The Dignity of Work and the Rights of Workers (Chapter 7)

- In your own jobs, be diligent in your efforts in order to give honest work in return for the pay you are receiving.

- Be assiduous in school work and develop your skills and talents now to be able to secure future employment that will bring you joy and help support your family.

- Support families with parents who are unemployed.

- Fight against injustices in the workplace, such as discrimination and child labor.

6. Solidarity (Chapter 8)

- Try to develop more than a vague compassion for the less fortunate; rather, grow in solidarity with others through a true, active empathy. Often this involves becoming educated about others' life situations, without jumping to conclusions or making uninformed judgments.

- Strive for peace within your own life and contest unjust wars.

- Root out any prejudice you may have toward those different than yourself.

7. Care for God's Creation (Chapter 9)

- Respect God-given resources by living a life that is simple, not wasteful. This includes recycling, conserving energy, and avoiding unnecessary pollution through taking public transportation or riding your bike when you can.

This eight-year-old child, part of the Christian minority in Pakistan, works daily at a local brickyard.

Praying as a Disciple

It is important to note that the first "step" in living these themes of Catholic social teaching is always *prayer*. Sometimes injustices seem so much bigger than what you have the power to control, which is true. Often the best thing you can do is prayerfully intercede for those suffering from these injustices. One of the patron saints of social justice is St. Thérèse of Lisieux, who never left her convent in France. However, she constantly prayed for missionary efforts of others, thus giving you an example of the power of intercessory prayer for social woes.

You should also seek out the intercession of Mary, the Mother of God, who was the first and greatest disciple. You can ask for the grace to follow her example of "may it be done to me according to your word" (Lk 1:38) when faced with a challenging situation, especially in transforming society and culture.

The *Compendium of the Social Doctrine of the Church* says, "Love must be present in and permeate every social relationship."[5] Your human nature as a social being is ultimately fulfilled when you are in true communion with others; through this communion, society can become what St. John Paul II deemed a "civilization of love,"[6] in which justice and charity prevail. The world needs more than just ideas and words about justice: it needs Jesus Christ. "No, we shall not be saved by a formula but by a Person and the assurance that he gives us: I am with you!"[7] The task of bringing Christ into every element of society lies with each one of you. And yet, he promises you that, "I am with you always, until the end of the age" (Mt 28:20).

NOTES

1. Social Persons Called to Justice

1. http://catholicdioceseofwichita.org/guadalupe-clinic.

2. *Gaudium et Spes* (*GS*), 22.

3. *Evangelium Vitae* (*EV*), 36.

4. *Compendium of the Social Doctrine of the Church* (*CSDC*), 36.

5. *Lumen Gentium* (*LG*), 1.

6. *Sacrosanctum Concilium* (*SC*), 10.

7. *Mater et Magistra* (*MM*), 1.

8. John Hardon, "Social Justice," in *Modern Catholic Dictionary,* http://www.catholicculture.org/culture/library/dictionary/index.cfm?id=36529 (accessed November 8, 2011).

9. *GS*, 26.

10. *Caritas in Veritate* (*CV*), 2.

11. St. Thomas Aquinas, "Question 57" in *Summa Theologiae*, http://www.newadvent.org/summa/3057.htm (accessed November 8, 2011).

12. *CSDC*, 199.

2. Catholic Social Teaching: Definition and History

1. *GS*, 23, § 1.

2. *LG*, 1.

3. *Veritatis Splendor* (*VS*), 12.

4. St. Ambrose in Paul VI, "On the Development of Peoples (*Populorum Progressio*)," http://www.vatican.va/holy_father/paul_vi/encyclicals/documents/hf_p-vi_enc_26031967_populorum_en.html (accessed November 9, 2011), 23.

5. St. Augustine, *Tractate* 1 John 8,8.

6. *Populorum Progressio,* § 41.

3. Life and Dignity of the Human Person

1. http://news.discovery.com/human/life/china-birth-rate-single-men.htm.

2. http://www.allgirlsallowed.org/blog/posts/2012-injustices-moved-world-action.

3. Karol Wojtyla, *Love and Responsibility* (San Francisco: Ignatius Press, 1993), 41.

4. *CSDC*, 144.

5. John Hardon, "Abortion," in *Modern Catholic Dictionary*, http://www.catholicculture.org/culture/library/dictionary/index.cfm?id=31582 (accessed November 8, 2011).

6. National Right to Life, "Abortion Techniques: Instillation Methods," http://www.nrlc.org/abortion/ASMF/asmf9.html (accessed October 2011).

7. Ibid.

8. Guttmacher Institute, "Facts on Induced Abortion in the United States," (August, 2011), http://www.guttmacher.org/pubs/fb_induced_abortion.html (accessed October 2011).

9. Ibid.

10. Ibid.

11. Religious Leaders Call for New Efforts to Lower the City's 'Chilling' Abortion Rate, *New York Times* (January 6, 2011).

12. *EV*, 12.

13. Norma's story is at this website, http://roenomore.org/ (accessed October 2011).

14. See, for example, St. John Paul II's *Evangelium Vitae* (1995) and the various statements of the American Bishops: http://www.usccb.org/issues-and-action/human-life-and-dignity/abortion/ (accessed October 2011).

15. *EV*, 11.

16. Pope Benedict XVI, "Address of his holiness Benedict XVI to the participants in the plenary session of the Congregation for the Doctrine of the Faith," (January 31, 2008), http://www.vatican.va/holy_father/benedict_xvi/speeches/2008/january/documents/hf_ben-xvi_spe_20080131_dottrina-fede_en.html.

17. Right to Life of Michigan Educational Fund, "Stem Cell Basics," http://www.stemcellresearchcures.com/stem-cells (accessed October 2011).

18. United States Conference of Catholic Bishops, "On Embryonic Stem Cell Research," *United States Conference of Catholic Bishops*, http://old.usccb.org/prolife/issues/bioethic/bishopsESCRstmt.pdf (accessed November 8, 2011).

19. Ibid., 29.

20. *EV*, §56, as cited in *CCC*, 2267.

4. Rewards and Challenges of Family Life

1. The phrase originated in John Donne's *Devotions Upon Emergent Occasions* (1624): "No man is an island, entire of itself; every man is a piece of the continent, a part of the main. If a clod be washed away by the sea, Europe is the less, as well as if a promontory were, as well as if a manor of thy friend's or of thine own were: any man's death diminishes me, because I am involved in mankind, and therefore never send to know for whom the bells tolls; it tolls for thee."

2. *CV*, 53.

3. Ibid.

4. *Christifideles Laici (CL)*, 40.

5. *Centesimus Annus (CA)*, 39.

6. *GS*, 48.

7. See *CSDC*, 217–218.

8. http://childrenatrisk.org/research/child-trafficking/ and http://www.havocscope.com/black-market/prostitution/.

9. *Humanae Vitae (HV)*, 16.

10. http://old.usccb.org/laity/marriage/cohabitation.shtml.

11. *CSDC*, 227.

12. http://www.vatican.va/holy_father/john_paul_ii/homilies/1986/documents/hf_jp-ii_hom_19861130_perth-australia_en.html.

13. *L'Osservatore Romano*, May 25, 1980, 19.

5. Rights and Responsibilities

1. *CA*, 47.

2. *CSDC*, 186.

3. *Quadregisimo Anno*, 80.

4. *CSDC*, 390.

5. *MM*, 53.

6. *EV*, 71.

7. *CSDC*, 214.

8. *CA*, 47.

9. *CSDC*, 407.

10. Ibid.

11. John Henry Newman, "Letter to the Duke of Norfolk," in Charles Chaput, *Render Unto Caesar* (New York: Doubleday, 2008), 148.

12. John Henry Newman, "Letter to Mrs. William Froude," in Charles Chaput, *Render Unto Caesar* (New York: Doubleday, 2008), 148.

13. Congregation for the Doctrine of the Faith, "Doctrinal Note on Some Questions Regarding the Participation of Catholics in Political Life," http://www.vatican.va/roman_curia/congregations/cfaith/documents/rc_con_cfaith_doc_20021124_politica_en.html (accessed November 8, 2011), 4.

14. USCCB, *Faithful Citizenship: A Catholic Call to Political Responsibility* (Washington, DC: USCCB Publishing, 2007).

6. Option for the Poor and Vulnerable

1. Each of these statistics were updated in 2010 and collated from various sources by Anup Shah in "Poverty Facts and Stats," http://www.globalissues.org/article/26/poverty-facts-and-stats (accessed October 2011).

2. US Census Bureau, http://www.census.gov/hhes/www/poverty/about/overview/index.html (accessed October 2011).

3. *CA*, 57.

4. United States Conference of Catholic Bishops, *Economic Justice for All: Pastoral Letter on Catholic Social Teaching and the US Economy*, http://www.usccb.org/upload/economic_justice_for_all.pdf

5. St. Rose of Lima in *CCC*, 2449.

6. Quoted in *GS*, 69.

7. The Food and Agriculture Organization of the United Nations, Economic and Social Development Department, "Global hunger declining, but still unacceptably high: International hunger targets difficult to reach," September 2010, http://www.fao.org/docrep/012/al390e/al390e00.pdf, cited in "Hunger Stats," World Food

Programme, http://www.wfp.org/hunger/stats (accessed January 2011).

8. Ibid.

9. *CA*, 32.

10. *CA*, 31.

11. *CSDC*, 171.

12. St. Gregory the Great in *CSDC*, 184.

13. *Rerum Novarum*, 22.

14. Ibid.

15. *Evangelii Nuntiandi (EN)*, 14.

16. *Hom. In Lazaro* 2, 5: *PG* 48, 992.

7. The Dignity of Work and the Rights of Workers

1. http://www.hrw.org/sites/default/files/reports/crd-0510webwcover_1.pdf.

2. *Laborem Exercens (LE)*, 4.

3. Ibid.

4. St. John Chrysostom in *CSDC*, 265.

5. *LE*, 10.

6. http://data.bls.gov/timeseries/LNS14000000.

7. *CSDC*, 289.

8. Ibid.

9. *CA*, 853.

10. *CSDC*, 301.

11. *LE*, 19.

12. Ibid., 20.

13. *CSDC*, 307.

14. Ibid., 296.

15. International Programme on the Elimination of Child Labour, "Worst forms of child labour," International Labour Organization website, http://www.ilo.org/ipec/facts/WorstFormsofChildLabour/lang--en/index.htm (accessed January 2011).

16. "Child Labor Used to Make Soccer Balls," Digital Journal website (October 16, 2008), http://www.digital-journal.com/article/261248 (accessed January 2011).

17. Reuters, "Human Rights Group Blasts US Meat Industry" (January 25, 2005), http://olympics.reuters.com/newsArticle.jhtml?type=domesticNews&storyID=7425340 (accessed February 2005).

18. *CV*, 37.

19. *CA*, 8.

20. *Deus Caritas Est*, 28.

21. *GS*, 63.

22. *Sollicitudo Rei Socialis (SRS)*, 28.

23. *Ibid.*

8. Solidarity

1. http://catholicreview.org/article/news/oregon-catholic-man-bares-his-soles-in-solidarity-with-worlds-poor#sthash.yehGd2MJ.dpuf.

2. United States Conference of Catholic Bishops, "Forming Consciences for Faithful Citizenship," *United States Conference of Catholic Bishops*, http://www.usccb.org/issues-and-action/faithful-citizenship/upload/forming-consciences-for-faithful-citizenship.pdf (accessed November 8, 2011), 53.

3. See *CA*, 10.

4. *CA*, 52.

5. http://www.catholicnewsagency.com/news/spiritual-generosity-is-form-of-solidarity-pope-states/.

6. *SRS*, 38.

7. Ibid.

8. *CSDC*, 196.

9. See *CCC*, 2439.

10. Martin Luther King Jr., "Christmas Sermon on Peace," *A Testament of Hope: The Essential Writings and Speeches of Martin Luther King Jr.*, ed. James M. Washington (New York: Harper-Collins, 1986), 254.

11. *CSDC*, 297.

12. St. John Paul II, "Message for World Migration Day 1996," http://www.vatican.va/holy_father/john_paul_ii/messages/migration/documents/hf_jp-ii_mes_25071995_undocumented_migrants_en.html (accessed November 8, 2011), 5.

13. http://judiciary.house.gov/hearings/pdf/Kicanas100714.pdf.

14. http://www.pewhispanic.org/2013/01/29/a-nation-of-immigrants/.

15. *CSDC*, 495.

16. USCCB, *The Harvest of Justice Is Sown in Peace*, http://www.usccb.org/beliefs-and-teachings/what-we-believe/catholic-social-teaching/the-harvest-of-justice-is-sown-in-peace.cfm p. 5.

17. *SRS*, 24.

18. Erna Putz, *Franz Jagerstatter: Letters and Writings from Prison*, tr. by Robert A. Krieg (New York: Orbis Books, 2009).

19. St. John XXIII, *Pacem in Terris*, "Encyclical of Pope John XIII on Establishing Universal Peace in Truth, Justice, Charity, and Liberty" (April 11, 1963), §171, http://www.vatican.va/holy_father/john_xxiii/encyclicals/documents/hf_j-xxiii_enc_11041963_pacem_en.html (accessed October 2011).

9. Care for God's Creation

1. USCCB, *Renewing the Earth*, http://www.usccb.org/issues-and-action/human-life-and-dignity/environment/renewing-the-earth.cfm, 4.

2. http://www.vatican.va/holy_father/benedict_xvi/speeches/2008/august/documents/hf_ben-xvi_spe_20080806_clero-bressanone_en.html.

3. http://www.vatican.va/holy_father/benedict_xvi/letters/2007/documents/hf_ben-xvi_let_20070901_symposium-environment_en.html.

4. http://water.org/water-crisis/water-facts/water/.

5. World Health Organization, "Fact Sheet: Air Quality and Health" (August 1, 2008), http://www.who.int/mediacentre/factsheets/fs313/en/index.html (accessed November 2011).

6. Kounteya Sinha, "'Indoor air pollution is the biggest killer," *The Times of India* (March 22, 2007), http://timesofindia.indiatimes.com/india/Indoor-air-pollution-is-the-biggest-killer/articleshow/1790711.cms (accessed January 2011).

7. Environmental Defense Action Fund, "Clean Air Facts" from *Clean Air Declaration*, http://www.edf.org/page.cfm?tagid=60634 (accessed January 2011).

8. The World Wide Fund for Nature, "Reducing Emissions from Deforestation," http://wwf.panda.org/what_we_do/footprint/climate_carbon_energy/forest_climate/forests_and_climate_change/ (accessed January 2011).

9. "Rainforest Facts," from *Raintree Nutrition*, http://www.rain-tree.com/facts.htm (accessed January 2011).

10. https://www.un.org/millennium/sg/report/ch4.htm.

11. Pope Benedict XVI, "Message for World Day of Peace 2010," http://www.vatican.va/holy_father/benedict_xvi/messages/peace/documents/hf_ben-xvi_mes_20091208_xliii-world-day-peace_en.html (accessed November 8, 2011), 4.

12. http://www.vatican.va/holy_father/benedict_xvi/messages/peace/documents/hf_ben-xvi_mes_20091208_xliii-world-day-peace_en.html.

13. *Renewing the Earth (RE)*, 4.

14. Ibid., 9.

15. *The Ecological Crisis: A Common Responsibility*, 13.

16. *RE*, 4.

17. *GS*, 69.

18. *SRS* 34.

19. For the text, see: http://www.zenit.org/en/articles/a-christian-view-of-man-and-nature Also, see *Ten Commandments for the Environment*, by Woodeene Koenig-Bricker (Notre Dame, IN: Ave Maria Press, 2009).

20. http://www.zenit.org/en articles/3-minute-showers-and-lots-of-walking.

21. http://water.org/water-crisis/water-facts/water/.

Epilogue

1. Pope Benedict XVI, "Papal Homily at Close of Eucharistic Congress: A Eucharistic Spirituality Is a Real Antidote to Individualism," *Zenit*, http://www.zenit.org/article-33405?l=english (accessed November 8, 2011).

2. See *Evangelium Vitae*.

3. *GS*, 58.

4. USCCB, Doctrinal Elements of a Curriculum Framework for the Development of Catechetical Materials for Young People of High School Age.

5. *CSDC*, 581.

6. St. John Paul II, "Message for World Day of Peace 2004," http://www.vatican.va/holy_father/john_paul_ii/messages/peace/documents/hf_jp-ii_mes_20031216_xxxvii-world-day-for-peace_en.html (accessed November 8, 2011), 10.

7. *Noro Millennio Ineunte*, 21.

Glossary

abortion The deliberate termination of a pregnancy by killing the unborn child.

adultery Marital infidelity, or sexual relations between two persons, at least one of whom is married to another (*CCC*, Glossary).

affirmative action Policies and programs established to correct past discrimination in educational and employment opportunities directed against women, African Americans, and members of other minorities.

almsgiving Freely giving money or goods to the poor as an act of penance or fraternal charity. Almsgiving, together with prayer and fasting, are traditionally recommended to foster the state of interior penance.

anarchy A state of lawlessness or political disorder due to the absence of governmental authority.

artificial contraception The use of mechanical, chemical, or medical means to prevent conception from taking place as a result of sexual intercourse (*CCC*, Glossary).

artificial insemination A fertility technique in which a man's sperm and a woman's egg are united through clinical means—most commonly by injecting sperm into a woman's cervical canal.

capital The natural resources God has given people to use as well as to all the means of producing and developing them.

capitalism An economic and political system in which trade and industry are controlled by private owners for profit.

Catholic social teaching The Church's social doctrine, which is articulated as she interprets events in the course of history, with the assistance of the Holy Spirit, in the light of the truth of Revelation.

charity The virtue by which people love God above all things for his own sake, and their neighbor as other selves for the love of God.

chastity The moral virtue which provides for the successful integration of sexuality within one's whole identity, leading to the inner unity of the physical and spiritual being (*CCC*, 2337).

civil allegiance Duty of respect and obedience owed by every person to the state of which he is a member. In the light of Christian principles, this does not mean that one must support his country in morally wrong ideologies or practices.

civil authority Leaders of public groups—particularly government leaders—or institutions that make laws.

civil society The sum of relationships and resources, cultural and associative, that are relatively independent from the political sphere and the economic sector.

cohabitation Living together in a sexual relationship without the lifelong commitment of a sacramental marriage.

communion of Persons A complete giving-of-self, shown perfectly in the life of the Trinity. The Trinity, as a communion of divine Persons, is a model for human relationships.

communism A social or political system in which all economic and social activity is controlled by a totalitarian government dominated by a single political party.

commutative justice The type of justice that governs exchanges between individuals and private groups.

concupiscence The human inclination toward sin, caused by Original Sin. More specifically, it means "the rebellion of the 'flesh' against the spirit" (*CCC*, 2515).

conscientious objection The moral right to refuse to follow laws or other social constructs based on moral or religious grounds. An example is choosing not to fight in an unjust war.

conscientious objectors People who refuse to join the military or participate in a war based on moral or religious grounds. Conscientious objectors must be open to other forms of service.

consumerism A social and economic order that encourages the purchase of goods in ever greater amounts.

culture The personality of a society. As understood in Catholic social philosophy, culture is the totality of a people's traditions (what they believe), attitudes (what they desire), customs (what they do), and institutions (how they live).

disciple A follower of Jesus Christ. The word disciple comes from a Latin word that means "learner."

distributive justice The type of justice that governs what the greater community owes individuals based on their contribution and needs.

domestic church A name for the Christian family. In the family, parents and children exercise their priesthood of the baptized by worshiping God, receiving the sacraments, and witnessing to Christ and the Church by living as faithful disciples.

euthanasia Any act or omission which, of itself or by intention, causes death in order to eliminate suffering.

evangelization The proclamation of Christ and his Gospel (Greek: *evangelion*) by word and the testimony of life in fulfillment of Christ's command.

fecundity Fruitfulness. In relation to marriage, fecundity refers to procreation and education of children as one of the purposes of marriage.

fidelity Faithfulness. In relation to marriage, fidelity refers to one of the purposes of marriage. Both spouses give of themselves definitively and totally to one another. They are no longer two; from now on they form one flesh. The covenant they freely contracted imposes on the spouses the obligation to preserve it as unique and indissoluble (*CCC*, 2364).

fornication Sexual intercourse between an unmarried man and an unmarried woman (*CCC*, Glossary).

greed Also known as avarice; the desire for earthly goods beyond what we need. Greed is a sin against the Tenth Commandment.

humility A virtue that avoids extreme ambition and pride and focuses rather on the acknowledgement that God is the author of all that is good.

in vitro fertilization The fertilization of a woman's ovum (egg) with a man's sperm through a clinical procedure, then implanting the fertilized egg in the woman's uterus. In vitro fertilization violates the dignity of procreation.

just wage Also called living wage, the basic wage needed to ensure wage earners' basic needs—such as food, shelter, education—are met, and that they and their families can live with dignity.

justice The cardinal or moral virtue that consists in the constant and firm will to give God and neighbor their due; the actions that flow from that virtue.

legal justice The type of justice that governs what individuals owe their country and society.

Magisterium The official teaching authority of the Church. Jesus bestowed the right and power to teach in his name on Peter and the Apostles and their successors, that is, the pope and College of Bishops. The authority of the Magisterium extends to specific precepts of the natural law because following these precepts is necessary for Salvation.

natural law Moral knowledge written in every human heart and that every human person innately possesses. It is universal, permanent, and unchanging.

objective dimension of work The product or outcome of work.

Original Sin The sin of the first human parents, by which they lost their original holiness. Original Sin is transmitted to every person born into the world, except Jesus and Mary.

participation The voluntary and generous engagement of a person in society.

Paschal Mystery Christ's work of Redemption, accomplished principally by his Passion, Death, Resurrection, and glorious Ascension. This mystery is commemorated and made present through the sacraments, especially the Eucharist.

personalistic norm The principle that maintains that a person is to be treated as a unique individual, never a means to another's end.

physician-assisted suicide The process of ending one's own life with the help of a doctor rather than directly by the doctor's hand.

pornography The written or visual depiction of sexual acts or nudity with the purpose of stimulating and gratifying lustful desires. Pornography debases human dignity by turning people into objects to be used for selfish gratification.

preferential option for the poor A preferential love for the poor that allows one to give priority to the needs of the poor and to make a commitment to transform unjust social structures that are the causes of poverty.

prejudice A preconceived opinion formulated without consideration of known factors and usually based on erroneous knowledge.

principle of double effect A formula used for evaluating the permissibility of an act that is morally good when the act causes an effect one is normally obliged to avoid.

principle of proportionality The rule that requires the damage inflicted and the costs incurred in a war (or a particular action in war) to be commensurate with the good expected.

prostitution The act of providing sexual services in exchange for money or other material gain.

prudence The moral virtue by which a person is inclined toward choosing to do good and avoiding evil.

racism A belief that race determines human traits and abilities and that a particular race is inherently superior or inferior to another; and the discrimination that stems from those beliefs.

rape The forcible violation of the sexual intimacy of another person (*CCC*, 2356).

relativism Believing that truth is dependent upon one's own perception or opinion; holding that there is no absolute or objective truth.

revealed law God's law made known in the Old Testament and the New Testament.

scandal An attitude or behavior that leads another person to sin.

social encyclical A letter from the Pope to the Church on issues related to human rights, social justice, and peace.

social justice The application of the virtue of justice. The defense of human dignity by ensuring that social structures and institutions on all levels—including political, cultural, and economic—provide for essential human needs and protect human rights.

social sin The effect that every personal sin has on others; sin that violates the freedom, dignity, or rights of others; the collective effect of such sins, which can affect society and its institutions to create structures of sin.

socialism A social-economic system based on the common ownership of the means of production and exchange of wealth.

solidarity The virtue of social charity, friendship, and responsible sharing whereby the interdependence among all people is recognized.

soul The innermost spiritual part of a person. The soul is the subject of human consciousness and freedom. Body and soul together form one human nature. The soul does not die with the body. It is eternal and will be reunited with the body in the final resurrection.

stewardship The proper use of the gifts God has given us, in particular, the care for creation that will allow the earth and its resources to flourish and last for future generations.

subjective dimension of work The human person and his or her involvement in work.

subsidiarity The moral principle that large organizations or governments should not interfere with, or take over, responsibilities that can be administered by individuals and local organizations, but rather should support them, always with a focus on the common good.

surrogate motherhood A medical process in which a woman becomes pregnant through artificial means and carries the child for someone else. The procedure separates intercourse from the act of procreation and is morally wrong.

terrorism A systematic use of subversive strategies aimed at the destruction of material goods or the killing of people in order to coerce certain actions or decisions.

totalitarian A society in which the state exercises total control of the life and conduct of the citizens.

vocation The call to holiness emanating from Baptism to live out your Christian destiny in this world and the next. Vocation also refers to a special call to share in the mission of the Church, especially as a priest or consecrated religious.

works of charity Actions that provide an immediate response to a person or group who is suffering or in need of the basic necessities for a dignified life.

works of mercy Charitable actions by which we provide for the physical and spiritual needs of others.

Subject Index

A

Abaire, Bekele, 302

Abortion, 73–82
    alternatives to, 81
    breakdown of family, 76, 78
    danger to health of mother, 79
    defined, 73
    factors that lead to, 76–78
    freedom as absolute value, 78
    healing from, 81
    history of, in United States, 74–76
    incidence of, 73, 75
    main types of, 74
    principle of double effect, 80
    promoting life, 82
    rape and, 79
    Roe v. Wade, 76
    SLED argument, 77
    as social sin, 19–20
    working to eliminate, 78–79

"A Call to Action" (Pope Paul VI), 52

Adam and Eve
    marriage as foundation of family, 109
    social nature of people, 7
    suffering and, 173
    work and, 213

Addition, poverty of, 172

Adultery, 113, 114

Affirmative action, 267

Air pollution, 288

Almsgiving, 190–191

Ambrose, St., 43

Amos, 179

Anarchy, 148

Aquinas, Thomas, St., 93

Aristotle, 111

Artificial contraception, 118–120
    health insurance mandate, 135

Artificial insemination, 120

Assisted suicide, 89–90

Augustine, St., 43–44
    on happiness, 4

Authority
    civil authority, 146
    defining legitimate, 148
    from God, 148
    guidelines for true, 148
    role of, 148–149

B

Basilica of Our Lady of Guadalupe, 100

Beatitudes
    peacemakers, 255
    poor of spirit, 172, 173

Beginning-of-life issues, 83–87
    abortion, 73–82
    cloning and genetic manipulation, 85–87
    stem cell use, 84–85

Benedict XVI, Pope, 8, 226, 234, 285, 299
    common good, 17
    dictatorship of relativism, 154
    environmental issues, 287, 289, 291, 299, 300, 304
    environmental refugees, 291
    on evangelization, 193
    on government control, 227
    as green pope, 279
    human ecology, 290
    "In Charity and Truth," 53
    "In Hope We Are Saved," 54
    on peace and justice, 255
    prayer for the unborn, 103
    on stem cells use, 83–84
    on world hunger, 183

Bernardin, Cardinal Joseph, 91

Bigamy, 125

Biodiversity, 289

Blesseds. *See also* Saints and Bl. Pope Paul VI
    Franz Jägerstätter, Bl., 273–274
    Frédéric Ozanam, Bl., 46
    Giovanni Battista Scalabrini, Bl., 163–164
    Louis and Zélie Martin, Bl., 129–130
    Mother Teresa of Calcutta, Bl., 46, 64
    Pier Giorgio Frassati, Bl., 47

Blessed Trinity, family life image, 108

BP oil spill, 303

Brewer, Jan, 252

Budget planning, 222

Burke, Cardinal Raymond, primacy of conscience, 156

C

Cain and Abel, 38

Calumny, 153

Canticle of the Sun prayer, 313

Capital, 212

Capitalism
    defined, 50
    unbridled, and exploitation of workers, 50, 212, 226–227

Capital punishment, 92–94

Crepaldi, Giampaolo, 299
Cross of Christ, work as share of, 215
Cultural rights, 138
Culture of Life and the Penalty of Death, 54
Culture of waste, 185

D

Daughters of Charity, 26
Day, Dorothy, 46
Death and dying
    assisted suicide, 89–90
    capital punishment, 92–94
    compassion for sick and dying, 91–92
    dignity of, 90–91
    euthanasia, 89–90
    right to die mentality, 90
Debt bondage, 223–224
"Declaration on Religious Freedom" (Vatican II), 54
Deforestation, 289
Democratic governments, 151–152
Detraction, 153
Discrimination
    prejudice, 266–267
    racism, 267–268
    solidarity principle, 266–268
Distributive justice, 13–14
Divine law, 149
Divine Revelation, natural law and, 35
Dolan, Cardinal Timothy M., 189
Domestic church, 108
Dostoevsky, Fyodor, 195
Double effect, principle of, 80

E

Ecclesiastical law, 149
Economic Justice for All, 54
Economic rights, 139
Economic systems
    capitalism, 226–227
    principles of economic life, 228
    socialism, 227
Eighth Commandment, 140, 153
Elizabeth Ann Seton, St., 46
Elizabeth of Hungary, St., 46
Emigration
    defined, 250
    right to, 140
End-of-life issues, 89–94

assisted suicide, 89–90
    capital punishment, 92–94
    compassion for sick and dying, 91–92
    dignity of dying and suffering, 90–91
    euthanasia, 89–90
    ordinary vs. extraordinary medical treatment, 91
Environmental issues
    air pollution, 288
    biodiversity, 289
    Catholic response to environmental disaster, 303
    clean water, 288, 302
    consumerism and, 291–292
    deforestation, 289
    goodness of God's creation, 281–285
    human ecology, 290
    link between environment and human life issues, 290
    population growth and, 291–292
    poverty and environmental offenses, 288, 290–291
    scope of modern, 286–289
    solidarity and subsidiarity, 292–293
    stewardship of environment, 294–297
    Ten Commandments for environment, 298–305
    Vatican City's environment-friendly initiatives, 279
Environmental refugees, 291
Equal dignity principle, 56
Eternal Law, 137
Eucharist, commitment to poor and, 197–198
Euthanasia
    assisted suicide, 89–90
    defined, 89
    development of mentality of, 90
    dignity of dying and suffering, 90–91
    as false mercy, 91–92
    Patient Refusal of Nutrition and Hydration (PRNH), 91
Evangelization, to end poverty, 193
"Evangelization in the Modern World" (Pope Paul VI), 54

F

"Faith and Reason" (St. John Paul II), 53
Family
    adultery and effect on, 114
    breakdown of, and abortion, 76, 78
    prayer for, 132
    relationship between government and, 150
    role of mothers, 232–233
    subsidiarity principle, 143, 150
    workplace promoting, 219
Family, community and participation principle
    adultery, 105–132, 114

as foundation and purpose of government, 146–147

humans as God's special creatures, 283

link between environment and human life issues, 290

personalistic norm, 70–71

progress of persons, 16

right to life, 69

SLED argument, 77

as ultimate purpose of society, 70–71

Human rights. *See also* Rights and responsibilities principle

fundamental, 137–141

inalienable, 138

inviolable, 137–138

natural law and, 137

before scientific advances, 301

source of, 141

universal, 137

Humility, 173

Hunger, world

changing culture of waste, 185

direct aid to poor through subsidiarity, 185–187

factors contributing to, 184

facts and statistics on, 182–183

malnourishment, 182

scandal of, 182–187

self-examination to help, 186

works of mercy and feeding hungry, 182

I

Ignatius of Loyola, St., 111, 207

Immigration

case study on, 252–254

Catholic perspective on, 250–252

compared to emigration, 250

defined, 250

immigrants in workplace, 219, 251

right to, 140

solidarity principle and, 250–254

welcome the stranger, 250

Immunity of noncombatants, in standard of restraint, 260

"In Charity and Truth" (Pope Benedict XVI), 53

Individual citizen, responsibilities of, 147

Individuality of human beings, 7

Infertility, 120–121

"In Hope We Are Saved" (Pope Benedict XVI), 54

Innocent II, Pope, 311

International Labor Organization, 223

In vitro fertilization, 120

Israelites, care for the poor, 178–179

J

Jesus Christ

Church as Mystical Body of Christ, 9

life of, and care for poor, 179–181, 188, 196

as man of work, 214

as model of justice, 40–42

poor in spirit and, 173

poverty and need for, 173, 176

reconciles creation to Father, 283–284

teaches meaning of good stewardship, 284–285

true identity in, 6

work as share in Cross of Christ, 215

John Chrysostom, St., 196, 197

on work, 213

John of the Cross, St., 111

John Paul II, St., 298

artificial contraception, 119

care for gifts of creation, 283

The Catechism of the Catholic Church, 53

Church's love for the poor, 177

on consumerism, 227, 229, 291

death penalty, 94

on economic freedom, 227

environmental issues, 286, 290, 292, 295, 297

euthanasia as false mercy, 91–92

exaltation of weekends, 231

"Faith and Reason," 53

family wage, 220

helping the poor, 187, 190

human ecology, 290

on immigration, 251–252

individuality of human being, 7

need for justice, 12

"On Human Work," 52

"On Social Concern," 52

"On the Hundredth Year," 53

personalistic norm, 70

prayer for families, 132

"Redeemer of Mankind," 54

on relativism, 154

on religious freedom, 141

"Rich in Mercy," 54

role of mother, 232–233

on same-sex unions, 125

sexual act in marriage, 114

solidarity, 245, 248

stewardship, 295, 297

on terrorism, 264

"The Gospel of Life," 53

true identity in Christ, 6

on war, 257

women who have had abortions, 81

on work, 213

John XXIII, St.
   Church as teacher, 10
   fundamental human rights, 138–140
   "On Christianity and Social Progress," 51
   "Peace on Earth," 51
   prayer for peace, 276
   on war, 257

Joseph, St., 294
   life of, 215
   prayer to, 241

Jubilee Year, 178–179

Judgment, criteria for, 34

Just cause, as criteria for just war, 258

Justice
   charity and, 18–19
   common good and, 16–17
   commutative, 12–13
   defined, 11
   distributive, 13–14
   to end poverty, 190–191
   legal, 14
   need for, 12
   in New Testament, 40–42
   in Old Testament, 37–40
   saints and laypeople living justly, 43–44, 46–47
   social, 14–15

"Justice in the World" (Synod of Bishops), 52

Just wage, 220

Just war doctrine, 258–265
   criteria for, 258–259
   defined, 258
   standard of restraint in, 260
   war on terrorism and, 264–265

K

Katharine Drexel, St., 47

Kicanas, Gerald, 253

King, Martin Luther, Jr., 247

L

Ladies of Charity, 25

Laity, 232

Last resort, as criteria for just war, 259

Law
   civil, 149
   definitions of, 149
   Divine, 149
   ecclesiastical, 149
   Eternal, 137
   natural, 34, 35, 137, 149
   revealed, 149

Lawrence, St., 46

Lazarists, 25

Legal justice, 14

Legitimate authority, as criteria for just war, 258

Leo XIII, Pope, 14–15, 191
   on capitalism, 50, 226–227
   child labor, 223
   "On Capital and Labor," 50, 51
   origin of modern social teaching and, 49–50
   on socialism, 50, 227
   solidarity, 245

Liberia, nonviolent action in, 262

Life
   right to choose freely one's state of life, 139
   right to life, 138
   simplicity of, 195–196

Life and dignity of human person principle, 67–103
   abortion, 73–82
   capital punishment, 92–94
   cloning and genetic manipulation, 85–87
   compassion for sick and dying, 91–92
   dignity and equality of every person, 71
   dignity of dying and suffering, 90–91
   end-of-life concerns, 89–94
   euthanasia, 89–90
   ordinary vs. extraordinary medical treatment, 91
   other beginning-of-life issues, 83–87
   overview of, 55
   personalistic norm, 70–71
   stem cell use, 83–85

"The Light of Faith" (Pope Francis), 53

Lord's Day, 231–232

Louise de Marillac, St., 25–26

Love
   conjugal, 114
   God as, 8

M

Magisterium
   defined, 34
   response to justice issues, 44–45

Malnourishment, 182

Marcos, Ferdinand, 262

Marriage
   adultery, 114
   attacks against dignity of, 122–125
   characteristics of, 109–110
   cohabitation, 122–123

complementarity of sexes, 110
as foundation of family, 109–111
regulations on, 125
sacrament of, 110
same-sex unions, 123–125
sexual act in, 114
Martin, Louis, Bl., 129–130
Martin, Zélie, Bl., 129–130
Martin de Porres, St., 111
life of, 46
Marx, Karl, 50
Marxism, 50
Mary, Our Lady of Guadalupe, 99–100
Masturbation, 115
Materialism, balance with nature, 299
Material poverty, 172, 174–175
Medical treatment, ordinary vs. extraordinary, 91
Meeting and association, right to, 140
Missionaries of Charity, 47
Money, love of, 227
Moral law, 34
Moral rights, 138
Mothers, role of, 232–233

N

Natural Family Planning (NFP), 119–120
Natural law
defined, 34, 149
Divine Revelation and, 35
human rights and, 137
Newman, John Henry, St., on conscience, 155
New Testament
care for the poor, 179–180
justice in, 40–42
Ninth Commandment, 113
Noncombatants, immunity of, 260, 261
Nonviolence
preference for, 261–263
successful examples of, 262
suggestions for promoting, 263
Nuclear war, 262

O

Objective dimension of work, 212
Old Testament
care for the poor, 178–179
justice in, 37–40
"On Capital and Labor" (Pope Leo XIII), 50, 51

"On Christianity and Social Progress" (St. John XXIII), 51
"On Human Work" (St. John Paul II), 52
"On Social Concern" (St. John Paul II), 52
"On the Church in the Modern World" (Vatican II), 52
"On the Development of Peoples" (Pope Paul VI), 52
"On the Hundredth Year" (St. John Paul II), 53
"On the Reconstruction of the Social Order" (Pope Pius XI), 51
Original Sin, 6, 173
Our Lady of Guadalupe, 99–100

P

Participation, call to, 157–158
The Participation of Catholics in Political Life, 54
Paschal Mystery, 6
Pastoral Letters
The Challenge of Peace: God's Promise and Our Response, 54
Culture of Life and the Penalty of Death, 54
Economic Justice for All, 54
Sowing Weapons of War, 54
Statement: To End the Death Penalty, 54
Patient Refusal of Nutrition and Hydration (PRNH), 91
Paul, St.
authority, 148
on greed, 227
solidarity, 245–246
on work, 213
Paul VI, Pope Bl., 49, 298
"A Call to Action," 52
artificial contraception, 118–119
civilization of love, 245
"Evangelization in the Modern World," 54
Holy Family, 108–109
"On the Development of Peoples," 52
on peace and justice, 255
on war, 257
Peace
defining, 256
just war doctrine, 258–265
legitimate circumstances for war, 257
more than absence of war, 255, 256
prayer for, 257, 276
preference for nonviolence, 261–263
solidarity principle and, 255–265
virtues that help, 257
in your life, 256–257
"Peace on Earth" (St. John XXIII), 51
Pensions, 221

Relativism, 154

Religious fanaticism, 153

Religious freedom, 141
    prayer for protection of religious liberty, 166
    right to worship God, 139

Religious sister, 232

Reproduction issues
    abortion, 73–82
    artificial conception, 120–121
    artificial contraception, 118–120, 135
    artificial insemination, 120
    China's one-child policy, 67
    cloning and genetic manipulation, 85–87
    infertility, 120
    Natural Family Planning (NFP), 119–120
    stem cell use, 83–85
    surrogate motherhood, 105, 120
    in vitro fertilization, 120

Revealed law, 149

"Rich in Mercy" (St. John Paul II), 54

Right intention
    as criteria for just war, 259
    in standard of restraint, 260

Right of meeting and association, 140

Rights and responsibilities principle, 135–166
    call to participate, 157–158
    Catholic understanding of government, 151–154
    conscientious objection, 156–157
    corruption in political society, 152–153
    democratic governments, 151–152
    fundamental human rights, 137–141
    humans as foundation and purpose of government, 146–147
    overview of, 55
    politics and conscience, 155–158
    relationship between government and family, 150
    relativism, 154
    responsibilities in civil society, 142–145
    role of authority, 148
    source of human rights, 141
    subsidiarity, 143–145
    totalitarianism, 153–154

Right to choose freely one's state of life, 139

Right to emigrate and immigrate, 140

Right to life, 138, 140

Right to private property, 192

Right to worship God, 139

Roe v. Wade, 20, 76

Rose of Lima, St., 111, 180

S

Sabbath rest, 220, 231–232

Sabbatical Year, 178–179

Saints. See also Blesseds; specific saints
    Elizabeth Ann Seton, 46
    Elizabeth of Hungary, 46
    Francis of Assisi, 310–311
    Gaspar, 46
    Gemma Galgani, 204–205
    Gianna Beretta Molla, 46
    Giuseppe Moscati, 238–239
    Joseph, 215
    Katharine Drexel, 47
    Lawrence, 46
    living mission of social justice, 46–47
    Louise de Marillac, 25–26
    Martin de Porres, 46
    Peter Claver, 61
    Vincent de Paul, 25–26

Salt poisoning, 74

Same-sex unions, 123–125

Santiago, Robert, 243

Satan, poverty and, 188

Scandal
    defined, 268
    solidarity principle and, 268

Seal of confession, 153

Self-defense, capital punishment and, 92–93

Serbia, nonviolent action in, 262

Seventh Commandment, 185

Sexuality issues
    adultery, 114
    artificial contraception, 118–120
    chastity, 113–114
    fornication, 114–115
    homosexual acts, 117–118
    masturbation, 115
    pornography, 116
    prostitution, 115–116
    rape, 115
    sexual act in marriage, 114

Sharing Catholic Social Teaching (USCCB), 56

Sick
    compassion for sick and dying, 91–92
    ordinary vs. extraordinary medical treatment, 91

Simplicity of life, 195–196

Sin
    concupiscence, 4
    leading human to abuse gift of creation, 283
    Original Sin, 6

U

Unemployment, 217–218, 221
Unions, 221
Universal destination of goods, 191–192
Utility, friendship of, 111

V

Vatican City, environment-friendly initiatives, 279
Vatican II
    "Declaration on Religious Freedom," 54
    "On the Church in the Modern World," 52
Vincent de Paul, St., 46
    life story of, 25–26
Vincentians, 25
Virtue, friendship of, 111
Vocations, 232–233
Vote, duty to, 157–158

W

Walesa, Lech, 156, 262
War
    criteria for just war, 258–259
    just war doctrine, 258–265
    legitimate circumstances for, 257
    nuclear war, 262
    preference for nonviolence, 261–263
    principle of proportionality, 261
    standard of restraint, 260
    on terrorism and just war doctrine, 264–265
Waste, culture of, 185
White collar crime, 224
Women, in workplace, 219
Work
    abuses in adult labor, 224
    as an idol, 230
    child labor, 223–224
    choosing a career, 233–234
    duties and benefits of, 213
    Jesus as man of, 214
    nature of, 211–215
    objective dimension of, 212
    origins of, 213
    as share in cross of Christ, 215
    subjective dimension of, 212
    white collar crime, 224
Workers' rights and dignity of work principle, 209–241
    abuses against dignity of, 223–225
    assemble and associations of, 221

    careers and vocations, 232–234
    child labor, 209
    economic systems and, 226–229
    full employment, 217–218
    just wage, 220
    keeping the Lord's Day, 231–232
    maternity leave, 221
    nature of work, 211–215
    overview, 55–56
    pensions and health care insurance, 221
    rest from work, 220, 231–232
    rights overview, 217–222
    safe workplace, 220–221
    special concerns in workplace, 219
    strikes, 221–222
    unemployment, 217–218, 221
Works of charity, 185
Works of mercy
    corporal, 189–190
    defined, 182
    to end poverty, 189–190
    spiritual, 189–190
World hunger, 182–187
    changing culture of waste, 185
    direct aid to poor through subsidiarity, 185–187
    factors contributing to, 184
    facts and statistics on, 182–183
    malnourishment, 182
    self-examination to help, 186
    works of mercy and feeding hungry, 182
Worship, right to worship God, 139

Z

Zechariah, 179

Church Documents Index

Scripture Index
Old Testament

Pentateuch
Genesis

Gn 1:1–5, 37
Gn 1:28, 118, 191, 213, 299
Gn 1:31, 282
Gn 2:2–3, 220
Gn 2:15, 213, 283, 294
Gn 2:18, 7, 109
Gn 2:24, 109
Gn 3:19, 213
Gn 4:1–15, 98
Gn 4:9, 38, 252
Gn 15:2, 120
Gn 30:1, 120

Exodus

Ex 3:7–8, 38
Ex 20:15, 185
Ex 22, 250

Leviticus

Lv 25:35, 38

Deuteronomy

Dt 10:18, 38
Dt 10:19, 38
Dt 14:28–29, 38

Wisdom Books
Psalms

Ps 8, 284
Ps 72, 98
Ps 103:6, 12
Ps 104, 284
Ps 104:24–25, 27–30, 305
Ps 104:30, 299
Ps 127:3, 118
Ps 139, 95, 98
Ps 139:13–15, 70
Ps 146:6–9, 39

Ps 148, 284

Proverbs

Prv 6:6–11, 235
Prv 22:22–23, 179
Prv 24:8–12, 98
Prv 31:9, 39

Sirach

Sir 4:1–9, 39
Sir 6:14, 111
Sir 6:15, 111

Prophetic Books
Isaiah

Is 1:17, 40

Jeremiah

Jer 1:5, 84

Hosea

Hos 4:1–3, 283

Amos

Am 5:24, 37
Am 8:4, 10, 179

Micah

Mi 6:8, 40

Zechariah

Zec 7:9–10, 179

New Testament
Gospels
Matthew

Mk 2:27–28, 214
Mk 6:30–44, 179
Mk 12:41–44, 196
Mt 5–7, 40
Mt 5:3, 6, 40, 173
Mt 5:6, 12
Mt 5:9, 255
Mt 5:28, 113

Catechism of the Catholic Church Index

Photo Credits